The Power of Apartheid
State, power and space in South African cities

Policy, Planning and Critical Theory

Series Editor: **Paul Cloke**
University of Bristol, UK

This major new series focuses on the relevance of critical social theory to important contemporary processes and practices in planning and policy-making. It demonstrates the need to incorporate state and governmental activities within these new theoretical approaches, and focuses on current trends in governmental policy in Western states, with particular reference to the relationship between the centre and the locality, the provision of services, and the formulation of government policy.

Titles published in the series include:

Policy and Change in Thatcher's Britain
Paul Cloke

The Global Region: Production, State Policies and Uneven Development
David Sadler

Selling Places: The City as Cultural Capital, Past and Present
C Philo and G Kearns

Globalized Agriculture: Political Choice
Richard Le Heron

Gender, Planning and the Policy Process
Jo Little

Uneven Re-Production: Industry, Space and Society
Andy Pratt

The Power of Apartheid
State, power and space in South African cities

Jennifer Robinson

Department of Geographical and Environmental Sciences, University of
Natal, Durban, South Africa

Butterworth-Heinemann Ltd
Linacre House, Jordan Hill, Oxford OX2 8DP

_R_ A member of the Reed Elsevier plc group

OXFORD   LONDON   BOSTON
NEW DELHI   SINGAPORE   SYDNEY
TOKYO   TORONTO   WELLINGTON

First published 1996

British Library Cataloguing in Publication Data

Robinson, Jennifer
  Power of Apartheid: State, Power and
  Space in South African Cities – (Policy
  Planning & Critical Theory Series)
  I. Title   II. Series
  320.968
ISBN 0 7506 2689 5

Library of Congress Cataloguing in Publication Data

Robinson, Jennifer.
  The power of apartheid: state, power, and space in South African
  cities / Jennifer Robinson.
  p.   cm. – (Policy, planning, and critical theory)
  Includes bibliographical references and index.
  ISBN 0 7506 2689 5 (pbk.)
  1. Municipal government – South Africa – History.   2. Federal–city
  relations – South Africa – History.   3. Apartheid – South Africa –
  History.   I. Title.   II. Series.
  JS7533.A3R62   1995   95–39072
                                                           CIP

Composition by Scribe Design, Gillingham, Kent
Printed in Great Britain

Contents

Acknowledgements

Many people helped me with the research and the thinking that went into this book, and others helped put me on the path that led to it being written. In this regard, I need to thank Jeff McCarthy, who first inspired me to become a geographer, and to find honourable ways to understand the South African political predicament. My path to study at Cambridge was suggested by friends, especially by Jonathan Taylor and his family and by Sheldon Rankin, both of whom have been important sources of moral support and inspiration. The numerous friends and colleagues in Cambridge who helped make a strange place home for a while were an integral part of my thinking and the project itself. I must especially thank Graham Smith, my supervisor, and Chris Philo who, in addition to plenty of intellectual and general support, also did a lot of proof-reading at one stage. Since being at the University of Natal, my intellectual and emotional survival has been dependent upon a small but lively group of feminist scholars, amongst whom I want to thank Debby Bonnin, Cathy Campbell, Rob Morrell, Cherryl Walker and Roger Deacon especially as well as Raphael de Kadt. Mark Devenney shared the traumas of the final editing stages.

Central to this study were the people in the Eastern Cape who assisted with tracking down archival material, in helping me to understand Port Elizabeth under very difficult political circumstances, and in making my stay in the region a comradely and sociable one. I must thank especially Bill Davies and A.J. Christopher; Melanie, Debbie, Mbo and Jeremiah who helped me explore New Brighton, security police notwithstanding; Claudia and Don who looked after me so often; and Jenny, who I stayed with during my time in the city. The history of Port Elizabeth had not been studied very much at all when I began my thesis, but during the course of my research, Gary Baines, Janet Cherry and Bev Taylor were also beginning work about Port Elizabeth. Having people to discuss the finer details of local history with was wonderful, and our mutual learnings are very evident in what follows. We hope that the people of Port Elizabeth, and of New Brighton in particular, will find much to reflect upon in our recording of their past as they seek to transform the city that apartheid has bequeathed to them.

I wish to dedicate this book to Jonathan Taylor, who played a large role in shaping my political and moral motivations for this study and whose untimely death is still mourned by all his friends.

Acknowledgements for funding at various stages of this project must be made to the Human Sciences Research Council, the University of Natal Research Fund and the Geography Department at Cambridge University. Of course all opinions and errors are my own.

Parts of this material have been published elsewhere. Acknowledgements to publishers for the following extracts:

Chapter 2, pp. 41–55 include adaptations from parts of 'A Perfect System of Control? State power and "native locations" in South Africa'. *Environment and Planning D. Society and Space* (1990) **8**: 135–162.

Chapter 3, pp 65–72 include adaptations from 'Power, space and the city: historical reflections on Apartheid and post-Apartheid urban orders'. In D. Smith (ed.) *The Apartheid City and Beyond* (1992), London: Routledge. Pages 72–76 include adaptations from 'Administrative strategies and political power in South Africa's black townships, 1930–1960'. *Urban Forum (1992)*, **2**: 63–80.

Chapter 4 includes a fairly substantial adaptation of 'Progressive Port Elizabeth: Liberal politics, local economic development and the territorial basis of racial domination, 1923–1935'. *GeoJournal* (1990) **22**: 293–303.

Chapter 5, pp. 123–145 include material from 'The Politics of Urban Form: Differential Citizenship and Township Formation in Port Elizabeth 1925–1945'. *Kronos: Journal of Cape History* (1993) **20**: 44–65.

Abbreviations

ANC	African National Congress
CA	Cape Archives
DNA	Department of Native Affairs (central)
EPH	Eastern Province Herald
HSlEl	Housing and Slum Elimination Committee
MM	Mayor's Minutes, Port Elizabeth
MOH	Medical Officer of Health, Port Elizabeth
NAC	Native Affairs Commission
NABd	Native Advisory Board
NAD	Native Affairs Department (local)
PE	Port Elizabeth
PEIA	Port Elizabeth Intermediate Archives
SA	South Africa
SANAC	South African Native Affairs Commision
SANCO	South African National Civic Organization
TA	Transvaal Archives

Introduction

Apartheid, a universal signifier of political and racial domination, has a specific literal meaning as well, 'apartness'. It is a social system founded upon the 'setting apart'[1] in space of different race groups. The power of apartheid, I will argue, was crucially dependent upon this spatiality. Apartheid – setting apart – was itself constitutive of the power of the South African racial order. But the spatial technology upon which this political order rested was invented long before the term 'apartheid' became popular – indeed, even before its predecessor, segregation, emerged as a coherent political platform. And, unfortunately, the spatiality of apartheid persists to confound post-apartheid urban managers in their project of repairing the damages of the past. This book traces the history and considers the present implications of the spatiality of apartheid power.

The argument I want to make is somewhat different from previous efforts to understand the spatiality of South African cities. Where others have emphasized capital accumulation, a docile workforce, white agitation or just plain racism, I would suggest that the organization of urban space into racially segregated living areas was central to the persistence of the racial state – indeed, it was one of the key technologies which enabled the more or less effective implementation of state power in South Africa's urban areas. Urban apartheid, then, was a particular historical form of a spatial technology of power which emerged in the arena of state intervention in the city. Without a gathering of the racially defined African population into spatially contained areas and the evolution of specific methods of administration and governance in these areas, the implementation of various racial policies would have been held hostage to the racial and physical 'chaos' of the early twentieth century city. In addition, in the face of a rapidly growing and politically disruptive African urban population, the location represented a more efficient and simpler method of surveillance than traditional strategies of state surveillance in the West. The racial South African state survived for decades at least partly as a result of its ability to implement routine governance by means of what I have called the 'location strategy' – for early African townships were known as locations (a term which persists to this day in the vernacular – in Zulu, *ilokshini*). The power of apartheid, of the setting apart of racial groups, was therefore rooted in the spatial practices referenced in its very name: much more than simply an expression of a political order, the spaces of apartheid constituted and sustained that order.

The primary focus of this study, then, is the emergence and evolution of the 'location strategy'. A detailed case study of the Port Elizabeth locations is the main vehicle which I use here for exploring this strategy. Evidence of its evolution at a wider national scale is also presented, but it is on the ground, at the interface between employees of the state and African urban residents, that the dynamics of this strategy of control can best be identified and its operations demonstrated.

Although the power of apartheid rested in the spatial arrangements of the city which we have come to see as characteristic of this political order, the location strategy was not simply a unique and oppressive outcome of South African politics. This is because in synthesizing a number of normalizing Western practices and discourses of urban government, the location as residential area was also designed to solve crises of accommodation which racked South African cities periodically through the twentieth century. The rather perverse character of the solutions chosen represents the particular amalgam of ideas and practices which generated the 'native location'. Not only contemporary house design and planning ideas, or the growing medical concern with public health, but also the racial discourses of the time and the practices of 'native administration' which had emerged during colonial times contributed to the emergence of this spatial technology.[2] By spending some time exploring the history of its development in Port Elizabeth, we will be able to capture these various dimensions of modernity as they contributed to the shaping of South Africa's cities. We are reminded then of Gilroy's (1993) claim that racial domination has been intrinsic to the path of modernity – not an aberration. The substance of my argument concerning the strategic role of the location in urban government is set out in Chapters 2 and 3, where I trace the emergence of the idea of the location in South Africa and the tactics and discourses of administration which came to be associated with it.

My case study of Port Elizabeth (Chapters 4 to 7) is a tale of a place somewhat distant from the more elevated and acceptable accounts of grand and epochal cities (Los Angeles, San Francisco, London, Chicago, World Cities) or of the central (economic) mechanisms of global transformation. But I would contest the self-serving strategy of western geography in labelling Third World or colonial cities as other – somehow different from and unconnected to the trajectory of cities in the West. Histories of cities 'out there' are also histories of the West, as well as of its transformation. Not just reflective of the 'dark side' of modernity, then, the apartheid city is perhaps archetypically modern – contrary to popular claims as to the archaic character of racism. The landscapes of racial segregation in South Africa, for example, were described, created and managed by well-intentioned citizens, not very dissimilar from those who housed the poor in Western cities and certainly strongly influenced by these earlier reformers. Similarly, as some writers have demonstrated, the styles and influences of colonial planning also found their way back to the centre (Rabinow, 1989a; King, 1990).

The key agent of urban segregation in South Africa was the state. Yet the history of segregation is conventionally portrayed as the outcome of racist white agitation, or of the demands and needs of capital. Instead, I develop an argument which not only considers the modernizing impulses which gave rise to the apartheid city form but also establishes the state's own motivations for intervention in the city. Here I draw upon an institutional account of the state, which I present in Chapter 1. The state is, I suggest, best seen as an institution, with particular interests associated with the territorial sovereignty of modern states. However, it is an institution which is deeply divided within itself, both vertically and horizontally. Not only do different sections of the state jostle for position and seek to prolong their institutional life but the fragmentation of territorial responsibility within the state (between local and central or regional government) also makes the centralized co-ordination of state actions across the entire territory an important strategic concern of state managers. Historically, the creation of effective powers of governance has been associated with the expansion of bureaucratic powers of routine surveillance – many of which were linked to the development of professional discourses and competences. These also provide grounds for division within the state even as they contribute to the enhancement of the modern state's capacities. Most significantly for our purposes, a number of these professional activities were closely dependent upon the territorial organization of society (I discuss this further in Chapter 1).

The Port Elizabeth case study shows the central state to be concerned with problems of national political order and economic accumulation, as well as with the generation of the knowledge and information necessary for state planning and political regulation. Certain general state interests are also present in the local state – especially a concern with governability and political domination. But the territorial specificity of the local state, and the particular history of Port Elizabeth, provide for the emergence of important differences between central and local state interests. The fragmentary nature of the state at both central and local state levels is also well illustrated by the complex of professional discourses and state apparatuses which came into play in the creation of a landscape of control in Port Elizabeth.

In addition, state power is clearly demonstrated to be bound up with spatiality, in terms of the implementation of the location strategy, the exercise of administrative power, and the particularity of building state capacity in the locality of Port Elizabeth. From the 1920s, the local council professed a liberal political disposition, but also had a keen entrepreneurial eye for the economic advancement of the town. This resulted in an ambiguous stance with respect to the location strategy in the 1920s and 1930s. Keenly aware of the value of the location and its administration in exercising control over the African population of the town, the council was nonetheless not eager to expend time or money on its upkeep. Other priorities, such as promoting local economic development and shielding white ratepayers from the costs of their racial privilege, took precedence. The contradiction between the desire for control and a reluctance to bear any financial burden – common to all local authorities in the country – resulted in instances of resistance from the local African population as excessive rents were levied in an effort to reduce the costs of urban order to the state.

A further consequence of the council's interest in promoting local economic development was their effort to ensure that labour market conditions were attractive to international investors. As a result, they were ambivalent about the value of limiting the size of the African population in the town. This persisted as long as the council thought it feasible to control and to govern the African population via the location system rather than through the mechanisms offered by influx control legislation. Such mechanisms would have helped to limit the size of the potentially politically dangerous urban African proletariat – a major concern of the central state. Implementing the location strategy involved the removal of thousands of African people from the declared 'slum' of Korsten to a new extension to the location, McNamee Village. Conflict between the local and central states over the implementation of influx control legislation continued, however, and was resolved in favour of the central state in the 1950s. Nonetheless, council debates of the period confirm that there was in fact a great deal of unity of purpose between the local and central states in the area of 'native policy'. Both wished to ensure domination of the African population, and both saw the location as a central mechanism for achieving this. But self-imposed financial constraints meant that the location could not continue as the sole means of political control without substantial financial investment by the council. In addition, the added surveillance capacities generated by the influx control machinery became pressing in a situation of heightened political conflict. Port Elizabeth's council eventually and cautiously capitulated to the new legislation, although their caution was in the end due more to a healthy fear of the strength of African political organization in the town than to moral disgust or even specific plans for labour markets.

The new urban order which emerged in Port Elizabeth from the 1950s (described in Chapter 7) also depended upon the orderly organization of urban space. The location strategy continued to play a central role in political domination in the town. Thus although several authors have pointed out that the implementation of influx control was bound up with central state strategies for labour distribution and regulation in the context of a particular national accumulation strategy (Greenberg, 1987; Hindson, 1987; Posel, 1990), this study demonstrates that it also had much to do with the need for achieving urban control. The location strategy and influx control were both essential and complementary components of the apartheid urban regime. Indeed, without the effective implementation of the location strategy, influx control would have been impossible even to contemplate.

In some respects the history of segregation in Port Elizabeth replays themes common to studies of other South African towns. A significant addition in this account is the emphasis placed upon the role of space and place in the foundations of racial domination in South Africa's cities. I also hope that I offer a convincing explanation as to why the state was so interested in spatially and racially ordering cities: a state-centred account of urban segregation has been long overdue.

Of course it was not only African people who were segregated, or who experienced the ignominies of being removed from family homes to soulless and inadequate township accommodation. From the 1950s, under the Group Areas Act, Coloured and Indian people too were forced to live in segregated townships which bore strong resemblances to the African locations initiated earlier in the century. While the focus of this study is on the form and functioning of the African location, elsewhere I have reflected upon some parallel local initiatives to house Coloured people in model townships (Robinson, 1993). The particular relations between space, power and identity which were forged in these areas still need to be researched in detail (although see Western, 1981; Scott, 1992; Maharaj, 1993; Lupton, 1994). I have argued that the spaces of Coloured townships, while similar in some ways to African locations, represented a quite different set of relations with the state. In essence, a set of differential citizenships were being carved out in urban space. While African people were largely excluded from formal citizenship as represented not only by their lack of the franchise, but also by the high levels of surveillance and administration of their daily lives, Coloured people were incorporated into a different, less controlled relationship to the state. This relationship was nonetheless articulated through urban arrangements and, for long periods of this century, it was also marked by the absence of the right to vote. The creation of these different citizenship relations was bound up with a complex politics of racial identity and, I suspect, the creation of segregated residential spaces was implicated in the constitution of separate racial identities, even as they were a response to an evolving political discourse about racial difference.

In constructing a notion of differentiated citizenship, however, the gendering of citizens is a topic too often ignored. The current study was not begun with this issue in mind, but the gendered nature of both the conceptions of citizens and the practical arrangements made for their 'proper' incorporation into the city emerge very strongly during the course of the book. If citizens were to be properly controlled, the family was a key modal unit through which this control was to be exercised and proper citizens (or non-citizens, subjects) were to be created. Houses were built (if inadequately) for families, and only families could inhabit them. Women were persistently conceived of as 'housewives' by administrators in a community where women were frequently key breadwinners, even if through informal work rather than formal employment. And women contested the terms of their incorporation into the city through frequent conflicts with the administrators, and through the even more common (and more hidden) tactics of resistance necessary for the pursuit of life in these locations of surveillance. Perhaps most significant, however, and least remarked upon in most studies of the state, is the masculinity of the state apparatus itself (Connell, 1990). That the administrators were all men is perhaps unsurprising. But that images of fatherhood, and the punitive characteristics of this social and familial role, were central to the exercise of power in locations is a direct consequence of this masculine character of the state. As with questions of racialized political identity, the gendered character of apartheid (and post-apartheid) state power requires a lot more research, and the account here can only offer some suggestive guidelines.

If questions of gender threaten to disrupt too easy a reading of the history of South African cities as a dualistic encounter between (ungendered) oppressor and oppressed, writing from a place in the present (where these opposing positions have found an accommodation in a negotiated settlement) profoundly challenges the dualisms through which we have written much of our history. (I discuss this further towards the end of both Chapter 2 and Chapter 7). It also reminds us that many other aspects of our positionality have also been important in shaping not only what we write about, but also how we write it. Race, class and gender are of course not simply axes enabling us to mark off our position on a pre-given multi-dimensional social graph. They are clearly strongly mediated by our particular historical positioning. But the call to 'progressive' academics to engage with the history and geography of the oppressed people in South Africa – to write a history from below – and the persistent interest in the dark workings of the apartheid machine amongst liberal white academics can both be projected against the frequently erased positionality of these shapers of knowledge (Peckham, 1992). I have no doubt that my own interest in the history of the spatiality of apartheid was driven by a complex process of self-identification and disgust, a desire to escape my own implicatedness in the processes I was studying and to align myself with those who were oppressed by and who resisted the forces of domination. This alignment is in itself a significant (re-)positioning within the South African context, and it will not be difficult to see that this text is a product of the period of resistance during which it was conceived. But I also hope that while my own profoundly implicated imprint on this account may be most apparent to some of those reading it, we can learn much about power, space and the city at the same time.

The present also provides us with a place from which to celebrate the transformation of the history I have recorded here: a place where new visions of the city collide with the old; where leaders of the poor and dispossessed negotiate politely with the advocates of the wealthy and privileged; and where a fundamental transformation in the discourse of both is being captured in legal documents. Both sets of apartheid subjects, dominator and dominated, are transparently mediating a new vision, and giving new meaning to the cities they live in. But the history itself still has a part to play in the present. For we cannot easily escape from the entrapment of the already fixed concrete – or less securely, but just as difficult to change, wood, iron, cardboard and mud – form of the city. The socio-spatial dialectic, in the face of the enormity of the powerful effects of space in apartheid cities, seems more of a nightmare of entrapment than the ceaselessly transforming metaphor it started out as. But perhaps the physicality or materiality of much of the society – space literature (Werlen, 1993) weighs too heavily here. For the spatiality of the city – even under apartheid – was far from the simple, dualistic, monotonously imposing grid of power which its pure physical form might impress upon us. The struggle for the city was – and is – not only evident in the ordered landscapes created by ruling elites or in the disorderly transformations wrought in its fabric by those who lived there. It was also played out through resistant imaginings of the meaning and future of the city, through the absence of closure in the identities and actions of even those responsible for domination, and in the practices and tactics of the oppressed themselves, who challenged the dominant order both in the interstices of everyday lives and spaces and in mass public assaults on the very icons and sites of power. Competing discourses about urban meaning, form, government, practice and future emerged through the long history of our cities, si(gh)ting one another in violent confrontations until their meeting during the course of negotiations. I have taken the opportunity to explore the place of apartheid history in shaping the post-apartheid/post-colonial present (and vice versa) in a 'postscript'. Negotiations around a post-apartheid form of urban government enable us to assess the meaning of this denouement to a long and conflictual struggle for the South African city. I do not only wish to consider the possible place(s) of the past in the present form of the city, however; I also wish to suggest how our (dualistic, apartheid-inspired) interpretations of the past are being challenged by the post-apartheid present.

At the same time as disrupting the prevalent dualisms of interpretation which contrasted insistent and single-minded dominators with the coherent resistances of the oppressed, I hope to redress something of an imbalance in the recent historiography of South African politics. For the social history school has left one side of this dualism substantially underexplored. It has been the resistances of the oppressed, both individual and collective, which have attracted most attention, and correctly so, since the celebration and affirmation of the struggles of the poor in the darkest days of oppression were an important and courageous writing of the past. As a result, however, we have explored less effectively the practices of the dominator, those tactics and disciplines which meant that white power endured. And the central role of spatiality here is something which has sometimes been intuited, but never exposed to systematic enquiry. The key task of this book, then, is to explore analytically and substantively the ways in which the racially separated character of social life in the city was connected to the persistence of the racial state. I will argue that this was not only because the state was racist (although being a racial state was of course important) but because the demands of statehood itself, and the rationalities of government, were important motivations in the organization of race and space in the South African context.

Notes

1   The title of a recent innovative exhibition (by Hilton Judin, Deborah Posel and Sue Parnell in the Gertrude Posel Gallery,

University of the Witwatersrand) about the history of spatiality in the South African city.

2   I cannot avoid commenting here on recent accounts which draw far too simple a comparison between racial segregation in Western cities and the form of the apartheid city (for example, S. J. Smith, 1989; Goldberg, 1993). Of course 'white supremacy' or racism in different countries may have found similar uses for the spatial strategies of planning which have regulated and divided cities around the world. But perhaps noting these similarities is to say something about the ubiquity of racism in the world and the universal character of town and city planning. As I trust this book will demonstrate, the creation of the segregated or apartheid city was at least partly the outcome of normalizing Western practices of planning and government, and partly the result of a very particular (and very severe) racial political order. While the former set of courses may well explain some similarities between the South African city and the forms of contemporary Western racial segregation, the latter should caution us to explore the particularities of the spatiality of different racisms and not glibly assert their universal character.

1

States, power and spatiality

The relationship between society and space has come to be a central theme – if not a truism – of contemporary human geography. Somewhat less extensively explored has been the relationship between power and spatiality, especially the strategic use of territory in the exercise of power (although see for example Wolch and Dear, 1989). This chapter will address a number of issues concerning the relationships between power and spatiality, especially in so far as these offer us some insights into the links between spatial organization and state power in South Africa, the focus of this book. The discussion, however, also has some wider ramifications. First of all, for political geographers the analysis of power offers a productive agenda for research within the context of a broader, theoretically informed contemporary human geography (Smith, 1985). This agenda expands the traditional scope of the sub-discipline, which has largely been confined to questions of state and government.[1] At the same time, and more importantly for this book and for my argument here, a focus on power and spatiality enables a non-reductionist, non-functionalist and spatially sensitive analysis of the state. Frustrated with the functionalist and reductionist tendencies in state theory and in the analysis of the South African state in particular (on this see the next chapter), I have followed emerging 'institutional' accounts of the state in order to understand the role of the state in shaping urban space. By linking these analyses to a more general consideration of power relations, the spatiality of state power and of the state itself is brought more clearly into view.

Spatiality, I argue, is a central component of state power. Not only does the territorial expression of the state provide grounds for a conception of the state as an autonomous organization (Mann, 1984), but it also encourages us to consider the relevance of spatiality in the exercise of state power. The last section of this chapter sets out a theory of the state as an autonomous institution. I also outline two aspects of state power which are of interest to me in this study and which are both profoundly spatial in their operations. Although these are by no means the only areas of state power which are so spatialized, they have both been crucial to the growth of modern states and of modern power. One, administrative power – or, in the terminology to be employed here, administrative capacity – captures the internal organization of state apparatuses. The geography of these apparatuses has been an important part of both the growth and the functioning of state power. The regionalization of government departments, problems with communication and hierarchical co-ordination, as well as the local–central tensions which hamper many administrations, are all important here.

The second form of power which has been central to the modern state is what Foucault (1977) has termed 'biopower'. Dreyfus and Rabinow (1982) define 'biopower' as 'the increasing ordering in all realms [of society] under the guise of improving the welfare of the individual and the population. To the genealogist this order reveals itself to be a strategy, with no one directing it and everyone increasingly enmeshed in it, whose only end is the increase of power and order itself.' Gordon (1987: 299) defines 'biopolitics' as when 'the individual and collective life of human populations, or even of the human species, becomes an explicit object of practices of government'. This form of power, operating at the level of society, has come to be at the centre of relations between the modern state and its citizens. While 'biopower' it is most certainly a concern of central policy makers, Foucault (1986) suggests that if we wish to understand both the application and the transformation of biopower, we need to look at the very edges of its operation, at those sites where people – citizens or subjects – are drawn into its activities. Although the study of the normalizing tactics of the modern (Western) state may seem a touch removed from an analysis of the strategies of domination in apartheid South Africa, I will be arguing, especially in Chapters 2 and 3 and at length in the case study of Port Elizabeth, that the South African state drew upon many of the tactics of modern biopower in its administration of African people in cities. Similarly disturbing for our understanding of modernity is the conclusion that the reasons for implementing these strategies had a lot to do with the interests of the South African state in routine governance – the particular province of modern states.

Of course the South African state's interest in governance was strongly mediated by its concern with securing racial domination. And here we are compelled to face some aporias in my proposed conceptual framework. For it could be argued that in following a Foucauldian analysis of power I am evacuating my interpretation of South African society of the moral assessment which it has universally demanded. In addition, in subscribing to an interpretation of the anonymity of modern power, I could conveniently erase the place of individuals in shaping the system of domination in South Africa. The following section, as it seeks to establish the grounds for an analysis of domination which is central to specifying the autonomous powers of the state separately from economic exploitation, will also attempt to develop some (necessarily contingent) pathways through these questions.

A question of power: definitions, differentiations and dilemmas

Despite the many protestations found in the contemporary literature against a negative interpretation of power, against asserting a negative connotation for concepts such as domination and exploitation, and stressing instead the many productive or constitutive characteristics of power (Foucault, 1986: 242; Galbraith, 1984: 7), these concepts continue to be widely used, both popularly and analytically. Indeed, as I will argue below, asserting the role of domination and exploitation in 'producing' – subjects, actions, texts – need not restrict us to a non-critical interpretation of the nature of these social relations. Foucault himself, who is cited above all as emphasizing the productive qualities of power, suggests elsewhere that we can distinguish between three types of struggles against power relations: against forms of domination (ethnic, social, religious), against forms of exploitation 'which separate individuals from what they produce', and against 'that which ties the individual to himself [*sic*] and submits him to others in this way (struggles against subjection, against forms of subjectivity and submission)' (Foucault, 1982: 212). In response to this suggestion, and for reasons which I will elaborate upon below, I wish to work with a threefold differentiation of generalized power relations. Of course this is only one among many possible divisions, but for the purposes of the present discussion, I would propose that we distinguish between dominative, exploitative and emancipatory power relations.

There are two reasons for doing this. The first is to establish that – *contra* Marxists – exploitation is not the primary or only relevant form of power in society. This is essential if we are to argue that the state is an autonomous agent in society. Secondly, I want to work towards an understanding of power which allows moral judgments about the nature of power relations and which can incorporate notions of human agency in the exercise of power. This need not dismiss Foucauldian arguments concerning the often anonymous trajectories of modern power and should also allow for earlier notions about the unintended consequences of human action or the ways in which power operates 'behind the backs' of (and outside the control of) individual agents.

In deriving this threefold distinction of power, a useful place to begin is with the formulations of Max Weber. This is not because of his definition of power itself, which is both one-dimensional (Lukes, 1974) and unambiguously rooted in human intentionality (Clegg, 1989), but rather because he develops some definitions of domination as a special case of power which will be helpful in distinguishing amongst the different forms of power which I have proposed here. His analysis also leads very easily to a definition of the state which does not reduce it to economic logics or social pressures. In the broadest sense, Weber defines power as:

> the probability that an actor will be in a position to carry out his [*sic*] own will despite resistance, regardless of the basis on which this probability rests. (1948: 152)

Clearly this places the human agent firmly at the centre of the exercise of power. By contrast, more recent commentators have suggested that the factors which determine the probability of an agent's success may be beyond the individual's control, and on some accounts may even operate 'behind the backs' of human agents. Weber also implies that as one agent gains power, another must lose power – a zero-sum situation, which is similarly untenable (Lukes, 1974).

Although Weber understood that the exercise of power permeates human life, being found in personal, institutional and social settings, he also insisted that this very broad definition of power be narrowed down to produce what he considered to be a 'sociologically useful' understanding of 'domination'. This term he restricted to use in situations of power in which 'authority' or institutionalized social power, as opposed to collective interests (a 'constellation of interests'), formed the source of power. Domination, then, he ascribed to 'actors where they claim and to a socially relevant degree find obedience to commands given and received as such' (1968: 948).

Weber's interest in deriving such a definition was in order to understand different systems of rule and administration, which for him culminated historically in a rational, hierarchical bureaucratic form of administration. He also thought it important to distinguish amongst the different forms of legitimation of authority – or the different reasons for securing 'obedience', which included a category for non-legitimated obedience acquired through coercion and force. This analysis has been influential in theorizing states and forms of government, who rely upon a wide variety of forms of legitimation, including the ultimate and unique final recourse to the legitimate use of the means of violence.

The distinction between power in general and domination sets the ground for a more general account of power relations which, unlike that in Marxist accounts, is not restricted to economic power or class power. It is in the spirit of such a critique of Marxist accounts of power that Anthony Giddens (1981) developed his distinction between 'authoritative' and 'allocative' power resources, the latter entailing 'command over objects or material phenomena' and the former referring to 'capabilities generating command over persons' (p.47).[2] Authoritative power resources have been especially important in the rise of states and nations (Giddens, 1985). However, as Giddens himself notes, 'this is a wholly analytical distinction' and in historical analysis one must consider not only the 'intersection' (1981: 105) of these two sets of power resources, but also the role of 'symbolic orders' and various 'modes of sanction' (including law) (1981: 47). More generally, Giddens (1981) outlines an interpretative framework in which authoritative and allocative power resources are recursively drawn upon in human relations, which can then take the form of exploitative, dominative or emancipatory relations.

Following Weber and Giddens, then, we can understand power relations to be inherent in many social interactions. Both theorists would probably concur with Foucault's statement that 'relations of power are not in a position of exteriority with respect to other types of relationships (economic processes, knowledge relationships, sexual relationships), but are immanent in the latter' (1980: 94). Of course this does not mean that all of society can be reduced to power relations, as Habermas (1987) points out. In addition, power relations can be differentiated with regard to their sources, objects, purposes and forms of legitimation. However, where Giddens concentrates on power relations as 'reproduced relations of autonomy and dependence in interaction' (1981: 50) – that is, firmly within the domain of conscious and knowledgeable human agents – Foucault (1980: 93) suggests that power's conditions of possibility consist in 'the moving substrate of force relations which, by virtue of their inequality, constantly engender states of power'. One could see a similarity between these 'force relations' and Giddens' 'power resources', but the centrality of human agency and social structure in Giddens' account is most certainly inappropriate in the case of Foucault, who characteristically sidesteps human relations to assert that power 'is the name that one attributes to a complex strategical situation in a particular society' (Foucault, 1980: 93). Whereas Giddens and Foucault are therefore agreed upon the comprehensiveness of power in social life and its multiple forms, Foucault's account of power does not rest upon the conscious actions of Giddens''competent human agents'. But this is to elevate Foucault's programmatic statements about power above his complex histories of specific domains of modern power where the creative transformation of power is articulated by individual thinkers and practitioners.

This question of the responsibility of human agents in shaping power relations is at least partly linked to some serious concerns about the moral consequences of Foucault's account of power. Fraser (1982) finds Foucault guilty of 'normative confusion' for his wide and apparently undiscriminating definition of power. As she comments, 'Granted, there can be no social practices without power, but it does not follow that all forms of power are normatively equivalent, nor that any social practices are as good as any other' (Fraser, 1982: 286). She directs our attention to the Weberian project of distinguishing between power, authority, domination, violence and so on instead of settling for the 'catch-all concept of power'.

Fraser (1982) points to what is arguably one of the most important problems with Foucault's account of power, namely, its apparent lack of a general normative or moral sensitivity. Although, as I pointed out at the beginning of this section, Foucault does address the problem of assessing and categorizing power relations – distinguishing between domination, exploitation and self-subjectification – he does not offer us a universal foundation for such moral judgments. As Dews (1984) argues, without an account of the intrinsic nature and worth of the human subject, determining what is domination or exploitation remains an intractable problem. And perhaps it must remain so. For as Laclau (1994) observes, such a universal foundation can only ever be an 'empty signifier'. Siting something specific in the place of this universal closes and limits the possibilities for critique and resistance, attempting to universalize what can only ever be particular. Thus while we can – and in Laclau's view, should – persistently struggle against that which dominates and exploits (as Foucault has suggested), to impose a universal vision of what should replace this or against which to test it is to pre-empt historical actions and to run the risk of reimposing a new form of domination through this prescription.

These debates are somewhat outside the compass of the present study (although they can by no means be side-stepped altogether), but what they point us to is the possibility of identifying and resisting domination and exploitation – without necessarily demanding an identifiable universal foundation on which to ground that resistance (as Fraser, 1982; Dews, 1984; and Habermas, 1987 seem to be demanding). Concretely, and in terms of the present case study, a specific form of domination, such as apartheid, can be identified, resisted and overthrown, without there being a universal moral basis for this and every other political action. Thus while I would like to pursue Giddens' distinction between the 'liberating and productive' and the 'repressive and destructive' aspects of power, and to attempt to distinguish dominative from exploitative power relations, I mean to give these terms a particular, historical and (contestable) political meaning, since, as I have suggested, we cannot rely upon the determination of a universal foundation for moral or political judgment.

Firstly, exploitation. There are certainly some merits within the context of Marxist theory for retaining the technical definition of exploitation as the extraction of surplus value by capital from the overall production of value by labour, who retain only a socially determined exchange value for their productive efforts. The merits lie in pointing most clearly to at least one of the otherwise hidden sources of capitalism's inequities. But contemporary theorists have developed an expanded, although still materially oriented, conception of exploitation. Amongst these theorists John Roemer (1988) has focused upon the moral issues entailed in the usually unequal distribution of the economic products of society. He suggests that some unequal economic outcomes cannot be considered to be morally repugnant and are thus not exploitative, such as those which result from inherent variations amongst people in terms of personality characteristics, inclinations and abilities. But he suggests that exploitation does exist if 'in a given economy some agents must work more time than is socially necessary (longer than the socially necessary labour time) to earn their consumption bundles and others work less time than is socially necessary to earn their bundles' (1988: 20). Such morally unacceptable economic distributions are based upon systemically unequal distributions of power (thus, 'structurally asymmetrical power resources' of various kinds). Social relations where there is a direct interaction between the economic advantages of some and the economic disadvantages of others could therefore be considered to entail exploitation. In no sense can this situation be divorced from very complex 'strategic constellations' or power resources (involving property rights, law, gender, race, knowledge), but the direct or indirect (Barbalet, 1988: 544) human relationship involving exploitative power and drawing upon a multitude of power resources can be at least loosely identified. And retaining the broadly economic meaning of the term 'exploitation', as first employed within Marxist theory, is I think appropriate (contrary to Miller et al., 1989: 4ff).

By contrast, the term 'domination', or dominative power (Cocks, 1989), can be used in order to describe situations in which human power relations entail predominantly control, command or authority in relation to other human beings, whether associated with coercion, consensus, routine or hegemony. This could be described very generally, following Foucault (1982: 224), as 'the government of men (and women) by one another'. This is a broad conception, but if we wish to capture the many forms of contemporary and historical dominative relations and the many resources employed in securing domination as defined, this breadth is necessary. Cocks helpfully distinguishes between 'two very different forms (of power) – one legal–political and based at root on physical coercion, one moral–cultural and based on habituation and spontaneous consent' (Cocks, 1989: 42). These two forms of power are by no means entirely separate from one another – as the case study in this book also illustrates – for cultural practices and moral systems of signification are bound up with all aspects of social life, including political institutions and physical violence.

Indeed, what we have called dominative and exploitative power relations are also entwined with one another. Dominative power relations certainly exist within the context of exploitation, as the significance of disciplinary power in the workplace illustrates (O'Neill, 1986). But for our purposes it is important to note that domination also exists independently of economic motivations.

The third category of emancipatory power is intended to capture those aspects of power relations which are productive of individual and collective capacity and human 'good' and those aspects of exploitative and dominative power relations which, despite other outcomes, also secure some helpful effects. It has been a primary assertion of contemporary theorists of power that the traditional negative interpretation of power relations fails to understand the productive nature of power and, in Foucault's words, 'neglect[s]... its productive effectiveness, its strategic resourcefulness, its positivity' (1980: 86). I would argue that this productive quality is a general aspect of most forms of power, and that what I am proposing in making this distinction is something rather different. What Mann (1993) calls 'collective power' captures something of the socially useful powers I would include here – those powers resulting from the growth of infrastructural powers and capacities in society generally. But Arendt's (1986) notion of the empowerment of rulers by the people would also be relevant, as would attempts to improve human capacities for self-direction, and the powers which permit the liberation of human potential from domination[3].

Spatiality and social power

> Space is fundamental in any exercise of power. (Foucault, 1984: 252)

If proponents of contemporary human geography are to be believed, the profound changes in western society in the last two decades have enticed social theorists to consider anew the role of space in shaping both social processes and our understandings of the social world (Dear, 1988; Gregory, 1989; Soja, 1989). But while the spatiality of the 'postmodern' West may be the inspiration for such a retheorizing (Jameson, 1984; Harvey, 1989), the implications of a spatialized social theory stretch far beyond these concerns, both historically and geographically. And outside the economic literature detailing the restructuring of the landscape of production, modern theory's interest in space has often turned out to be more metaphorical than the materialist focus of human geography might have suggested (Werlen, 1993; Pratt, 1993).

Although Foucault's questioners from *Heredote* commented on his 'profuse use of spatial metaphors – position, displacement, site, field; sometimes geographical metaphors even – territory, domain, soil, horizon, archipelago, geopolitics, region, landscape' (in Gordon, 1980: 68), Foucault explains spatial distributions and the division and arrangement of space in much more than a purely metaphorical sense. Spatial strategies are seen to operate as key mechanisms for the exercise of power in modern society. He observes this in the cases of prisons, asylums and hospitals, and his concern with the space of the body and its associated disciplining and subjectifying technologies indicates a micro-sensitivity to spatial order. Even when he claims that there are 'absolutely no architectural dimensions' to issues of sexuality, he suggests the importance of a sensitivity to places of social encounter and the significance of public and private locations for sexual relations, in the form, for example, of public baths (Foucault, 1984: 251); and much more significantly for feminist theorists of power, he has identified the body as the primary site for the exercise of modern power (see for example Butler, 1990).

The production of space and place is not always associated with strategies of power, of course, although general processes such as the circulation of capital or investment in productive, reproductive and speculative aspects of the built environment produce spaces and places which mediate and facilitate power relations, especially those of exploitation (Harvey, 1985). But Robert Sack has summarized the strategic use of space in the concept of 'territoriality' which he defines as 'the attempt by an individual or group (x) to influence, affect, or control objects, people and relationships (y) by delimiting and asserting control over geographic area. This area is the territory' (1983: 56). He explores the way in which territory can be delimited, sub-divided, reorganized and so forth in order to achieve a multitude of human ambitions. Clearly the enforcement of forms of territoriality relies upon various power resources, but within this context it also constitutes a source of power – even though in itself it is inseparable from these general social power sources (Soja, 1971). Sack's identification of this strategic usefulness of spatial delimitations is helpful, but its value within the context of explaining social power (and all forms of social action) depends upon reintegrating this aspect of spatiality into appropriate social and political concepts. For 'territoriality' cannot be understood outside particular social and political relations. In the following section of this chapter, the strategic use of territory will be shown to be an important element of the growth of state power as well as of the various social powers which have been drawn into the constitution of the modern state. And in Chapters 2 and 3, the strategic use of territorial delimitation in the production of segregated areas for African people in South African cities will be explored.

Within the context of his methodological focus upon the 'how' of power, Foucault comments that 'space is fundamental in any exercise of power' (1984: 252). This is most obviously true when strategies entailing territoriality are realized in space. Thus, Bentham's Panopticon, aside from offering a metaphor and exemplar of a more generalized, internal and anonymous form of power (Dreyfus and Rabinow, 1982: 192), was itself a system of spatial organization (architecture) which was intrinsically bound up with the exercise of power. Observation – the 'gaze' – or at least the possibility of being observed, and the subsequent individual internalization of the disciplinary ethos, constituted a mode of power in both disciplinary and medical contexts (Foucault, 1977; 1980) and was 'architecturally congealed in the Panopticon sketched out by Bentham' (Habermas, 1987: 245). Both a disciplinary and a moral component to the exercise of power in the Panopticon can therefore be distinguished – constant observation inviting moral self-reflection and self-control (Driver, 1985c).

The physical division of space which assists authorities in the processes of 'fixing, dividing, recording' (Foucault, 1977: 304) has taken a variety of forms apart from the archetypical Panopticon with its observer tower and always potentially visible individual cells. Many institutions designed to effect power relations, such as hospitals, asylums and orphanages, have an intentional internal geography which is seen to be helpful to the authorities (Driver, 1987; Philo, 1988; Prior, 1988). At an urban scale, the opening up of places – homes and public spaces – to the gaze of power (Mitchell, 1988) and to the possible physical presence of the authorities suggests a technology of power operating at the level of the general population rather than specific 'deviant' individuals (Rabinow, 1989). Such an argument sits well with the notion of the Panopticon as a model of a form of power deployed throughout modern society (Dreyfus and Rabinow, 1982: 192–3). And it is not surprising that many technologies of social power have been accumulated by the state in its efforts to govern society. Before exploring this process and particularly the ways in which the organization of space has been involved in the growth of state power, the following section establishes a framework for a non-reductionist account of the state. For to assert that state power and actions are simply derivative of economic logics or pressures from social agents would be to miss the central argument of this book: that the South African state became involved in the social and spatial regulation of African people's lives in cities for reasons of statehood or governance, and not simply in response to some underlying economic logic or racist pressures.

State power and territory

Turning now to consider the relationships between the state and spatiality, as a specific case of the broader embeddedness of power relations in space, it is the relationship between state power and territory, or territoriality, which is of particular significance. Not only is the basic definition of the state linked to its territorially based claims to sovereignty, but the construction and exercise of state power take place within and across this territory, giving geography a heightened significance in most of the state's activities. It is Michael Mann (1986) who has given at least the first of these the most attention. He does so in a way which fits neatly into the distinction – borrowed from Giddens (1981) – between power relations and power resources and also bears out the significance of geography to both.

Mann (1986; 1993) suggests that there are four sources of social power – ideological, economic, military and political power – which he argues give rise to historically varying power organizations. These organizations are 'functionally promiscuous' (1986: 17) and usually draw upon more than one power source. The first two power sources (ideological and economic) operate usually as forms of 'diffused' power which, he argues, 'spread in a more spontaneous, unconscious, decentred way throughout a population, resulting in similar social practices that embody power relations but are not explicitly commanded' (1986: 8). He contrasts these with military and political power, which operate authoritatively and comprise 'definite commands and conscious obedience' (1986: 8) and which have a specific and contained territorial expression.

Unfortunately Mann insists that what he terms 'political' power should be firmly linked to the state as an organization. In his view this form of power is confined to the 'centre': as he writes, 'political power is located in that centre and exercised outward. Political power is necessarily centralized and territorial, and in these respects differs from other power sources' (1986: 27). This definition relies upon the archetypical organizational form of political power embodied in the modern Western state and its geographical specificity. Following Mann's own arguments about the functional promiscuity of organizations, hierarchical and spatially confined non-violent authoritative power is clearly not restricted to states – although this has proved to be an important and distinctive feature of modern states. But to name this as 'political' power could serve to reinforce a definition of politics as limited to the state. Rather, we could suggest that political power occurs throughout society and is drawn upon by economic organizations such as industries, corporations and banks, by ideological organizations, especially churches, as well as by military organizations. It is clear that the peculiar strength of the modern state is its confinement of this political power within very clear and unique boundaries within which internationally accorded sovereign rights may be exercised. But, following Mann's own argument, we must separate out the power resources from the state as a power organization – especially since not all states successfully embody the form of power that Mann describes in this context.[4] We might thus rename these 'administrative power' resources,[5] which are drawn upon to create authoritative domination in a variety of circumstances.

The second caution with respect to Mann's schema of power resources concerns his methodological focus upon organizations. While this has some attraction for cutting through persistent theoretical debates concerning the relations between economy, society and politics, his relative neglect of the domain of individual human strategies[6] in favour of a focus upon 'emergent organizational power sources' (1986: 6) leaves unexplored those forms of power which do not attain any clear organizational focus. This is particularly true of ideological power, but might also be pertinent to some forms of non-organizational resistance politics (Scott, 1985) or violence (Bourdieu, 1977). Mann (1986: 22–3) considers three sociological phenomena – meaning, norms and aesthetic/ritual practices – to form the domain of ideological power. He argues that

> where meaning, norms and aesthetic and ritual practices are monopolised by a distinctive group, it may possess considerable extensive and intensive power. It can exploit its functionality and build distributive on top of collective power. (1986: 23)

Embodied in institutions such as religious bodies, or evident as a form of 'morale' for governing social groups, this conceptualization of ideological power pays scant attention to the way in which cultural practices create forms of domination below the level of organizations or without any conscious collective direction. Here work in the area of sexual politics (see Cocks, 1989; Butler, 1990) is most pertinent, as individual men and women re-create and transform the gender order associated with certain cultural practices but which have no organizational embodiment and no co-ordinating strategist (Foucault, 1980: 95).

Although Mann (1986: 30) insists that societies – and therefore our theories – are 'messy', and shows that he is alert to the complexity of human societies, these comments indicate that in at least some situations Mann's account could be even more 'messy' (and no doubt he would agree with this). Although one could make similar comments with regard to his theory of the state and state power (and I will return to this point below), Mann (1984) has made a distinctive and helpful contribution to the long-standing theoretical problem of specifying the autonomous interests of the state. And it is here that the question of territory is crucial.

The twin weaknesses of Marxist theories of the state have been widely cited as economic reductionism and functionalism, which together undermine an effective account of state autonomy (Skocpol, 1979; 1985; Lovering, 1987). But Marxist scholarship has nonetheless considerably advanced our understanding of the relationships between states and the economy, and between states and certain class aspects of society (for example, Miliband, 1969; Habermas, 1976; Esping-Andersen et al., 1976). In addition, Marxist accounts, in conceding a degree of relative autonomy to the state have helped to set out some of the parameters for a non-reductionist state theory. An important manoeuvre here has been to focus upon the state as an organization. Thus, for Poulantzas (1978), the inscription of class struggles within the 'institutional materiality' of the state (a crystallisation of the 'relations of production and social division of labour') describes the specific nature of the state's constitutive role in economic and other social relations. But Skocpol considers this account to rest too much upon the economy and prefers to emphasize the organizational network of the state *per se* in her explanations:

> the state properly conceived is no mere arena in which socio-economic struggles are fought out. It is, rather, a set of administrative, policing, and military organisations headed, and more or less well co-ordinated by, an executive authority. (1979: 29)

Eschewing the reductionism of Poulantzas' argument, but pursuing his concern with the organizational materiality of the modern state and its centralized, hierarchical form, Mann (1984) offers an account of state autonomy which places territory at the heart of state power. He also implies that territorial arrangements will be of crucial significance to the operation of state power. He observes that within an international system of states, individual states have come to be accorded sovereign rights within their defined territory: no other body can lay claim to such rights (Held, 1989: Chapter 8). This sovereignty is centralized in the highest executive authority within the state and is exercisable throughout the territory. In addition, within the state area, the state is seen to confront various classes and social groups with differing spatial extents and usually a more diffuse power organization than that available to the state. The state, in effect, he argues, stands in a Bonapartist fashion above 'warring class factions' and is also in this sense able to establish an autonomous presence, distinct from other social groupings. Mann (1984) argues, then, that it is precisely because the state is an arena – a place, the state area – that it is autonomous, distinct from all other social actors and organizations. The unique, centralized form of state authority and organization across a particular territory is the power resource distinctively available to the modern state, whose sovereignty is externally guaranteed by the international system of states.

If this account adequately delineates the organizational and territorial bases of state autonomy, it should be possible to identify some of the 'interests' of states which are independent of and perhaps different from those of other social actors. Central state interests have been said to derive from the 'national interest' ideology of state managers (Miliband, 1983) and their self-interest in maximizing national prestige, including economic and military strength, in their position as a sovereign power within an international system of sovereign states (Block, 1981). The state's interest in promoting capital accumulation can also be derived from its dependence upon taxation revenue for finances (Offe and Ronge, 1975; Held, 1989: Chapter 2). Without finances the state cannot pursue its internal strategies and ambitions, and neither can it support international policies and activities. This reverses the line of dependence stressed in most Marxist accounts where the economy determines, in a variety of ways, state policies and practices. Here, for its own reasons of 'institutional self-interest', the state will protect and advance the economy in particular ways (Block, 1977)[7].

Alongside finances, the ability to govern and a measure of administrative capacity are essential for states to realize their interests (Moulakis, 1986: 3). While seemingly rudimentary, and often overlooked by state theorists, I would suggest that such motivations frequently constitute a powerful autonomous incentive for state action. They form an important part of the reasons for South African state intervention in cities during the course of this century. Accumulation of knowledge, surveillance capacities and the ability to carry out policy choices (the existence and mobilization of an apparatus) provide a substratum of state interests which, in some situations, can be very significant (see Croock, 1989 for an informative example from the African context). In other situations, where state power has been very effectively secured, as in modern Western democracies (Giddens, 1985), such skeletal motivations for developing state capacities are perhaps less easily observable.

In his later years, Foucault (1979) directed his attention towards what he termed 'governmentality' (Gordon, 1987), by which he meant to capture the specific practices of state managers and statecraft. Over time state managers developed a set of practices and ideas, which Foucault (1979) has linked to a form of power he has designated as 'pastoral' – harking back to Church practices and even to Jewish theories of kingship (1981). He sees in the anti-Machiavellian literature of some three centuries the search for a 'kind of rationality which was intrinsic to the art of government' (1979: 7) rather than bound up with the person and pleasures of the Prince. Many of the resultant practices were associated with activities such as information collection and storage, taxation, surveillance and economic management (Giddens, 1985) which have become central to the power of modern states (Gordon et al., 1992) . Thus a genealogy of 'statecraft' or 'governmentality' provides one (historical) approach to identifying some of the *sui generis* or autonomous interests of the state.

Securing these interests has entailed a process of the historical accrual of many different powers to the state and their consolidation into state apparatuses (Clark and Dear, 1984). This has been a geographically variable process, with state sovereignty often very weakly implemented, especially in many Third World countries (Jackson and Rosberg, 1982; Azarya and Chazan, 1987; Heper, 1987). But, according to Mann (1984), the organizational form of the state plays an important part in determining its autonomous power and as a result is both a basis for and an outcome of independent state interests. It is in this respect that the geography of administrative capacity takes on a renewed significance in the analysis of states. Such an emphasis also has the potential to undermine a unitary interpretation of the state and state interests, such as that which Mann's emphasis on the centralizing nature of state power would encourage. The different organizations or apparatuses within the state embody a wide variety of orientations, rationalities and ideologies, which need not be in step with those of the central authority. On this, Poulantzas (1978) and Skocpol (1985:15) agree, and Poulantzas especially stresses the conflict-ridden nature of the state, describing state policy as a set of 'conjunctural, conflictual and compensatory measures responding to the problems of the now' (1978: 134). Such fragmentation occurs both territorially in terms of the areal division of state power, and within state apparatuses at all levels as different professional, departmental, substantive or even class interests are embodied in different hierarchies. The former (areal divisions) concern the administrative geography of the state including divisions between central, regional and local levels of the state. Contra Duncan et al. (1988), then, these differences within the state are not only the consequence of particular social and economic geographies; they are also a consequence of administrative dynamics within the state, as well as the different territorial attachments of various tiers of the state (something of these dynamics will emerge during the course of the case study below).

Similarly important, and much less discussed, is the contribution of the multiple strategies associated with 'biopower' to the emergence of a variety of (frequently conflicting) state apparatuses. Contrary to Mann's (1984; 1986) emphasis upon the central role of territory in undergirding the autonomy of the state, Foucault's writings on the state direct us away from a concern with territory to a focus upon population. The modern state, he argues, is 'no longer defined essentially in terms of its territoriality, of its surface area, but in terms of the mass of its population with its volume and density' (1979: 21). His claims do not require that we reject Mann's arguments as outlined above, but they do point us towards a distinctive and very important set of practices which are bound up with state power and which, in a different sense, have their own territoriality.

Foucault coins the term 'bio-power' to refer to the 'multifarious strategies concerned with the subjugation of bodies and the control of populations' (Foucault, 1980: 140). His own historical work dwelt upon several 'disciplines' or techniques of power – such as medical knowledge, law and punishment, treatment of the mentally ill – which, he observed 'have come more and more under state control...[they] have been progressively governmentalized, that is to say, elaborated, rationalized and centralized in the form of, or under the auspices of, state institutions' (1982: 224). As Gordon (1987: 296) comments, Foucault's work concerned with government 'designates a continuity between micro- and macro- levels of political analysis' and postulates a direct relationship between government and a 'micro-physics' of power at the individual level.

Among these disciplines, the prison system and the Benthamite Panopticon have been most associated with the development of the modern state. The replacement of sovereign punishment by the modern practices of routine (self-)discipline epitomizes the creation of the modern Western state, where the emphasis of power has come to be in the domain of the techniques and strategies for producing disciplined and 'docile' bodies rather than in the realm of law and sovereignty. Foucault, then, sees the modern state as being closely intertwined with the population in its territory, with individuals who have been 'shaped in a new form and submitted to a new set of very specific processes' (1982: 213). This contemporary process of 'subjectification', which Foucault has explored in both disciplinary and sexual/moral dimensions, was initiated into the realm of statecraft, he argues, during the course of the eighteenth century when the Western state confronted a growing population, which it sought to harness to the production of wealth and security.

The study of South Africa presented below embarks upon an attempt to suggest how, in this particular place and historical period, strategies associated with biopower were co-ordinated by the state to secure the domination of African people. However, the particular strategies to be explored here do not fall easily into the domains of disciplinary power or self-subjectification. Rather, they are better captured by Foucault's discussion of the 'carceral city' (1977: 307). This city – the product of an early nineteenth century author's imaginings – consists of a series of 'carceral' institutions and mechanisms which work individually and in concert to 'exercise a power of normalisation', producing the 'disciplinary individual' (1977: 308). A transformation of this image to include modes of disciplinary power which also have the spatial organization of groups of individuals as their target is necessary if we are to begin to 'translate' Foucault's intentions to a broader urban and regional scale. In his criticism of Foucault for over-extending the Panopticon model beyond the prison – to the factory, the workplace and elsewhere – Giddens (1985: 185–6) reminds us that many different forms of power have a spatiality intrinsic to their deployment and that not all of these employ the twin aspects of the Panopticon model of power, being the discipline of the individual body and the exercise of surveillance. It is this latter aspect of Panoptic power which is most easily observed in the urban arena and which has been of value to the state in its broader construction of administrative power through the accumulation of knowledge.

Some colonial states, for example, in their bald efforts to control subject populations, embarked upon programmes to render living areas – previously hidden by the chaotic organization of traditional houses – open to the 'gaze' of the government (Mitchell, 1988; Thomas, 1990). And, as Rabinow (1989b) demonstrates for the French case, the history of urban planning in both the centre and the metropole is comprehensively bound up with the problematic of social regulation and the tasks of government surveillance, even as planning itself came to be an important rationality within the state apparatuses. Along with the legal system, then, planning, medicine, social welfare and many other 'professions' have been included within the apparatus of the modern state, and the many territorial strategies associated with these formalized 'disciplines' or rationalities have been incorporated in the scope of the state.

These observations concerning biopower have some important implications for our understanding of the state. The various state apparatuses with which these forms of power have been associated constitute potentially multiple bases of power within the state and lead to competing interests, strategies and ideologies (Jessop, 1983; 1985; 1990). These varying logics and rationalities within the state can have significant independent influences upon policy outcomes (Shannon, 1982) and – as frequently occurs in the case of military apparatuses and military coups – these separate rationalities can fundamentally affect the entire political terrain (Stepan, 1979). The interests of the centre, then, are frequently counterposed to this fragmentation of rationalities which have come to be embodied in the state – although administrative obstacles to central state co-ordination have many sources and are not only due to the differential historical and professional origins of techniques of power with which some apparatuses are associated.

An adequate account of the state should therefore take cognizance of the dynamics of both centralization (co-ordination of state activities over its territory) and fragmentation (the diversity of apparatuses which make this co-ordination ever problematic). What Mann (1993: 53) calls the 'cock-up foul-up' theory of the state (stressing fragmentation and a lack of organizational coherence) is belied by the measure of co-ordination and significance which the modern state has historically achieved. In the South African case, the tension between these two accounts of the state is readily apparent. Was apartheid a grand plan, implemented by a large and well co-ordinated repressive state bureaucracy? Or was it a haphazard, conflict-ridden and historically contingent outcome of a disorganized state? The answer I would prefer involves an ongoing tension between the two. This means that we need to conceptualize the central state as a (more or less effective) co-ordinating institution in particular societies and at the same time to be sensitive to competing and fragmenting tendencies within the institutional apparatus. The historically specific form of any given state is also going to be shaped by the crystallization of a variety of social and political processes in the state (Mann, 1993). Thus while my account of the location strategy as a normalizing spatial technology implemented by the state suggests that it embodied a complex set of governmental ambitions associated with ordering the residential and political domains of African people in cities and that it was certainly an outcome of the complex internal dynamics of state power, it was of course also a product of a historically specific state intent upon securing and protecting racial domination. The next chapter presents an analysis of the South African state which enables a more grounded account of the emergence of this particular technique of power.

Notes

1   Far from closing off politics around a concern with government, both Leftwich (1983) and Held (1989) have an expansive definition of politics, asserting its persistent centrality to human existence

and claiming that 'It is found in all societies, institutions and groups, and is hence much wider and more important than its usual identification with "government" and associated activities' (Leftwich, 1983: 26).

2   Echoed in Foucault's use of the term the 'accumulation of men'.

3   Of course, these concepts fall prey to the demand for universal concepts of human nature – and need to be interpreted politically within particular conjunctures, and also themselves subjected to criticism, especially if institutionalized, as strategies for liberation can quickly become incorporated within new regimes of domination, even those based upon notions of self-empowerment.

4   Especially what Jackson and Rosberg (1982) identify amongst African states as a form of juridical rather than empirical statehood. The state as power organization is replaced by a notional state gaining international stature through its recognition as sovereign but being unable to effectively exercise that sovereignty within its designated territory.

5   Graham Smith suggested this helpful distinction to me.

6   He does comment though that, underneath relatively stable social networks, 'human beings are tunnelling ahead to achieve their goals, forming new networks, extending old ones, and emerging most clearly into our view with rival configurations of one or more of the principal power networks' (Mann, 1986: 16). This would suggest that we do need to move beyond the organizational forms of power in order to understand some important social phenomena.

7   Unfortunately, in many accounts the questions of 'independence' and 'autonomy' have become confused (see especially Skocpol, 1985: 9; Stepan, 1979; Evans et al., 1985). For states, as with all social organizations, will always exhibit changing dependencies upon various social, economic and political processes (Stepan, 1985), or as Skocpol (1985: 14) somewhat confusingly puts it, ' "state autonomy" is not a fixed structural feature of any government system. It can come and go'. But this does not negate the existence of states as autonomous entities in societies, with logics, interests and configurations resulting from their unique organizational presence. The task, then, is twofold: to establish the bases of state autonomy and associated potential state interests and dynamics, as well as to establish the nature of the dependencies which will determine or influence many state actions.

2

The location strategy: the geography of state power and racial domination in South Africa

The spatiality of South African cities is apparent to even the most casual observer. Urban racial segregation has created starkly divided landscapes with sprawling, infrastructurally poor black townships severed from the high-rise commercial city centre and salubrious suburban areas. It is my argument here that these different places 'mattered' not simply as contrasting contexts for social life but because, in themselves, they constituted a making of state power. In contrast to other accounts of urban segregation which have stressed the importance of racism or economic interest in explaining this phenomenon, I wish to understand why the state itself chose to intervene in the urban arena in this way. This habit of reducing state actions to economic or other social processes has been as characteristic of studies of the South African state as it has of accounts of states elsewhere. Before exploring some of the detailed history of the segregated African location, then, I offer a critique of the literature concerned with the South African state, and propose a preliminary specification of the interests which have characterized this particular state over the years.

Autonomy and dependence in the analysis of the South African state

Despite the importance of both geography and the state in the South African context, the nature of the relationship between the two constitutes an important 'blind spot' in South African studies. Both the geographic foundations of state power and the autonomous interests of the state have been neglected, as the following review of recent accounts of the state in South Africa indicates. Although there has been a revival of interest in the independent dynamics of the South African state, not unconnected with its recent contemporary political significance, it will be argued that a strong theoretical grounding for such a state-centred approach has yet to be developed. Thus we need to establish, within the framework of power and spatiality outlined in the first chapter, the particular historical interests of the South African apartheid state.

Amongst those who have explored the nature of the South African state it has been the relationship between the state and the economy which has attracted by far the most theoretical attention. As Wolpe (1988: 39) observes, this 'inherent economism' has resulted in a 'paradoxical neglect of the state structures and the political terrain in work concerned with the state'. This generated an exclusive preoccupation with the intervention of the state in the economy and has produced what Dubow (1986a) terms a 'capital-state centric' view of South African history. Although there have been recent efforts to move beyond this limited focus of analysis (notably Yudelman, 1983; Dubow, 1986a,b; Posel, 1987; Greenberg, 1988; James, 1990; Swilling, 1990), a coherent theoretical specification of the state, its autonomy, interests and relations with citizens and subjects has not yet been offered. In fact, most analyses continue to address primarily the state-economy relationship and have not theoretically explored the specifically political content of the state's projects.

The earliest attempts by Marxist writers to describe the South African state employed an unambiguously reductionist, instrumentalist and functionalist view of the state (Legassick, 1974; Wolpe, 1974). From their perspective, the state's policies and ideologies unproblematically met the 'needs' of capital for cheap labour power either in the form of the reserves policy, migrant labour and influx control or through job colour bars and the suppression of working-class organization (Lacey, 1982; Levy, 1982). Later contributions made use of the early Poulantzian (Jessop, 1985) concepts of hegemony and class fractions (Poulantzas, 1973) in an attempt to periodize the South African state's interventions on behalf of different fractions of capital. The interests of agricultural, mining and manufacturing capital were considered to be competing for hegemony within a power bloc – a hegemony which, once achieved, was seen to be translated quite unproblematically into state policies and practices (Davies et al., 1976). More specifically, these writers identified a shift in this intra-power-bloc hegemony from imperial (mining) to national (agriculture and manufacturing) capital around 1924. This was exemplified by the succession of the Pact government to power.

Several contributions have since been made to a debate over the details and problems of this periodization and the 'fractions of capital' approach. These have criticized, amongst other things, the absence of both working-class struggle (Innes and Plaut, 1978) and the dynamics of capital accumulation (Clarke, 1978) from earlier analyses. Bozzoli (1978), for example, suggested that the project of forging a class hegemony (rather than a fraction-of-class hegemony) was undertaken by the fraction of capital most closely resembling the objective interests of capital in general at the time. But – and although these contributions did problematize the nature of capital's interests and the process whereby hegemony was achieved – their assumption that the state necessarily operated in the interests of capital has been shown to be both theoretically and historically unfounded. More recently, authors have cast doubt on the persistent economic functionality of apartheid policies (Lipton, 1986; Gelb, 1987) and have also turned their attention to a major absence in the neo-Poulantzian analysis: namely, the neglect of state forms (Wolpe, 1988) or of what the later Poulantzas (1978) termed the 'institutional materiality' of the state.

Many recent accounts have accorded the state an active role in economic and political developments. Thus both the formulation of legislation and the implementation of policies are seen to be influenced by dynamics internal to the state. Dubow (1986b), for example, discusses the impact of administrative organization and administrative ideology upon 'native' policy in the 1920s and 1930s. Personal and bureaucratic ambitions, the status and relative capacities of various administrative departments, as well as the concrete administrative problems confronted by, in this case, the Native Affairs Department, all influenced the timing and content of legislation. More significantly, the implementation of various laws concerning 'native affairs' (such as the 1927 Native Laws Amendment Act) was shaped by the state personnel and administrative organizations concerned. It is this disjuncture between political and legislative intent and administrative practice which Posel (1987) emphasizes in her study of urbanization policy during the 1950s and 1960s. She argues that during the 1950s a programme of 'practical apartheid' was implemented in place of the grand 'territorial segregation' promised in the National Party's 1948 electoral programme. This reflected the ideas and concerns of the native administration apparatus, including the local managers of urban 'native locations'. Thus, in place of the Stallardist doctrine, whereby no African people would be allowed in urban areas except to fulfil labour requirements, residence rights (provided for under Section 10 of the 1945 Natives (Urban Areas) Act) were conferred on those who had lived or worked in urban areas for long periods of time. However, the contradictions generated by this 'practical' programme mounted during the 1950s. Administrative failure at the local level, together with the growing strength of the central Native Affairs Department, and heightened resistance (Sharpeville and Cato

Manor), led to the state initiating a 'second phase' of apartheid in the 1960s. This was more centralized, more repressive and associated with Bantustan development. It also partially undermined the limited residence rights which urbanized African people had secured in the previous phase. Conflicts within the state made this process of change historically contingent and its implementation depended crucially upon increased state capacity (see Chapters 6 and 7 for details in the context of Port Elizabeth).

In contrast to earlier theorists, Evans (1986: 15) stressed the important role which the growth in central state apparatuses played in enabling the implementation of apartheid policies. And yet, despite his protestations to the contrary, he portrays the state as being 'operated upon'. His 'weak version' of state-centred theory considers state managers to be 'bounded by the limits placed by the imperatives of capital accumulation' (1986: 14) and much of his argument rests upon too simplistic a linkage between state actions and economic growth (he often stresses the direct impact upon the state of particular economic interests). Dubow (1986a) and Posel (1987: 410) similarly, but more subtly, postulate that in the long term the state acts to promote the survival of capitalism as a system. Why this should result from complex and contradictory historical processes is not made clear (cf. Jessop, 1985: 143), although Posel (1987) agrees, following Offe, that the state's 'institutional self-interest' in supporting capital accumulation is an important factor here.

The question of the political and autonomous interests of the state, then, remains to be addressed by South African scholars. Wolpe (1988) discusses at length the effects which particular state forms and policies have had in structuring political struggle (both mass political organizations and workers' struggles), and thus he makes a significant contribution to a more clearly political analysis. Yet he does not deal with the internal dynamics of the state and neither does he discuss the foundations of its autonomy and dependencies. In this regard, Yudelman (1983) employs Habermas' (1976) characterization of the state's actions as falling into the two spheres of legitimation and accumulation. These, he claims, can specify the motivations of what he takes to be a strongly autonomous state. But clearly in the South African context, the concept of legitimacy is somewhat problematic (Adam and Moodley, 1986; Greenberg, 1987). Yudelman (1983) very inappropriately applies his analysis of the state's hegemonic and nation-building efforts with respect to the white working class (especially mine-workers) during the 1920s to an interpretation of reform initiatives directed at African people during the 1980s. But, as Greenberg (1988: 8) comments, 'for the excluded groups in South Africa, compliance represent[ed] little more than a dulled necessity, without trace of supportive sentiments'.[1] Rather than attempting to preserve legitimacy, then, in South Africa the state's 'balancing act' was to defend white supremacy and secure the domination of African people at the same time as ensuring political support amongst the white population (especially amongst the power bloc and state officials). The search for external, international legitimacy for reform efforts has also been important, as has the pursuit of an at least adequate (if frequently poorly informed: see Moll, 1990) accumulation strategy.

But in seeking to achieve these ends, the state encompassed a variety of competing 'hegemonic projects' and 'accumulation strategies' (Jessop, 1983; Evans, 1986; Morris and Padayachee, 1990). Inter-departmental conflict (Dubow, 1986b), contested local – central relations and different visionary formulations (Lazar, 1986) all fragmented the state's initiatives. Practical problems of implementation, inadequate state capacity, disjunctures between central and local administrative ideologies and unintended consequences of state action (Greenberg, 1987) hampered the enactment of policies secured in this contradictory and conflictual manner. Thus not only do the interests of the state executive need to be specified, but so do the complex and competing interests and strategies of the different segments of the state apparatus. Incipient discourses shaping state policies and practices must also be accounted for (Jessop, 1990).

Recent state theory in South Africa, informed by concrete historical investigations (see especially Bonner et al., 1993), has therefore moved away from the class-reductionist and capital – logic accounts of the 1970s. Both state complexity and autonomy have received a great deal of attention. But, as was pointed out above, the persistent focus on state intervention in the economy and labour markets has left us with an impoverished view of the autonomous political interests of the state. Thus while either strong (Yudelman, 1983) or weak (Helliker, 1988; Evans, 1986) autonomy is now generally accorded to the state by most writers, the political dimensions of the state's interests have still been neglected. This is once again evidenced in the recent debates informed by regulation theory which consider the changing functionality of apartheid to capitalist growth (Gelb, 1987; Nattrass, 1989). Here the question of the political logics of state policies is subsumed under the consequences that they have had for economic growth. An adequate account of state policies and state power must also address the development of social and political insitutions and policies with respect to their own logics and dynamics. The following section seeks to derive some of the more basic interests of the state in South Africa from a historical review of its growth over time and the particular form which it has assumed.

Constructing the South African state: state-building and state interests

Modern state-builders have all tried to concentrate means of power, knowledge, surveillance and violence in a centralized state apparatus within contested territories. Their motivations have certainly been divergent, and yet building state capacities has occupied an important place in the political strategies of many governments. Warfare, systems of taxation, information collection and storage, economic and techno-logical developments, religion – and probably many other processes (Tilly, 1975; Hall, 1986; Mann, 1986) – were central to the story of state-building in the West. But we cannot expect that similar processes were necessarily involved in the rise of the South African state (especially those which were historically specific, such as the significant role of warfare amongst relatively equal and competitive states in eighteenth century Western Europe). The distinctiveness of the South African state form and state interests which emerged as its managers sought to achieve 'stateness' (Nettl, 1968) must therefore be explored historically. Most especially, the racial form of the state needs to be accounted for. Since concerns with rudimentary state-building persisted well into the 1950s in South Africa, a review of this process must cover some 300 or more years, and hence can only be something of a broad sketch of relevant dynamics.

Early state forms

The pre-capitalist indigenous societies which existed within what is today South Africa assumed a variety of forms. Some were associated with relatively strong embryonic states governed by chiefs and kings, and rested upon various forms of surplus extractions, such as the labour demands made of young men in the Zulu kingdom (Guy, 1980; Bonner, 1982; Freund, 1980). Others, particularly the Khoi-khoi and the San people, had loose kin group and clan associations, and lived as pastoral-ists and hunter-gatherers respectively (Elphick and Malherbe, 1989). These varying political forms were of crucial significance in the later conflicts which emerged between indigenous people and the European colonizers (Marks, 1986; Beinart and Bundy, 1987) and in the strategies which were developed for asserting colonial dominance and later white supremacy.

   First among the colonizing powers were the Dutch, in the form of the trading company, the VOC (Dutch East India Company), which occupied the Cape in the mid seventeenth century. The company was given sovereign rights within territories which they governed. The form of administration which they employed partly reflected that of the

Dutch state, and partly reflected choices made in the interests of their trading venture. The most striking aspects of this 'state' form were the absence of representation for those under the authority of the company administration (although this was the case in Holland as well), and the tolerance shown for the practice of exploiting official positions for personal gain (Schutte, 1989). This continued in the early years of British rule (1806 onwards) when the first Governor of the Cape, Lord Somerset, notoriously made liberal use of existing latitudes (Freund, 1989; Peires, 1989). The process of building a modern, 'rational' state in the expanding colonized area began slowly in the 1820s following 'the inevitable dismantling of the old Dutch mercantilist system and the integration of the colony into the liberal political and economic order of the nineteenth century British Empire' (Peires, 1989: 495).

An independent legislature, together with economic (anti-mercantilist) and administrative reforms, as well as improved central control of outlying regions (Green, 1957: 5–6) formed the major thrusts of these changes and, apart from the issues of representation and labour regulation, laid the foundations for a modern form of state in the Cape, as well as for the emergence of capitalist markets (Peires, 1989: 511). But as British colonial state-building proceeded slowly and somewhat problematically in the Cape and Natal, the migration of Afrikaners (Dutch settlers) beyond the Cape borders to escape new British land and labour policies, and the closing off of opportunities which the 'corrupt' early Cape government had permitted (Fredrickson, 1981: 166–167) re-established a form of state reliant upon patrimonialism and upon contractual schemes for economic monopolies in the Boer republics (see Figure 2.1) (Trapido, 1980).

The demise of these states as a result of the Boer War has been the subject of some debate concerning the relationship between the economic demands of the gold mines, imperial interests and colonization (Marks and Trapido, 1979; Denoon, 1973; Mawby, 1974). But the British victory was an important spur for state-building and, soon after that, for the unification of the various colonies and republics into present-day South Africa.

However, long before this time, the racial exclusivity of the political and economic order had been laid. In the Cape during the eighteenth century, European racial attitudes and colonial practices of identifying and naming different groups – which formed a basis for racial divisions – were transformed into a socially regulated racial hierarchy, albeit one with considerable 'mixing' in the middle levels of the social and economic order. Historians suggest that labour shortages, experiences of extensive slave ownership and coerced labour, as well as the relative population imbalance between the more numerous Europeans and the indigenes and slaves in the eighteenth century Cape Colony, permitted

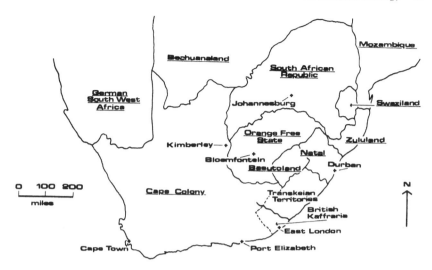

Figure 2.1 Southern Africa *c.* 1900 (after Frederickson, 1982: 92)

a relatively strict racial order to emerge in South Africa as compared to that in Brazil, for example (Elphick and Giliomee, 1989). Thus, although political representation in the Cape, when it was granted, was based upon 'class' criteria such as wealth and land ownership rather than on 'race' (unlike the situation in the northern republics: see Tatz, 1962), the racial structure of colonial society and economy effectively excluded Coloured and African people from state power. This exclusion was reinforced by the policy at the eastern frontier where Xhosa tribes were successively conquered and incorporated into a colonial administration designed to ensure domination by the Cape state (Beinart and Bundy, 1987). Towards the late nineteenth century, then, this practical experience of violent confrontation, followed by the replacement of 'incorporationist' ideas by broadly eugenicist or social Darwinian ideas (Dubow, 1987) and the coercive labour policies employed to support the demand of the new mines for labour (Levy, 1982), cemented a particular racialized state form.

The rise of a modern state

Many of the 'rationalities' of the twentieth century South African state had begun to evolve in the various constituent societies during the course of the nineteenth century: most importantly, strategies for labour procurement and control (Turrel, 1987; Worger, 1983). Government had also assumed an administrative form derived directly from British state practices, and the beginnings of a more effective communications and transport network – essential for a growth in state capacity – were appearing. In addition, formal procedures for urban and rural government and administration were formulated. But a strong contribution to state-building in the region came from two related sources: firstly, from Milner's reconstruction of the Transvaal administration after the Boer War, and secondly, from the unification of the colonies and republics in 1910.

In his efforts to replace the patrimonial Boer Republics, Lord Milner embarked upon a conscious and highly directed exercise in state-building. As van Onselen (1982: 26) comments of the several post-war administrations, it was Milner's 'that intervened most directly to lay the foundations of modern industrial society on the Witwatersrand'. Milner had been strongly influenced by state socialist arguments and was fully convinced of the 'creative role of political power' (Stokes, 1962: 52). He and his 'kindergarten', a group of young British assistants (Nimocks, 1968), embarked upon the reconstruction of the social and political order in the Transvaal, primarily by means of thoroughgoing administrative reforms (Denoon, 1973: 34). Thus, in the context of municipal government, as well as in the general administration of the Republic, one of Milner's aides, Lionel Curtis, saw himself as getting rid of 'corrupt heirlooms from the old administration' to be replaced by 'competent new officials' (Curtis, 1951: 237).

The influence of Milner and his assistants went far beyond mere administrative reform, though, as both Nimocks (1968: 360) and van Onselen (1982: 29–30) observe. Far-reaching policies for urban government (Green, 1957: Chapter 12) and urban social control were also elaborated. And, even more widely, Milner's imperialist vision for a united settler state in South Africa was motivated both by his political orientations and by a growing concern that political and administrative disunity in the region was constraining economic growth. He co-ordinated the 1903 Customs Union Conference in Bloemfontein, whose agenda was expanded to include rail tariffs, the 'native question' and the issue of Union. The strong economic interdependence of the four colonies provided some justification for this thrust (Newton, 1968: vol. II, 154). Research remains to be conducted into the extent to which the unification of South Africa was motivated by state-building ambitions *per se*, as well as into the specific state ideologies which underpinned this important period in the history of the South African state (although see Cope, 1989). But the construction of a rational-bureaucratic Western-style state was promoted by these developments, as was the racial exclusivity which had been laid down in the nineteenth century. Cell (1982) sees the growth of the state as having been an important contributing factor to the consolidation of the political ideology of segregation which dominated the state from Union in 1910. Certainly it was the electoral and policy-centred discourses which resulted from the expansion and consolidation of a unified South African state which cemented segregation as both a system of practices and a state ideology (SANAC, 1903–5; Dubow, 1986b).

At the time of Union, though, the process of state-building had only just begun and advances in this direction were to be somewhat halting. A major preoccupation of the Union government was to build support amongst the white electorate (Yudelman, 1986; Dubow, 1986a: 23–4) in the face of working-class struggles and Afrikaner discontent. But state-building received setbacks from a shortage of suitable staff (especially during the world wars) and the consolidation of state power with respect to African people, especially in urban areas, was very slow. In terms of state-building the Afrikaner Nationalists made a substantial contribution to the construction of a large modern state. We will be concerned with some of the details of this state-building process, especially in urban areas, in the chapters which follow.

The interests of the modern South African state

From the perspective of state-builders one of the foundational interests of all states lies in securing the basic capacity to act. This is probably an appropriate conceptualization of most states, bureaucratic-hierarchical or otherwise.[2] Information gathering, communication networks, surveillance mechanisms and record-keeping form an indispensable part of modern 'stateness' (Giddens, 1985; Tilly, 1975), and securing these capacities guides, or at least shapes the growth (or rationalization) of state apparatuses, and the particular forms which policy measures take. Both the colonial states and the unified South African state faced a situation where the exercise of their powers through infrastructural, despotic or clientist means was severely hampered. Travel and communications especially placed severe restraints on government, particularly during the colonial period. Long journeys on horseback, rivers to be waded, language and cultural barriers all made administering colonial society immensely difficult. The parsimony of the imperial state and the shortage of officials compounded these problems (Welsh, 1971), but the colonial states as well as the South African and apartheid states had a strong and autonomous interest in building the capacities to govern.

Clearly such capacities were also desired to achieve specific policy ends, which would be associated with social and economic interests. But as I have argued, and contrary to many Marxist state theorists, the state's motivations for action in the form of economic and social policies can also be construed as autonomous, derived from 'institutional self-interest', the state's position and role in the international arena, particular state ideologies or rationalities, and a concern for social order. In the South African case, the historically racial form of the state gave rise to some specific state interests. Whereas democratic states exhibit a concern with legitimation – or at least with what Held (1989: 132) calls 'conditional consent or pragmatic acceptance' – states with little or no foundations in popular support must rely upon different methods to secure authoritative domination, often entailing violence and coercion. In South Africa, the racial state ensured the exclusion of African people from the political realm of the state while simultaneously incorporating and building hegemonic relations with the included white citizens. The latter has involved a considerable amount of state-building, along similar lines to those prevailing in Western democratic states. But preserving the racial character of the state, a fundamental imperative of the South African state, has also entailed securing at least rudimentary governmental capacities with respect to African people to ensure compliance with the prevailing social order, if not consent. And here I will argue that the deployment of the location strategy was crucial.

Forging state domination along racial lines does not exhaust the practice and ideology of racial domination, of course. Racist domination in the home, workplace, street, popular culture and so forth are important to the racial order in South Africa, and are not at all reducible to the state. But the particular relation between the racial state and the dominated population is also very important. This has not taken the form of hegemonic or consensual relations and, contrary to more popular interpretations of apartheid, has not relied solely upon violence. The routine application of repressive legislation (Frankel, 1979; Posel, 1987) and a routine compliance derived from dire economic need and daily survival (Adam and Moodley, 1986) were certainly supplemented by efforts at the co-optation of the small urban petty-bourgeois population during the last years of the apartheid regime. But the power of the apartheid state has also depended upon building basic state capacities with respect to African people, and it is this process which we will be examining in some detail in this study. An important influence on the development of these capacities has been the form of the state itself. Motivated by interests in state-building and racial exclusion (amongst others), the process of constructing state power has been complicated by its territorial form. This is especially true in the context of urban government and native administration, the two themes central to this study.

Native administration and the geography of state power

In the first chapter I argued that the territorial nature of modern states has important consequences not only for their autonomy and internal coherence (Mann, 1984), but also for their fragmentation and incoherence. As a state seeks to ensure that policies and governmental capacity are secured throughout the territory, areal and functional sub-divisions and decentralization of tasks become important (Clark and Dear, 1984; Paddison, 1983). At the same time, the uneven development of society often encourages states to vary the form and style of government between places, regionally or locally (Duncan and Goodwin, 1988). These processes of fragmentation are important for understanding both the nature of states in general and the form of a particular state. Historical arrangements and place–specific conflicts shape the set of relationships between central and local states, for example, or the distribution of state powers between the centre and regions. We cannot simply deduce the substance or significance of these relationships in South Africa from studies in other countries. Thus this section sets out a broad context within which we can understand the historical meaning of local – central state relations and the territorial fragmentation of the state in South Africa.

The brief history of state-building presented above has already pointed to some important sources of fragmentation within the South African state. Firstly, the pre-Union history of the area which today falls within the South African state entailed four diverse colonies, each with different state forms and policies. At the time of Union, the sense of distinctiveness prevailing amongst the political elites in each of these four areas contributed to the retention of some administrative powers and certainly for a time some independent policies for the various colonies, then designated as provinces. While many aspects of this division of responsibility remain unexplored, the impact of unification on 'native policy' has (helpfully for this study) received some attention.

At Union, the four colonies had different systems of political representation. In the Cape and Natal, some African, Coloured and Indian people could gain the right to vote on the basis of wealth and property criteria, while in the Transvaal and the Orange Free State the vote was reserved purely for white people (Tatz, 1962). Accommodating these differences, as well as preserving the variety of administrative procedures employed in the government of African people living in the four provinces, occurred through the granting of a measure of independence to provincial bodies (Thompson, 1971). In addition, for a time different laws relating to African administration, land ownership and occupation were enacted in the four provinces. In the field of native administration, therefore, divergent administrative ideologies and practices prevailed (Dubow, 1986b: 229).

In conjunction with an ongoing bureaucratic process of increasing state efficiency and co-ordination, the creation of uniform central state policies was pursued, certainly in the area of 'native policy'. This was not achieved without some difficulty, however. After Union the 'native question' was approached with some caution by the central state in an effort to avoid divisions within white politics (Dubow, 1986a: 23–4). But its 'solution' also played an important role in solidifying a white national identity and in facilitating the construction of a stronger central state apparatus in the area of native affairs (Dubow, 1986a). In the urban areas, the process of constructing a homogeneous, central-ized administration was complicated by the division of responsibility for African government between the central state and local authorities. Just as provincial bodies in South Africa had no sovereign rights, so the rights of local authorities in South Africa were dependent upon the proclamations of the central state (Cameron, 1986: 18). As a result the level of independence and the functions of local authorities have changed substantially over time – most would argue in the direction of decreasing independence and greater centralization (Marquard, 1968: 94; Cameron, 1988; Heymans, 1988). However, in the period immedi-ately following Union during which central state power was very weakly developed, the local authorities were essential to the exercise of state power, especially in urban areas (McMillan, 1917: 4). This is apparent in the field of 'urban native administration' where the central Department of Native Affairs depended upon the local authorities to implement policies (Rich, 1980b) and was only in a position to assert central directives in the 1950s (Evans, 1986).

In addition to this territorial fragmentation of state power, all levels of the state – central, regional and local – are in their turn cross-cut with divisions, including those between professional interests and technologies associated with particular state apparatuses. The process of crafting and implementing a uniform policy across the state appara-tuses is therefore frequently conflict-ridden. But during the course of the twentieth century, a number of professional and bureaucratic 'interests' embedded in the South African state converged around the notion of the location as the most appropriate and useful strategy for enhancing state capacity with respect to African people in the cities. The rest of this chapter focuses upon the early emergence of the location strategy as a result of the imperatives of colonial governance, while Chapter 3 explores the different professional discourses and state imperatives which shaped the deployment of the location strategy through the twentieth century. All these groups contributed to the construction of a discourse of urban native administration which was most influential in shaping the form and content of state interventions in twentieth century South African cities. It is important to recall here that these discourses were not outside modernity. Rather the tactics and rationalities which emerged to regulate urban space in South Africa were closely allied to normalizing and modernizing strategies throughout the West. As Gilroy (1993: 163) has suggested with respect to slavery, 'racial subordination is integral to the processes of development and social and technological progress known as modernization.'

The territorial basis of state power: locations and administration in urban areas

> How on earth can I take charge of Natives [*sic*] that are allowed to squat in every yard, hole and corner in Durban, where everyone is allowed to go except a policeman? (SANAC, 1905, Evidence, Vol. 2: 652).

Thus complained the exasperated superintendent of the Durban police on 17 May 1904 before the South African Native Affairs Commissioners. He stressed the urgent need to have a location in Durban, 'just the same as they do in East London'. In some senses his vision of this proposed location sits uneasily alongside images of twentieth century black townships, since he envisaged it being on what he described as

> a magnificent site; you have got the Umgeni River running down on one side, the Indian Ocean close by, and the whole of your 100 acres as level as can be, with lovely trees. You could make a town there a perfect picture, with the glorious sun shining all day long on it. They would lie under the trees, or swim in the river as long as they liked. They would be perfectly happy, and away from all temptations. (1905: 653).

But, despite this fairly utopian vision, Mr Alexander was also pleased to note that:

> The Indian Ocean would guard them on one side, the Umgeni on the other, and the borough police on the third. I would put my Natives in barracks and let them march into town as they do with soldiers. That has been my ambition for 25 years, and I have not altered it. (1905:653)

The municipal official may have had a quaint vision of sun-kissed happiness for 'his natives', but his primary reason for building a location was in order to control 'them' more effectively. Attempts to ensure the effective control of African people through the creation of particular ordered and segregated spaces pre-dated Mr Alexander's vision by some decades and outlived him for several more. It is a central argument of this book that important aspects of South Africa's contemporary urban form – especially segregated residential areas for African people, with an associated administrative apparatus – developed out of visions such as that expressed above by the Durban superintendent of police. Indeed, the account which follows traces this nexus of segregation and state power to efforts by the colonial state[4] to conquer and govern the indigenous inhabitants of the land.

Long before urban segregation was articulated as part of a relatively coherent ideology of segregation, the essential form assumed by residential segregation in the case of African people in South Africa had been well established. Whereas the formal political ideology of segregation only took shape after the turn of the century (Cell, 1982; Dubow, 1986a), and it was only in the 1880s that white racist agitation over African living conditions had emerged in towns (Saunders, 1978; Kinkead-Weakes, 1985), the location strategy was first implemented in the 1830s in rural areas and the late 1840s in urban areas in the eastern Cape (Baines, 1989). The search by historians for the 'origins' of segregation in South Africa (Swanson, 1976; Baines, 1989) has, inevitably, been influenced by the particular theoretical and empirical lenses they have adopted. Thus, the general neglect in South African studies of the interests of the state and of the importance of spatiality in power relations has partially obscured the early history of the location strategy in South Africa. My sense is that by focusing upon the demands of capital in recounting the history of urban segregation, the continuity of purpose (effective government and political domination) in the location strategy has been understated in favour of the variety of immediate causes motivating the implementation of the strategy in different times and places.

The rural location in South Africa

Although various territorial strategies probably surfaced in a variety of situations prior to the mid nineteenth century (most likely, for example, in slave-owning situations), the defeat of African tribes in what were then the 'frontier' regions of the eastern Cape resulted in the emergence of the first 'locations' together with associated administrative structures and social policies. This territorial strategy has been associated with a variety of purposes over time but the following account hopes to show that a common effect (and clear purpose) of locations as they were developed for African people in South Africa has been to enhance the capacity to govern of both relatively weak colonial states and – at a later date – of the more powerful but frequently beleaguered apartheid state.

One of the earliest uses of the term 'location' in South Africa has been noted at the time of the settlement of 'refugee' Mfengu people on the colonial side of the Kei River after the frontier war of 1835–6 (McMillan, 1963: 149–52). McMillan comments that this 'ill-omened term' later came to be more commonly applied to urban locations rather than to their rural antecedents. However, although these settlements clearly reflected the later controlling purposes of urban locations, the term itself was applied to earlier areas which had been demarcated for parties of British settlers on the eastern frontier in 1820, as well as to 'Hottentot' locations of about the same time (Cory, 1913). Both of these settlements were created as human buffer zones in the ongoing wars over land rights, and were by no means benign state creations (see Figure 2.1). The use of these demarcated areas of land in conscious strategies of control, though, does seem to have begun with the founding of the Mfengu locations in the 1830s and 1840s, as MacMillan suggested. The frontier wars in the eastern Cape were spread over one hundred years, and Davenport (1977) sees them as having promoted the crystallization of a policy for the government of the indigenous people:

> Far more than any other frontier, it was the one on which policies were thought out and deliberately applied. The blockhouse system and the military village; the buffer strip, the frontier of no outlets and the trading pass; the trade fair, mission station, hospital and school; the spoor law, the treaty system, the government agent, and the magistrate – all these were tried in various combinations. (Davenport, 1977: 99)

Several international influences came to bear upon the policies which those in authority implemented, including the Indian treaty system and the Canadian experience, as well as policies formulated in local mission stations. Legal and administrative aspects of colonial policy were also important, as was the general background understanding of the colonial mission as one involving the 'uplifting' and 'civilizing' of the conquered populations (Du Toit, 1954: Chapters 2–4; Davenport, 1977: 99; Schreuder, 1976). After the war of 1835–6, 17,000 Mfengu people were removed across the colonial border and settled near Peddie in an area administered by a 'resident agent'. However, British treatment of these people was in the worst tradition and they were left to defend themselves against the tribes they had deserted, and in the process to act as a human buffer protecting the colonists from attack (Moyer, 1974). While a similar 'security' motive lay behind later Mfengu settlements in the colony, a system of government was also being designed to maintain generalized control in the area as well as to 'uplift' the inhabitants. The Reverend Calderwood, then civil commissioner of the (short-lived) frontier province of Victoria, was responsible for drawing up the recommendations and regulations for the locations established in 1847. He had previously been a missionary, responsible for Birklands mission station close to Fort Beaufort (Soga, 1930: 210), and this – together with questions of military strategy and government – informed his suggestions for the organization of these defined spaces (Du Toit, 1954: 36). As with earlier relations with tribes in the area, a white official was to be assigned to the new settlements. Calderwood's instructions to these officials began as follows:

1 In the successful working of the Fingoe locations, both as it regards the people themselves and the security of the frontier, very much must depend upon the activity and discretion of the superintendents. Their whole energies will require to be given to the work.

2 Superintendents will see and communicate with the headmen of locations, inquiring into the state of the location at least once a week. Frequent personal communication is of the greatest consequence, both for the encouragement and stirring up of the people, and the information of the superintendents. Superintendents will personally visit every village or kraal at least once a-month. (Correspondence with the Governor of the Cape of Good Hope, 1849(a))

Implementing a strategy he had seen as useful in a mission context – namely, the carefully supervised use of 'native agents' (Calderwood, 1858: 115) – he recommended that a native headman be appointed for each location and commented that 'a great deal may be done through a native agency of this kind, if managed with liberality and diligence' (Correspondence with the Governor of the Cape of Good Hope, 1850). The white superintendents were to be crucial in this scheme, and their regular presence and oversight was seen as essential for its success:

An authority capable of diffusing life and diligence throughout the system must be on the spot, else a very large amount of efficiency will be sacrificed. (1850)

The Governor of the time (Sir H.G. Smith) was suitably impressed with this scheme of 'dividing them [the Mfengu] into four townships, under the charge of a British superintendent', and remarked upon Mr Calderwood's 'zealous endeavours to establish rule and order'. His enthusiasm reflected his general concerns with government, as he noted after a tour of the area:

This is a measure fraught with good; for one of the greatest evils to contend with upon this frontier, is the existence of a vagrant set of the coloured classes, having no fixed residence and knowing no rule or self-control. (Correspondence with the Governor of the Cape of Good Hope, 1849(b))

The usefulness of this confinement of Mfengu people to particular places, under the direct personal oversight of a white superintendent, was thus fully appreciated by those in authority.

In addition to such benefits this territorial strategy was also infused with the senses of mission and of civilization which prevailed in both missionary and official circles at the time. Although strictly religious matters were to be out of the hands of the superintendents, they were instructed to attempt to prevent 'heathen rites and practices...injurious to morals and offensive to decency', and to discourage 'as far as is in their power', secular employment on the Sabbath (Correspondence with the Governor of the Cape of Good Hope, 1849(b)). Calderwood also declared his intention to announce prizes for people who achieved certain standards of civilization: for example, prizes were to be awarded to the 'most respectably and decently clothed man/woman/child throughout the year' or for the 'best and cleanest and best furnished house', as well as for agricultural achievements.

A similar form of government – spatial confinement, together with some superintendence, and measures for 'civilization' – was also applied by T.S. Shepstone in Natal (see Figure 2.2). Shepstone had previously been a resident agent in Peddie, the first area of Mfengu settlement, and probably brought ideas on possible strategies for 'native' government from these earlier experiences to his appointment in Natal as 'diplomatic agent' in 1845 (Brookes, 1974; Welsh, 1971). Brookes (1974: Chapter 4) makes the claim that without Shepstone's territorial strategy for governing the disparate groupings in the area claimed as the colony of Natal, it would have been impossible to exert any control at all over the local people. Shepstone was hampered by the problem of limited imperial financial support and so devised a scheme which relied on chiefs (traditional or appointed) exercising authority in their areas rather than on white superintendents overseeing the locations. With these territorial devices set alongside military and moral sanctions (Brookes, 1974: 57), an exceptionally weak colonial government was able to maintain a semblance of control in places it otherwise could not have reached. The scheme was devised with several purposes in mind. One was to 'divide and rule' the various chiefdoms in the area; a second – as some perceived it – was to use the scheme as a means of protecting tribal lands from alienation by settlers; and a third was to enable rudimentary supervision of the population (Brookes, 1974: 42–3). 'Civilizing' measures, such as industrial schools and missions, were planned but never properly implemented, supposedly due to a lack of sufficient funds.

Natal offers us an important example of the embeddedness of administrative spatial outcomes in the more general political economy. While creating an effective administration or at least allowing some sense of colonial control over African inhabitants was an important motivation for creating locations in this colony (Welsh, 1971: 12), they became the subject of some controversy amongst the white settlers and colonial authorities, and there was also a measure of resistance from the African communities. With the arrival of groups of white settlers after 1849, a protracted debate ensued amongst the settlers over the questions of land and of a suitable policy for 'native' inhabitants. The government's defence of its locations policy (in the face of settler demands to break up the locations and thereby release both a larger labour supply and more land) reflected not only some of the administrative concerns outlined above but – according to Harries (1987) – the government's direct interest in protecting African agricultural productivity was in order to ensure the ability of the African people to pay

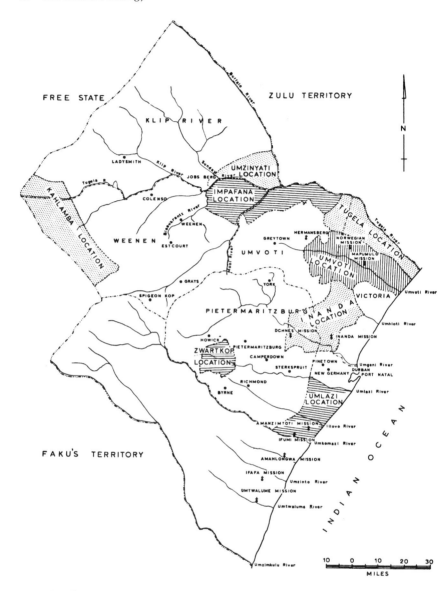

Figure 2.2 African locations in nineteenth century Natal

taxes which, in the face of imperial reluctance to fund the administration of the colony, were an important source of the government's income. In a disagreement with Shepstone, Lieutenant-Governor Pine argued a case for building up the economic capacities and level of civilization of the Africans by breaking down the reserves, dispersing Africans amongst Europeans and granting them individual title to some land. Earl Grey in the Colonial Office agreed with these objectives – civilization, promotion of industry and some measure of assimilation – but for him the imperative to maintain order and government using as few resources as possible prevailed, and the locations and what later came to be termed 'indirect rule' were perpetuated (Correspondence Relating to the Settlement of Natal, 1852).

This system of rule by means of chiefs, white agents and locations was extended to the Transkei territories as these were annexed to the Cape Colony between 1879 and 1894, and a collection of papers by Beinart and Bundy (1987) provides an insight into the detailed workings of this system of administration – its motivations, variations in time and space, conflicts and personal and community actions. Despite what they term the 'overwhelming power and technological superiority of the colonial state' (1987: 32) *vis-à-vis* the capacities of the local population, they still assess it to have been administratively weak, with a 'thin line' of white officials, making the use of African subsidiaries and 'loyals' essential (1987: 8). Administrators (or magistrates) of the magisterial districts also depended to a large extent upon their 'local knowledge' (1987: 1), which was acquired through personal contacts, native headmen, spies or police.

Debates over land distribution and over the relative merits and demerits of establishing locations or dispersing black people across the countryside also occurred in what is now the Transvaal and the Orange Free State (Keegan, 1987). These republics both had far less systematic native policies than the two British colonies, but locations and other spatial methods of 'native' administration also formed part of their network of control (see Table 2.1). Administrators and politicians from these areas emphasized before the South African Native Affairs Commission in 1903 the need for a more consistent application of some of their land policies, and an improved administrative network. As one member of the Transvaal legislative council put it:

TABLE 2.1 *Territorial distribution of African people in the various colonies*, c. 1903

Colony	Private	Town farms	Crown locations	Reserves lands	Private locations
Cape Colony	218,834	113,828	nil	1,057,610	39,506
Natal	426,674	nil	13,985	463,382	nil
Transvaal	479,674	28,264	180,427	207,840	nil
Orange River Colony	195,494	22,972	nil	17,000	nil

Source: South African Native Affairs Commissions, 1903–5

more direct personal supervision, a closer supervision, should be maintained...There should be more officers, more control, more supervision. (SANAC, 1905, Evidence, Vol. 4: 629)

Pre-mining urban segregation

While the various colonial states were involved in formulating policies and strategies which would enable control and conquest of African people in rural areas, some Africans had begun to move to urban areas and principally to Cape Town, Durban, Port Elizabeth and other centres such as King William's Town, Grahamstown, East London and Bloemfontein. Urban settlements in South Africa were not an indigenous phenomenon (Davies, 1976), and white settlers established themselves in new centres which they then considered to be their own exclusive domain even when they were vastly outnumbered by African people. Here we encounter the two more important hypotheses concerning the emergence of segregation. The first is settler agitation (for example Parnell, 1991), the second the demands of capital and economic accumulation (for example Mabin, 1986a). While these two processes were both clearly important in the development of urban segregation, my contention is that the emergence of segregated locations pre-dated these historical factors, and also that the location strategy, while it was certainly enmeshed in the dynamics of the economy and settler politics, had a logic of its own, as well as considerable support from actors within the state apparatuses whose interests cannot be reduced to those of social and economic forces. We will draw upon evidence from towns in the Cape Colony for this, since it was here that urbanization was most advanced during the early nineteenth century.

Many of the earliest African inhabitants of Cape Town were brought there forcibly as slaves or prisoners, although the original inhabitants of the area – the Khoi-San people – also made up part of the population. But Saunders suggests that many 'became indistinguishable components of the "Coloured" [population]' (1980: 16), and he goes on to trace the settlement of African people in the town. Until the 1830s he found only scattered reference to individual Africans living and working in Cape Town, but from the late 1830s (probably as a result of the frontier wars and the abolition of slavery) records show a small settlement of Mfengu people on the slopes of Table Mountain. This period in the Cape was marked, according to Freund's (1976) argument, less by a racial structuring of the social order than by one based on social class and status. Bickford-Smith's (1981) analysis of 'dangerous classes' in nineteenth century Cape Town supports this argument, although Elphick and Giliomee (1989) suggest that both race and class were important in social differentiation. This was reflected in the relatively mixed racial geographies of South African cities until the early decades of the twentieth century, which saw the beginning of government action in the area of urban segregation (Scott, 1955; Christopher, 1988). Although there was a considerable degree of racial residential integration during the nineteenth century, in Cape Town congregations of Africans emerged on the outskirts of the town and at the docks (in accommodation provided by employers), but not as the result of any conscious state policy of 'segregation'. Saunders (1978) and Kinkead-Weakes (1985) locate the beginnings of such a policy in the late 1870s when the residents of Woodstock (now a suburb of Cape Town) objected to the settlement of Africans in their vicinity following an increased influx of Mfengu and Xhosa people after the cattle killing of 1857 (which drove many impoverished Africans to the towns in search of employment).

But segregation had already been implemented in various towns of the Eastern Cape by the 1850s, as well as in the Orange Free State. Baines (1988) for example, takes up a spirited critique of the theory that the origins of segregation are to be found in the mining-industrial revolution of the 1870s, and presents material relating to the settlement and relocation of Africans in Port Elizabeth (between 1840 and 1870). He argues that formal segregation was partly a result of the material interests of some white residents in promoting local property development but was also an outcome of a fear of urban disorder and violence which white residents imagined to be the consequence of the rapid inmigration of African people associated with the cattle killings of the 1850s. This example is especially instructive. Baines concentrates on the delimitation and subsequent removal of Africans from a settlement which had begun to obstruct the development of white housing, to a 'Native Strangers' location' further away from the built-up areas. But his study also reveals that both a mission station for 'Hottentots' and a 'Fingoe' location had already been established on the outskirts of the town. And, in the light of evidence presented so far in this chapter, it might be argued that each of these had served as important precedents for how African people were to be suitably housed and supervised in urban areas. In the new location, a superintendent was also appointed to oversee the location, to collect rents, to supervise house construction and to keep order (Baines, 1988).

In Port Elizabeth in the late 1840s, therefore, the assumption that a 'location' was the place where Africans should live was not challenged in principle. Only its siting was questioned by those whose immediate interests were at stake, such as employers of dock workers, for whom (not to mention the workers themselves) a location out of town was inconvenient (Baines, 1988). Similarly, in Bloemfontein and other Orange Free State towns, white residents resorted to the location and to regulations regarding African peoples' rights to live in the towns in their attempt to control and order people who they saw as different, inferior and a nuisance and yet also a source of cheap, exploitable labour (van Aswegen, 1971). Both rural and urban locations therefore arose as part of an emerging collection of appropriate procedures for creating and controlling regulated environments for black inhabitants of these colonies.

The ambitions of both the white population and the government were not easily met, however, and an inadequate state machinery coupled with an unwilling black population meant that many well-laid schemes for control were thwarted or failed and had to be improved upon. However, from the mid nineteenth century there existed in the location a possible spatial strategy for urban social control as well as a number of private individuals (missionaries, doctors, employers) and state officials (colonial and municipal) who claimed a special knowledge of the living conditions appropriate for black urban residents and who held opinions on how best to formulate and effect state policy. Their concerns filtered up the state apparatus in the form of reports and evidence which they were called upon to give before various commissions of enquiry.

My comments so far have demonstrated two main points. Firstly, the 'location' – residential segregation which took a specific supervisory form – definitely pre-dated the mining revolution in South Africa (although the meaning and detailed content of this strategy has varied considerably over time, and this requires a great deal more investigation). And secondly, alongside the economic and political conflicts which have been recounted by historians of this period, there seems to have been an awareness of methods and strategies relevant to achieving some measure of supervision (if not direct control) of the lives of subject populations by the state (Schreuder, 1976). However, the persistence of disorder which accompanied the slow creation of this mechanism of dominance, together with frequent resistance to this form of state intervention, should not be ignored. Nevertheless, the strategies of control which found embodiment in the landscape took a territorial form and entailed the creation of both a phenomenon and a term which came to be considered unique to South Africa – the 'location'.[4] Whilst influences from other situations of colonization and racial domination can be traced, this configuration of control, administration and, for a while, 'upliftment' of urban black people seems to have been peculiar to South Africa and, if anything, was exported to other parts of Africa (see for example, Pennat, 1983; Tipple, 1981; Ogilvie, 1946; Vasey, 1950; McNamee, 1946). After these suggestive glimpses of early examples of

the location strategy in urban areas, we turn now to consider the intersection of these tentative strategies with the mining revolution and the
growth of an industrial capitalist society in South Africa.

Compounds and townships

According to Cell (1982) the origins of the ideology of segregation can
be traced to the Natal system (Shepstonianism), the eastern Cape
administration, modern capitalist industrial society and the formation
of a central state. However, he contends that the Marxist 'revisionist'
concentration on capitalism as the primary source of segregationist
ideology is most accurate, and that although segregation may have had
roots in the distant past it only became 'a conscious, coherent system
and ideology...in the decades after the Boer War' (1982: 81). Such
ideological crystallization may have been important for fixing the limits
of the central state public policy debates (according to Cell's schema,
'segregation' came into being and has since coexisted with a national
state in South Africa), but I have suggested that separation and
attempts to control black people by territorial means had a definite
continuity within the administrative networks which had existed since
the mid nineteenth century. But the intensification of capitalism in
South Africa – with the discovery of minerals from the late 1860s
onwards – did lead to important developments in the methods and
strategies available for urban control, and also magnified the 'problem'
of urban disorder as the rate of urbanization increased rapidly.

The introduction of labour compounds in Kimberley's diamond
mines has been referred to as a central impetus in the development of
both 'native policy' and modern strategies of control (Rex, 1974; Crush,
1993). Davenport notes that:

> As a control device, the lesson of the Kimberley companies was not lost. The
> Durban municipality discovered at the beginning of the twentieth century that
> an open compound system could be used for the control of casual (`togt') labour-
> ers. It was a short step from the municipal compound to the `native hostel',
> which became a common feature of municipal locations in the larger centres
> under the stimulus of the Urban Areas Act of 1923. (1977: 355–6).

And Mabin argues that:

> Compound and hostel were essentially the first rigid form of residential segre-
> gation applied in the development of the South African city. Ordered townships
> were created in the wake of that experience' (1986a: 22).

These forms of urban organization (compounds, locations and
townships) were, Mabin suggests, 'generated in the specific process of

capitalist development in South Africa' (1986: 22). There can be little doubt that the development of the compound was an integral part of capital accumulation and class struggle in Kimberley, as has been demonstrated by Worger (1983) and Turrell (1984; 1987). Worger's account is particularly compelling. He sets out to show that 'By the time the owners of the diamond mines gained firm control over their labourers, they had created the most basic institutions that were to shape the lives of black workers in South African cities: the labour registration office, the location, the compound and the jail' (1983: 51). Capital, together with the state, came to assert 'slowly and with great difficulty, control over the space and time through which black workers moved' (1983: 50). Worger also stresses the significant growth in state structures to assist in establishing controls over labour, even though he argues that these controls were initially instituted as a result of pressure brought to bear on the young settler state by the powerful influence of mining capitalists. In this early stage of proletarianization, a labour force had to be created and disciplined and it is clear that labour entrapment and control – rather than the much paraded problems of illicit diamond buying (see, Williams, 1902; Smalberger, 1974) – were the reasons behind the establishment of closed compounds in a place like Kimberley (Turrell, 1987).

Moreover, together with their strategy of compounding workers – so these narrators argue – the mining capitalists evidenced a concern for the general control and supervision of black people in cities. By ensuring control and order throughout the city, the mining bosses argued, 'desertion would be prevented because there would be no unregulated area within the town to which to escape' (Worger, 1983: 71). Conflicts amongst employers and the limitations of state capacity both hampered the implementation of this ideal, however.

Nevertheless, and in spite of the many situations of poor urban control which were to be found at the turn of the century, state intervention in some towns soon after 1900 showed that practices and ideas from earlier times had been supplemented by lessons learned from industrialization, and from Kimberley's mines (see for example Moffat, 1901; Saunders, 1978: 45; Mabin, 1986a). New locations built during this period displayed a qualitative increase in regulation and regimentation which was mostly achieved by having state-built rather than owner-built houses. The location also became a place where rudimentary social services were provided. Thus the health and well-being of African people came to be of at least some concern to the state, in addition to their various pre-existing interests in creating a 'moral' environment (for a parallel argument with respect to the compounds see Turrell, 1987: Chapter 8). The officers responsible for location supervision expanded in number and, together with the location inspector and his assistants, medical doctors, nurses and public works engineers became involved in location administration.

The construction of townships in the midst of the 'sanitation syndrome' (Swanson, 1977) – a fear of the public health effects of slums and poor living conditions which swept South Africa in the wake of the plague in the first decade of the twentieth century – was an attempt to create modern, streamlined and more effective locations than had previously existed. In addition to being a response to more immediate imperatives such as the perceived need to control the spread of plague amongst black people, they were also a response to problems of general social control that resulted, in the authorities' opinion, from Africans living 'all about the town'. New ideas about urban planning, health and various technical advances current in the British metropole at the time were also important here, increasingly articulated through an emerging professional grouping of planners and medical health officers (King, 1976; Parnell, 1993). The Cape locations constructed in 1901 (Uitvlugt, or Ndabeni, at Cape Town) and 1903 (New Brighton, just outside Port Elizabeth) and administered under the Native Reserve Location Act of 1902 by the Cape government were perceived to be 'model locations', and played an important role in the systematization of 'urban native management' as well as its incorporation into the central state apparatus. These townships served as an illustration of how other cities could solve their 'native' problems. The South African Native Affairs Commission chairman, for example, asked the resident magistrate for Ndabeni location whether he felt any improvements could be made 'from an administrative point of view' since

> this experiment of locations is one which is of extreme interest to the various territories of South Africa, as they wish to learn whether it is a success in order to profit by it, and whether there are any modifications or improvements which suggest themselves to those who are in charge of the locations. (SANAC, Evidence, Vol.2: 418)

The resident magistrate of Ndabeni replied:

> I certainly think that it is advantageous from a health point of view to have the natives congregated out there, instead of allowing them to live in Cape Town. From an administrative point of view, as far as the natives are concerned, it is a splendid thing, and I think it is beneficial in every way to the natives themselves. (W.G.W. Wright, Resident Magistrate, Ndabeni Location, SANAC, Evidence, Vol.2: 416)

To the authorities in Cape Town, however, removing as many of the native inhabitants of Cape Town as possible to a location was not an entirely new idea when the plague arrived in February 1901 (Stanford, 1962). Swanson points out that even before the onset of plague a commission had been established to consider an 'African reserve or residential location beyond the borders of Cape Town and its suburbs', and he suggests that the swift territorial response to plague fears reflected 'the development of government powers and public health administration' since an earlier smallpox epidemic in 1882–3 (1977: 393). Furthermore, he acknowledges that

> the underlying question was one of overall political control: how to organise society to provide for the mutual access of black labourers and white employers in the coming industrial age without having to pay the heavy social costs of urbanization or losing the dominance of whites over blacks. (1977: 394)

The implementation of the location strategy did not take place without resistance, however, and rent protests, abscondments and refusals to move into the location significantly undermined its effectiveness as a strategy of control in both Port Elizabeth and Cape Town. If the location strategy was to be more effectively implemented, 'black spaces' (Cohen, 1986) would have to be more rigorously defined and policed. The confusion of authority systems responsible for native administration would also need to be streamlined: Port Elizabeth, for instance, had a government location at New Brighton, private locations within the city limits and uncontrolled settlements on the outskirts of the city (Christopher, 1987). Police action with respect to African residence outside locations was sporadic and legal and administrative problems combined with the lack of systematic city-wide control measures meant that, despite a clear idea of what was required for effective administration, black resistance and inadequate state capacity and knowledge led to a situation which seemed disorderly and chaotic. This certainly made subsequent rounds of state intervention – which became increasingly effective – appear more innovative than they actually were.[5] Instead, I will argue that through the twentieth century, as in 1902, the authorities 'tended to follow established patterns of thought in facing new and very great problems of social organization and control' (Swanson, 1968: 32). The location, then, was to remain central to state urban policy for much of the twentieth century. The following chapter explores the elaboration of this strategy within the discourses of administration and planning during the middle decades of the twentieth century when South Africa's urban areas were being radically transformed.

Notes

1   The contrast between legitimacy and domination is, in my opinion, somewhat too starkly drawn: for the securing of domination (apart from the use of brute force) always depends upon some measure of mutual agreement. In the context of urban African local govern-

ment, the elaboration of agreed-upon meanings and norms, Atkinson (1991) argues, were important in sustaining apartheid power.

2   States which rely, for example, upon what observers of the African situation have termed 'pathological patrimonialism' may give rise to state managers who wish to achieve very different ends (self-prestige, wealth, survival) or may prove less effective in realizing some stated ambitions – such as economic development – but an ability to act in some form will constitute a motivation for building certain state apparatuses, or for forging particular state–society relations (such as patronage).

3   Urban racial segregation, of course, is by no means unique to South Africa: indeed, some authors have suggested that this practice was ubiquitous in colonial situations (Simon, 1984: 501). By racial segregation is meant the residential separation of colonial officials or settlers from indigenous inhabitants and other intermediate groups as a result of either 'informal' or legislative and institutional practices. Whilst there is no denying the fact that racial segregation was a frequent and important component of colonial strategy generally (Christopher, 1988), it can be argued that this common urban form was the outcome of a wide variety of social processes. Of course each example of segregation was not unrelated to others, most especially since it was the general processes and ideals of colonialism which provided the context for such developments. Nevertheless, important nuances of process can easily be lost by positing too simple a relationship between the colonial domination of subject populations and urban racial segregation. Indeed, the particular process which is of interest in the South African situation, namely the connection of administrative imperatives with the demarcation of racially exclusive areas for the subject population, appears to be relatively distinctive from those operating to produce racial segregation in many other colonial situations (although territory and administration were certainly also linked in interesting ways in other places).

4   'Location' is a term which had currency in the South African context from the early nineteenth century until at least the mid twentieth century. A nineteenth century usage of the term referred to a 'demarcated area of land' – 'a tract of land with boundaries designated or marked out', according to the 1890 *Century Dictionary of English*. By the 1920s, though, the British dictionaries do not record this usage, but ascribed to South Africa the use of 'location' in connection with 'native settlements'.

5   Baines (1994: 40–52) offers an insight into this in the Port Elizabeth case with his account of the extension of legislation and state capacity to remove African people from the town and surrounding areas during the first decade of this century.

3

Continuity, control and the construction of state power: professional discourses in urban government

During the course of the twentieth century several state and professional interests coalesced around the discourses of 'urban native administration' and urban planning in South Africa. Central state managers, medical officials, planners and administrators all perceived the utility of the location to their professional projects and elaborated upon the form which this strategy should best assume. I will discuss the development of these ideas, firstly, from the perspective of the central state, in the context of its policy formulations. I will then establish the important role which actors outside the centre – including liberal activists, urban native administrators and urban planners – played in shaping the discourses of urban native administration and urban planning. I do not pretend to offer a detailed history of either the legislation or the professions discussed here: those are being ably pursued by others.[1] Rather, I hope to illustrate the continuity of the location strategy through time. That its character changed considerably during the course of its existence, I do not dispute. But my aim is to point to the continued strategic usefulness of the location through much of the century, and also to illustrate how the set of discourses and practices associated with the location came to represent something of a normalizing horizon in the thinking of officials and professionals from a wide range of backgrounds. Significantly, these discourses were strongly gendered, and during the course of this chapter fragments of an account of the role of gender in the creation of this politicized urban space emerges. I will draw these together towards the end of the chapter, as I discuss the paternalistic imagery used by location administrators in making sense of their position.

Urban policy and the location strategy

National urban policy may well emerge in response to particular local conflicts, or to pressures from the ruling classes and local governments (Stadler, 1979; Lodge, 1983; Parnell, 1990), but the content and timing of state policy initiatives also have much to do with the specific interests and ambitions of the central state itself. During the period discussed here (1920s to 1950s), two dominant central state interests were securing basic state capacities, and ensuring that political domination of the excluded and increasingly urbanized and resistant African population was maintained. These two ambitions were clearly reflected in urban policies of the time.

McCarthy (1983) has identified three phases in the evolution of state interventions in the urban arena. The first, he suggests, was primarily associated with public health and disease control, and was embodied in the Public Health Act (No. 36 of 1919) and the Slums Act (No. 53 of 1934). Under these provisions, housing could be declared 'unfit for human habitation' and the occupants removed or the buildings demolished. These (and related housing laws) were at least partially responses to influenza epidemics (1918) and widespread tuberculosis (Union of South Africa, 1914). Fears of plague (and actual outbreaks) were also contributing factors. Parallel legislation was concerned with the provision of alternative housing for inhabitants removed from slum areas. The Housing Act (No. 25 of 1920) and its amendments provided for central state supervision of the standard of housing provided locally, and also instituted some limited central state financing of housing. As Parnell (1993) has demonstrated, however, this legislation had been contemplated prior to the influenza epidemic, and was part of a growing concern amongst public health officials and urban managers to implement proper urban planning and slum control. In addition, political order was an ever present concern of the central state in its urban policies (see below).

A second 'phase' of legislation was more directly concerned with achieving control over African people living in towns. The pre-Union colonial and republic governments had instituted legislation directing African people in certain urban areas to live in declared 'locations' but, as we saw in the previous chapter, these regulations had not been very successfully applied. One of the main problems faced by the state in enforcing both this and the public health legislation was the lack of available alternative accommodation for those whom they wished to remove from certain areas. This problem was not successfully resolved until the 1950s, although the state persisted in its efforts to improve its capacity to implement these policies. After Union in 1910 the passage of centralized legislation for African urban control took some time.

This was partly due to the state's focus on the problem of ensuring white support (Yudelman, 1983) rather than on what came to be called the 'Native Question', but it was also because of interruptions caused by the First World War. Rising black political consciousness and organization spurred the South African state to consolidate a policy which would secure segregation and political control of black people, particularly in urban areas (Bonner, 1982).

The debates leading up to the passage of the 1923 Natives (Urban Areas) Act reflected a division between liberal and more conservative officials and politicians. There were some areas of substantial disagreement, especially over the issues of African land tenure in towns and the extent to which African movement to towns should be controlled (Davenport, 1970: 77). However, it could be argued that these different proposals were 'complementary rather than mutually exclusive' (Stadler, 1987: 93). Especially in practice, both the Stallard doctrine (restricting African entry to towns to the immediately necessary labour force) and the more permissive recommendations of the liberal-influenced Godley Commission, required some control of African influx to towns and a certain acceptance of the settlement of some African people in urban areas. As Davenport comments, there was in fact 'close agreement on what an Urban Areas Act should contain', (1971: 13).

The need for control over African people within the urban areas, and the measures to be employed to this end, were hence not greatly disputed. Even at the time of the Sauer and Fagan Commission Reports of 1948 and 1949, when the stark division between pre- and post-apartheid policies should have been most evident, there was considerable consensus over the form which African settlement should take and the methods which should be utilized in securing urban control. It was also agreed that African settlement in urban areas should be limited in order both to secure better control and to effect some state regulation of the distribution of the labour supply (Stadler, 1987: 92). It is in the area of state regulation of the labour supply that most of the conflicting opinions have been identified (Hindson, 1987). In practice, though, and as Posel (1987) demonstrates, the post-1948 state implemented a 'practical' version of apartheid which attenuated the polarization between the pre- and post-apartheid urbanization policies and appeased employers who objected to limitations being placed on local labour supplies.

The third phase of urban intervention – the apartheid phase – was in many respects a consolidation and streamlining of previous urban policies, and it saw the apartheid government finding solutions to the severe constraints on urban intervention and housing provision that had disabled the pre-1948 state. Research and policy changes led to substantial reductions in the cost of mass housing construction as well as a vast increase in the scale and speed of housing provision.

Legislation requiring African residence in locations could then be fully
enforced for the first time. However, segregated housing for defined
'Coloured' and 'White' people was also to be legally required under the
Group Areas Act. There had been forerunners to this Act, both legislative and customary. Under the Housing Act, for example, funds and
planning approval were only provided for segregated housing schemes;
racially restrictive clauses were frequently inserted into title deeds of
private housing developments (Christopher, 1988); and the Pegging Act
in Natal had been designed to resolve Indian–White competition for
residential and commercial land in favour of whites (Kuper et al.,
1958).

But the Group Areas Act effected an enormous transformation in
South African cities (on Port Elizabeth see Davies, 1971; Nel, 1986),
and signified an important shift in the relationship between 'Coloured'
and 'Indian' people and the state (Goldin, 1987). With respect to
African people, though, the Nationalist Party's era of intervention
meant only a more comprehensive implementation of various pieces of
legislation which the state had previously been unable to enforce. Thus
in terms of the location strategy a growth in state capacity was the
primary characteristic of this phase, alongside the extension and
consolidation of an ideology of racial separation which had important
implications for the broader spatial organization of urban areas
(Western, 1981; Mabin, 1991).

Central state interests in urban government

Throughout these legislative phases, central state managers displayed
a persistent awareness of the relationship between the planning of
urban areas and their ability to secure the capacity to govern those
living in cities. This was evident, for example, when in the 1920s,
central state officials began a concerted search for a solution to 'the
native question': 1923 saw the first consolidation of nation-wide legislation with respect to African people in cities (Davenport, 1971). Some
of the more obvious (but often neglected in the literature) concerns of
some of the committees and commissions associated with these deliberations were to do with the problems of identifying African people and
ensuring their efficient administration. The solutions offered invariably
centred around the organization of urban space: once again the location
strategy was to be deployed. An orderly distribution of black people
through the urban environment was the plan:

> We are of the opinion that the most satisfactory way of dealing with the matter
> [of 'undesirables' in the towns] is to provide suitable accommodation for natives,

and by suitable accommodation we mean attractive and properly controlled native townships or locations for the more permanent section of the native population, supplemented by efficiently conducted hostels and rest-houses for natives temporarily sojourning in these areas.[2]

These areas were to be efficiently administered by either state officials or recognized private bodies (such as employers or charitable institutions: see Gaitskell, 1979; Rich, 1984: Chapter 1). Yet, in their first report the Native Affairs Commission – which considered pass laws and the growing presence of Africans in urban areas to be 'pressing matters' – also expressed a disquiet about the state of urban native administration:

The Commission has been impressed with the ignorance of certain municipalities and officials of the possibilities of a happy and contented Native city life. Of such city life splendid examples are afforded by such progressive towns as Bloemfontein and Durban but owing to the isolation of Native affairs other towns are not aware of what could be done. The Commission is in favour of a conference at an early date of urban native officials at Bloemfontein where common problems could be discussed and mutual assistance given. From such a conference a professional body of location managers might spring with subsequent advantage to all concerned.[3]

The fragmented development of 'urban native administration' up until the time of this report (1923) had left a poorly co-ordinated body of officials in charge of urban locations. Partly as a result of this, the new central state (formed in 1910) was severely hampered by the absence of basic information concerning African people in the country. The Pass Laws Committee noted that

Europeans are...registered in many ways, notably at birth, through taxation records, directories and kindred compilations, parliamentary and municipal voters' rolls and under the Defence Act. They also almost invariably have fixed addresses at which they can be found or information obtained as to their whereabouts, and can usually produce documents or credible witnesses vouching for their identity at the shortest notice. On the other hand, apart from the pass laws, the only more or less general system of registration of native males is through tax records and these do not lend themselves to the ready and efficient tracing of natives even in their own districts.[4]

This concern (and others) provoked a recommendation for the rationalization of the existing pass laws, in the hope that:

By these means we consider that a record of all natives moving about the country would be built up at the Central Bureau and in the event of a native not being at his home or recorded at the local registration office as being in the district an enquiry at the Central Bureau should establish his whereabouts.[5]

The very basis for modern government – a rudimentary information collection mechanism – was absent with respect to the South African black population as late as 1920 and even into the 1950s. Although the recommendations of the Pass Laws Committee were not implemented until much later, they drew attention to the problem of actually distinguishing one 'Native' from another, and after noting that 'photography is not in itself a ready means of identification and particularly of natives'[6] they insisted on the need to record thumbprints, despite the acknowledged criminal associations of such a procedure.

I would argue that surveillance and enhanced administrative capacities were major achievements of both the location strategy and pass legislation from the point of view of the central state. But these policies were also significant in terms of both political domination and capital accumulation strategies. To quote G. H. Nicholls, a prominent member of the South African Party and an active participant in the legislative process described above, 'separate political representation, territorial separation and urban control go together...The towns constitute the front trenches of our position in South Africa' (quoted in Davenport, 1970: 91). And the undemocratic form of location administration together with the denial of property rights ensured that African people were excluded from representative government at both local and national levels, thus preserving the racial form of the state.

Liberal activists: reforming and refining the location

Similar concerns regarding state power – especially a fear of the political dangers which a growing urban African population might present to the white state – were reflected in the contributions of the liberal political movements and individuals[7] who assisted in the elaboration and institutionalization of the location strategy during the pre-apartheid period. Liberal intellectuals and academic institutions were an important locus for the consolidation of segregation generally, and of the location strategy in particular. The practice of segregation generated new areas for academic endeavour: 'Bantu studies' and 'native administration' both commanded departments and faculties in several South African Universities from the early 1920s. From the outset at least part of their task was conceived in applied terms, as it was felt that such studies could benefit missionaries, administrators, government officials and decision-makers, and others who 'worked with the natives' (Radcliffe-Brown, 1922). The government itself established an ethnological section within the Department of Native Affairs (Rogers, 1949). This growing body of knowledge reproduced and refined notions of tribal life and culture as well as concepts of cultural 'adaptation', especially that of black people to 'urban life'. Although by no means solely responsible, in the broadest possible sense much of the literature reinforced the concept of 'the native' as distinct, different from and certainly inferior to the 'European' population. Both the language and the project of 'Bantu studies' contributed to this reproduction of 'the native' as a particular and different subject about whom certain programmatic truths could be known ('the native mind', 'native civilization', 'native culture'). Alongside the creation and design of appropriate locations for African people, then, the discourses of urban management also participated in the attempt to create appropriate subjects to live there. Captured within the discourses of the dominant, the 'truth' of African urban life was constituted and transformed through practices associated with the location strategy.

Policy applications of such knowledge began to formalize what may be termed a technology of domination, and alongside their initiatives to improve race relations and the living conditions of African people in the city, liberal activists and organizations also facilitated the refinement of these dominative techniques.[8] Important here were the joint councils of Europeans and natives, first established in Johannesburg in 1921 and in some 26 other centres through the decade which followed. In 1929 the South African Institute of Race Relations (SAIRR) was founded to co-ordinate the work of these organizations. J.D. Rheinallt-Jones, a director of the SAIRR, and other members played an important role in the circulation and systematization of information regarding location administration practice, as well as that dealing with broader urban policies and planning (Dubow, 1989). Conferences provided an opportunity for practitioners to learn about new legislation, to be encouraged to study 'native administration' and to gain confidence with regard to their status and role in informing and goading their employers (the local authorities) into action.[9] Reinhallt-Jones' travels constituted an informal means of communication amongst administrators and municipalities, and with the formation of the SAIRR more regular methods of information circulation – journals, newsletters and frequent conferences – kept municipalities (many of whom affiliated to the Institute) and other interested professionals informed and involved in debates concerning urban 'native' policy. Two key concerns of the emerging discourse of urban native administration were the orderly arrangement and design of locations, and their proper administration. Here two emerging professions, planning and native administration, were central to the elaboration of the location strategy through the twentieth century.

Imagining geographies: order and the planning of townships

> The aim, in my opinion, should always be to convert the native into a real asset to the country. This ideal can be achieved, provided South Africans proceed on the right lines and take the steps that are necessary to cultivate amongst the natives a satisfied, peaceful, industrious community. (Language, 1950: 38)

As we have seen, the creation of 'peaceful', 'orderly' urban environments for black people has constituted a major ambition of white authorities in South Africa throughout the twentieth century. Clearly the motivations for these ambitions varied in both time and space, and of course depended upon who was conjuring up the vision. For example, in the early decades of the century a primary concern of many authorities was with the 'insanitary', 'overcrowded' and 'immoral' living conditions of many people in urban areas. Influenza epidemics (such as the one in 1918) and widespread tuberculosis encouraged a great deal of concern for the inadequately constructed and congested dwellings of the urban poor, especially those of African people, which in the minds of the authorities constituted a serious threat to the health of all inhabitants of the cities (South Africa, 1913; 1919; 1920). But as Parnell (1993) has argued, state intervention at this time was motivated as much by the evolving discourses of planning and public health as by immediate crises provoked by epidemics. Locally, medical officers of health began to play a central role in encouraging authorities to engage in slum elimination and housing construction – crucial in the implementation of the location strategy – and nationally, as we have seen, housing legislation and subsidies were introduced in an effort to redress this perceived problem.

Town planning was formally incorporated into the South African legislation at a relatively late stage, with the 1961 constitution (Scott, 1982: 220), but those concerned with housing and urban policy perceived its potential as an organizing schema able to address and provide coherent solutions to urban problems at a much earlier date. The 1920 Housing Commission, for example, while pointing out the lack of planning students or practitioners in the country, enthused about the potential that town planning offered for addressing the dual problems of housing the poor and of 'arranging' the rapidly growing towns (South Africa, 1920).

Others involved in the housing question, such as F. Walton Jameson, an engineer and a member of the Central Housing Board (CHB) as well as a Johannesburg city councillor, took careful note of 'planning principles' in designing and siting 'native' housing. By virtue of Walton Jameson's position on the CHB, his ideas had considerable influence in the planning and design of actual housing schemes (see Chapter 5). Together with other investigators in the 1930s and before, Walton Jameson found existing locations wanting in several respects. However, instead of being preoccupied with the sordid and insanitary conditions which prevailed in most African locations, he singled out for attention the 'barrack-type' dwellings which until that stage had been provided in most municipal locations. He commented that:

Until we get out of the rut of thinking and building in terms of barrack type of locations, the problem of providing for the health and well-being of Natives will remain unsolved. (Walton Jameson, 1937: 27)

His praises were reserved for a number of 'model' schemes around the country – Orlando, Langa, Batho, Lamont (see for example Torr, 1987) – which he argued 'in every way breathe an atmosphere of home life which is almost universally absent from other municipal schemes' (1937: 28).

The promotion of a stable home life was one of the most persistent ambitions of planners of housing schemes: somehow 'loose women' and 'delinquent children' were to be eradicated from the landscape by the remaking of the environments in which they lived. Local native administration departments attempted to foster this process by encouraging women in housewifely skills such as cooking, sewing, nutrition and health (Phillips, 1930; Janisch, 1940; IANEA, 1957), and, as a committee of the CHB commented hopefully in 1940, 'In by far the majority of cases [of re-housing] the woman becomes house-proud. The burden of keeping the home fires burning is largely upon her shoulders'. Until the mass housing schemes of the 1950s, the provision of a garden was seen as contributing to this 'atmosphere' of home life. Indeed, Walton Jameson thought that an extra 25 feet of land on the usual 50 ft by 50 ft plots would transform the 'barrack-like dwelling' into a 'homestead' and emphasized the 'beneficient sociological influence on family life due to physical and mental occupation in the cultivation of the soil' (1937: 32). The provision of family houses was also seen to have effects other than such 'sociological' benefits because 'neat little houses'[10] as opposed to congested and inaccessible slum areas effected a division and a more controlled distribution of the population. Even when overcrowded, such dwellings represented to Walton Jameson a 'lesser evil' than congested slum conditions (1937: 29).

Internal details of the houses built for black people also occasioned some debate. Liberal observers and planners were concerned to engender 'decency' and 'morality' into family lives by ensuring the separation of the sexes for sleeping purposes, and by also providing space for 'normal' family activities whilst not placing the costs of such accommodation beyond the means of very low-income families. The problem of providing for such 'sociological requirements' of African families was also taken up later as the apartheid state turned to deal with the urban crisis. This occasioned a number of studies into the 'living habits' of families – such as that reported in 1950 by Betty Spence, entitled 'How Our Urban Natives Live', which collected data from families in Orlando East, Johannesburg. Information was gathered on the furniture owned by the families, the sleeping and eating arrangements, places where children did homework and so on. This information was used in order to recommend changes in the layout and furnishing of the house: but the exercise only serves to illustrate the limits which such 'sociological' planning encountered in the poverty and low wages of Africans, and in the long-standing government policy of non-subsidization of black housing and administration (Guenault and Randall, 1940). As these researchers noted, two- or three-roomed houses were rapidly overcrowded, even when families were estimated to consist of four or five people. Since densities of eight to ten or more people were in fact much more common, their detailed calculations of the use of space in these houses were generally unrealistic.

Nevertheless, research into the planning and construction of houses for urban black people formed an important prong of the state's assault upon the 'housing problem', especially under the Nationalist government. Curiously enough, although this government was notorious for the anti-urbanism inherent in its influx control policies, it was also responsible for a large increase in the provision of formal urban housing and for partially resolving what had been a long-standing inertia in housing policy. Strongly interventionist, the state initiated research into building methods and, together with the application of a form of 'site-and-service' housing, building innovations permitted the construction of mass housing at cost levels which, in the government's view, fell within the financial means of urban black people. Minimum standards of accommodation and the cheapest methods of construction possible within the bounds of 'safeguarding family life and health' (CSIR, 1954: 2) were the subjects of investigation, and chief amongst the cost-cutting measures were the shift to the use of African building labourers and to the use of cheaper building materials and construction methods.

This austerity housing evoked an enthusiastic response from the authorities (e.g. in the government propaganda publication *Bantu*), a response which on many accounts was not shared by the inhabitants who had to endure cramped conditions and to live with the inevitable defects of cheap and quickly constructed mass housing. The criteria and concerns of planning went some way towards permitting such responses from the authorities, but in these schemes attempts at alleviating the monotony and inadequacies of the facilities were very weak. These included, for example, suggestions to position the 'little houses' in slightly different ways on each plot (see Figure 3.1); to provide open spaces; or to create sensitive landscaping which, according to Hector and Calderwood, 'does not constitute the camouflage, it is an art and should be used in the manner of art. Landscaping creates and should stimulate the senses of the observer to the point of undergoing a thrilling experience' (1951:5). Relieving monotony in the eyes of planners further involved such simple procedures as the colour co-ordinated painting of doors and window sills and some roofs. One

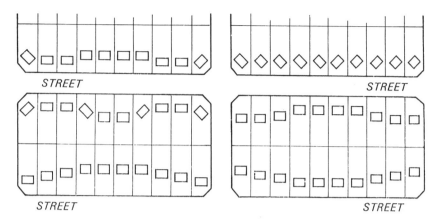

Figure 3.1 Relieving monotony in planning locations (Floyd, 1951: Figure 22)

planner noted that 'it is sufficient to paint one roof among twelve to fifty' (Merle Frean, 1957: 10) and suggested that this would contribute to creating 'a wholesome and beautiful human habitat' (1957: 2).

The organization of space not only provided a set of criteria by which to assess housing schemes quite apart from their human effects, but (and during the 1950s especially) quite obviously mediated and incorporated particular policies of the government of the time. An important case in point here is the organization of townships along ethnic grounds which reflected both the government's policy of Bantu education and their attempted resuscitation of tribal feelings as a strategy for urban social control. In Benoni an enthusiastic and efficient administrator of native affairs, Dr J.E. Matthewson, took up the 'rather interesting development' of ethnic grouping as part of the scheme for a new location in which Dr Verwoerd as Minister of Native Affairs was apparently both interested and involved. As he noted, 'Dr Verwoerd's personal interest in this scheme is no secret and he has given freely of his precious time and energy and has contributed tremendously towards its success' (Matthewson, 1956: Part III,39). In fact Verwoerd frequently referred to Benoni's township of Daveyton as a 'model', an example which other towns were exhorted to follow (Verwoerd in IANEA, 1956). Not only did the design of townships to ensure that different 'tribes' were grouped around educational facilities permit the co-ordination of government enforced 'mother tongue' instruction, but it was hoped that the reinforcement of tribal life would cultivate self-regulating 'discipline and order' and also allow tribally based headmen to operate within the local NADs (Matthewson, 1956:Parts I and III).

Urban black locations were not simply housing schemes, then, but sites for manipulation, domination and control – and this was more generally the case than the above example of ethnic grouping suggests. The intersection of administrative imperatives and location planning was appreciated by both planners and administrators. At the 1957 conference of the Institute of Administrators of Non-European Affairs (IANEA, see below), for example, one of the senior retired members raised some doubts as to whether they were 'right in creating these huge townships' and suggested instead that 'villages' might be more suitable. There, he implied, 'community responsibility' could be built up and 'you could have your headman and the people in that village playing an important part in the control of the activities of the people in that village under regulations which they are required to administer themselves' (IANEA, 1957: 79). A group of people in Johannesburg, including Colonel Bowling, a planner active in the design of African townships, also advocated a series of small, scattered townships associated with different white suburbs and industrial areas (Carr in IANEA, 1953: 86–7), and it was argued that this arrangement would provide easier access to employment and – given the shortage of land for large schemes at that time – would permit immediate and urgently needed action on the housing front.

One advocate of smaller schemes, A.J. Cutten, a Johannesburg city councillor, drew up a plan which clearly reflected this dual concern for administrative and spatial order (see Figure 3.2). He began by considering the South African housing problem within the same framework as nineteenth century British housing problems, and also discussed problems of plot size, street layout and service provision. His 'ideal township' employed the device of arranging the houses around a central point of interest (as was the case in the traditional African kraals, he noted) and this, he suggested, 'provides an admirable basis not only for planning but also for guiding and controlling the lives of the individuals in the township' (Cutten, 1951: 84).

The township was to be divided into precincts which were to be under the control of headmen who were responsible for law and order. These were then combined into blocks under 'blockmen' and further into superintendencies which were the responsibility of the white superintendent. As he noted, this was the usual practice in township administration but what he then asked was, 'how much more successful could it be in a township designed specifically with this end in view?' (1951: 85). In addition, each block would be centred around communal and social buildings which in his words would succeed in

> radiating their influence around them, they become pivots on which the lives of the surrounding residents may be hinged, and by this means is reborn in the African the sense of social union that previously existed only in his native kraal. (1951: 87)

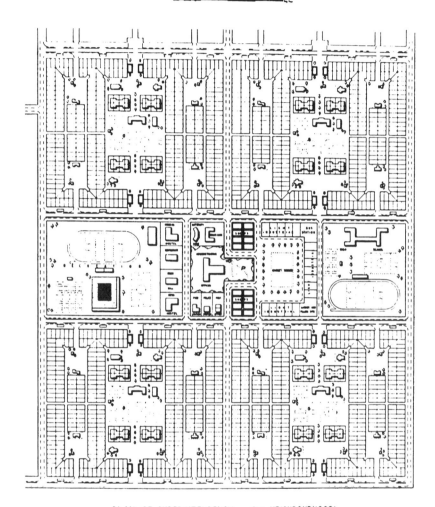

Figure 3.2 An administrative landscape (Cutten, 1951: 89)

This arrangement was one possible way of interpreting spatially the desire to reassert the values of the perceived stable and peaceful tribal life of the past alongside the implementation of an efficient administration which was responsible for overseeing and ordering the population. Other suggestions with similar ambitions were put forward and implemented; such as a traditional 'kraal' scheme at Vlakfontein, Pretoria. It was envisaged that this scheme would advance the restoration of the traditional system of Bantu rule. It was hoped that this would work to relieve the frustration which urban Bantu apparently felt at their lack of control over their existence, and would also serve to promote stability and morality in 'Bantu life'.

While these and other contributions reveal an acute awareness of the value of the organization and delimitation of space for administration, social control and political domination, some of them were never implemented because central government control of planning designs and layouts was practically complete by the 1950s. But state bodies were also concerned with these matters, as the Benoni example illustrated, and where actual planning failed to produce spatially appropriate townships, the practices of administrators were central to the effective functioning of the location strategy. Their subdivisions of residential areas for more effective surveillance, their 'local knowledge' and their regular movement into the environs in which the daily lives of inhabitants took place all represented a situated and strategic interaction (in which spatiality was once more important) between the human agent representative of state power and those individuals gathered together for their more efficient incorporation into the purview of the state. But because space itself does not automatically produce obedient citizens and because – in spite of their enforced residence in carefully ordered places – people continued to resist domination, the location administrator and his tactics and strategies formed an important part of the spatially organized subjugation of South Africa's black population.

'Speak gently, but carry the big stick'

From the establishment of the very first black location, white superintendents (and usually several black assistants) had been appointed to oversee the residents. But in the urban areas, unlike in the rural and reserve areas, a systematic or coherent national administrative ideology was not apparent by the 1920s (Dubow, 1986b). However, there was a growing concern to advance the study of the native races in order to assist administrators and, in time, a specific field of urban native administration was identified and came to constitute an independent body of knowledge with which administrators were expected to acquaint themselves (Reinallt-Jones, 1920). This supplemented an earlier emphasis upon the need simply for experience and understanding of 'the native' as suitable qualifications for a position as location superintendent.

There were a number of impulses behind this formalization of knowledge. One was the promulgation of legislation which the administrator was expected to understand and to implement, and which was accompanied by a growing regulation of local administration by the central state. Another involved the activities of 'liberal' activists who saw in urban native administration a means of promoting welfare and stability in the urban population and who encouraged the formation of links amongst the superintendents (Rich, 1978). But the administrators themselves saw the value in such networks and made a number of attempts to set up 'professional' bodies of urban native administrators. The first such national body (established in 1944) 'went defunct' (IANEA, 1957: 38), but its successor – the Institute of Administrators of Non-European Affairs – was founded in 1952 and outlasted many significant changes in the structure of urban black administration. One of its founding members, the administrator of native affairs in Durban, recalled that the IANEA was

> founded in 1952 for officers engaged on a career basis on Bantu Administration. Now that body was not only to look after the interests of its members such as many professional institutes do, but had as one of its main objectives the furtherance of the know-how, the techniques and the knowledge in regard to Bantu Administration.[11]

The establishment of an identifiable profession was itself of importance to the administrators, though, since departments of native affairs in municipalities were generally looked down upon by other officials and councillors and certainly did not carry with them a high status. Indeed, one participant at the second IANEA conference perceived their work to have been treated in a *stiefmoederlik* (step-childlike, literally stepmotherly) fashion and expressed the hope that through the Institute, native administrators would be brought 'to their rights as professional men' (van Schalkwyk, in IANEA, 1953: 10). A means by which they sought to promote their status was through the creation of a professional qualification – a diploma in native administration – which would enable people to become fellows of the Institute (Taljaard, in IANEA, 1963). This course incorporated material which was already taught at some universities at the time, and there was a shift to the specification of academic qualifications as prerequisites for the job of manager of native affairs. However, many members of the Institute became fellows prior to the introduction of these courses simply on the basis of their employment as managers of local NADs. And, whilst most managers of the NADs attended the conferences, oral evidence from Port Elizabeth suggests that the impact of the Institute upon other less senior members of local native affairs departments was negligible.

Something which the Institute did achieve, though, was the dissemination of research and information – the 'techniques' and 'knowledge' of native administration – to its members, most especially through the annual conferences. These gatherings also served to forge personal links which facilitated communication and the sharing of knowledge throughout the year and, in addition, such links created a shared experience and a shared interpretation of their tasks. From its founding in 1952, discussion at the IANEA included a strong concern for what was seen as a degenerating moral climate in the townships. Here, as in the planning discourses, the role of the family (and especially women) in stabilizing the community was seen to be crucial. But more conventional disciplinary measures were not eschewed: prisons, institutions for juvenile offenders – the problem of 'tsotsis' exercised the minds of the administrators on many an occasion – the more effective implementation of pass legislation, as well as the battery of rules and regulations governing township life were all harnessed in this struggle against what they perceived to be social anomie.

But to characterize the administrators as unambivalently controlling and dominating of those they governed is to misrepresent both their own sense of their work, and the dynamics of political domination. There was certainly a clear understanding that their work was central to the project of racial domination, as the Provincial Administrator of the Cape observed when opening the 1958 conference: 'You are the direct link between the authorities and the Bantu population in the white areas of the Union' (IANEA, 1958: 13). And the president in 1962, Mr S.F. Kingsley, tellingly described administrators as playing 'the part of sentries on a vitally important front' (IANEA, 1962: 10). But both the language used by the administrators to describe their position and their experiences in the townships hint at a greater ambiguity than this characterization allows.

The central theme in their discussions about the principles underlying their work was their role as 'fathers'. This notion has supported colonial interventions for generations, and obviously incorporates a vision of the black population as children, but – and apart from its obvious ideological roots – this idea of a father–child relationship provided administrators with a means of resolving some of the contradictions surrounding their dual role. They had both to administer unpleasant laws and also to defuse the conflicts which frequently resulted from their application. These problems were hence seen to be similar to the 'father's' dual responsibility for both care and discipline (Bourquin in IANEA, 1955: 97). However, the antagonism between these two functions remained a problem for individual administrators, some of whom saw the need to try to separate them out. Mr Marais (Boksburg) commented that combining the role of policeman and superintendent made it 'difficult for Bantu people to trust them', and Mr Smit (Virginia) suggested that managers and inspectors should deal with sensitive tasks (like rent collection), leaving the superintendent free to act as 'father to the natives' and to deal with matters directly affecting them (Buitendag in IANEA, 1959: 67). In order to gain the trust, friendship and support of the population what was required was tact, diplomacy, patience and 'the ability to apply the law in a manner that the people who are affected thereby do not feel wronged or have reason for complaint' (Roux in IANEA, 1960: 4).

Mr Ackerman of Witbank summarized the characteristics required of a location superintendent most eloquently:

> He must have the patience of a Job, he must have the wisdom of a Solomon, he must have the tact and the love of a supernatural creature, he must have the persistence to plead like an advocate, and the experience of a judge, and he must have ongoing personal contact with the inhabitants of the location which he administers. The manager and the city council who have such a location superintendent should truly value him. (IANEA, 1959: 65–6)

Personal knowledge of and friendship with the population were seen as being essential to their job, and were a source of some personal pride to the administrators. As the urban NADs grew in size some of the administrators felt that this became increasingly difficult to achieve, though, and as Mr Buitendag observed:

> One of the things that struck most forcibly in my young days when I learnt my profession at the knees of great men, was the fact that in a township of probably 20–25000 people, the superintendent knew every family living in that area by name and when he walked down the street he could say: 'That is Piet Chabalala, staying at stand so and so, he has got a wife, he has got five children, one of the daughters is married to so and so, that is related to that family around the corner'. That sort of knowledge I think is an absolute requisite for a superintendent to do his job...Today, I think, too often the superintendent does not stay on the job long enough to get to know the community, possibly because we do not pay them sufficient. (IANEA, 1959: 67)

Knowledge of the community served a more practical purpose than that of bolstering a superintendent's pride in his job and attachment to his subjects: it was also necessary in order to gain knowledge about the responses of people to the administration and also about other matters, including political organization and discontent. As well as personal observation, 'channels of information' existed in both black employees (wardsmen, or "chiefs") and white employees. Bourquin of Durban commented that the long-serving, Zulu-speaking white employees had been most useful in keeping in touch with the people: 'because they were sympathetic, mature men, because they had gained the confidence of the people, because they could speak the language fluently, these people were of inestimable value.[12]

It was often this local knowledge, a sense of attachment to the local population and a desire (even if only to a very limited extent) to temper the implementation of harsh laws with some humaneness, which led to some disagreements between the administrators and the central government. This was the subject of ongoing debate about the extent to which local administrators ought to exercise official discretion. For some commentators, such as E.H. Brookes, the idea of administrative discretion was anathema to the rule of law and parliament, and he argued that these institutions were being replaced by 'secret administrative decisions, where often no reasons are given, no evidence led in the presence of the sufferer or subject to his cross-examination, and where there is no guarantee of equity, objectivity or consistency' (1974: 1). Instead of court and parliament, he saw 'the thousand petty tyrants who rule the Bantu today' (1974: 3).

However, for the administrators official discretion represented the moment of sympathy and was also an important reflection of their personal expertise and special knowledge of their local area. Serious conflicts between administrators and the government over policy and administrative decisions did occur – such as that recorded by Edwards (1987) between Verwoerd and the then manager of the Durban NAD, Havemann. Central state representatives visiting the conferences tried to rally the local officials to their cause. Verwoerd, in 1956, for example, called upon them to be his allies – not, he said, because he had the right to instruct them, but because he was calling upon them simply to fulfil their 'ordinary duty'. He proceeded to chastise Johannesburg for failing to implement government policy, and held up Benoni as an example of what could be achieved through enthusiastic co-operation (IANEA, 1956: 110). But Havemann felt that administrators ought to have a great deal more say if not in the implementation of laws, then certainly in their framing (IANEA, 1953: 27). His successor, S.B. Bourquin, continued to insist that there needed to be space for local initiative or else, he commented, they may as well call themselves the 'Institute of Rubberstamps' (IANEA, 1958). Other officials, though, were quite content to leave flexibility to the central government (Marais in IANEA, 1958; 1961). While the personal political views of the administrators may have played a role in these disagreements, the local affiliation of managers meant that they had to tackle certain locally confined problems such as political opposition, and achieve certain locally important ends. This is partly borne out by the persistence of central–local conflicts even after the municipal administrations were transferred to solely central government control (Chaskalson, 1987; Humphries, 1983).

Paternalistic ambivalences

The men who administered African townships for much of this century are confusing historical subjects. The image of the father embodies the contradictions at the heart of their position, as much as it unambiguously reminds us that these processes of government and urban planning were profoundly gendered. For it was the 'father' who governed – contrary to the democratic myths of the fraternal contract – and the 'children' were invariably conceptualized as male.[13] As Manicom (1991) has argued, the 'Bantu' or 'native' was generally defined as male, and women's positions in the discourses of government were specified by strongly gendered concerns regarding sexuality and the family, as in the control demanded of 'loose women' (see Walker, 1991; Jeater, 1993). The organization of urban space was premised upon the existence of two types of individuals: married people, with the appropriate legal rights to settle in the urban areas; and single men, whose families remained in rural areas. And yet many accounts of the prominent role of single women and female-headed households remind us that the urban landscape and its administration was, for them, a constant terrain of struggle (Bradford, 1987a). Restrictions on single women's access to housing have only recently been dropped (despite the prominence of female-headed households in all areas of South Africa), and the urban livelihoods of women (beer brewing, prostitution, informal trade) have been under moral and legal threat for much of this century.

The image of the father also reminds us of the ambivalence of these administrators. Rulers of the daily lives of a large proportion of the African population under apartheid would seem to rank high in the demonology of South African history. And yet we have seen professions of attachment to their 'charges', instances of superintendents defending the interests of local African people against the strictures of state intervention and advocating improvements in their conditions of living: strange demons indeed! In exploring the relations between the dominator and the dominated in a historical situation as politically charged as South Africa, it is easy to forget that the effective implementation of power is usually mediated by some measure of consensus, if only partial and at times purely instrumental. Doreen Atkinson (1991) suggests that in particular townships 'moral communities' were forged in which administrators, the local state and urban communities together negotiated their understandings of the basis of governance, and of the nature and meaning of African people's place in the city. No zero-sum game, then, but a complex negotiation of the moral and substantive bases for the exercise of political power. The interface between the dominator and the dominated is a far more complicated phenomenon than a focus purely upon the exercise of power, even in its capillary and fragmented forms, permits.

That the relationship between 'colonizer' and 'colonized' is more complex than this is, of course, reinforced by the growing body of literature concerned to explore and specify the 'post-colonial' (Gilroy, 1993; Bhabha, 1993). Here we receive support for Atkinson's (1991) description of the ongoing mediation and negotiation of meaning between subjects embroiled in the colonization process: but we are also invited to take a more critical look at the kinds of subjects which our historical and geographical imaginations are conjuring up from the historical record. No longer inhabiting the rigidly separate domains of colonizer/dominator and colonial subject/dominated, the very constitution of these contesting subjects can be seen to be intertwined, and much more complex than dualistic apartheid or anti-apartheid historical accounts might imply.[14]

This argument is as true of the kinds of spaces which colonialism and apartheid have produced as it is of the interactions between the political and social (usually aspatial) subjects of history. For interpreting spaces of exclusion such as African townships as landscapes of control relies upon an account of subjects locked in dualistic opposition. These are captured through images of opposition: the moments of public conflict, when the oppositions are clearest – exactly those moments which are easiest to locate in the historical record associated with particular localities.

Our interpretations of the spaces of control should, then, also reflect the ambiguities of control which I have been discussing. And there is an emerging body of evidence to suggest that this is appropriate. Various types of state intervention under apartheid have, until recently, been seen as simply the products of a malevolent and dominative state. That form which these interventions adopted closely resembled both earlier segregationist policies and welfare state initiatives elsewhere has often been obscured – especially the latter relationship. But as Hyslop (1993: 401) argues in relation to apartheid (Bantu) education, 'The grossly racist and inegalitarian character of the new system should not obscure the fact that it introduced into South Africa a mass education system which effectively included the black working class. Important parallels can be drawn between the imposition of Bantu Education and the establishment of mass schooling in industrializing societies elsewhere.'

I would suggest that a similar argument could be made with respect to the provision of housing. While its particular segregated form and the separate administrative structures associated with African areas should not be divorced from the apartheid project of domination, houses were built, people were housed and state apparatuses were constructed which administered the intervention of the state in the everyday lives of ordinary people. As the chapters so far have demonstrated, these were quite unique structures in terms of both housing and administration. But that we need to take seriously the element of 'normality' (in a neatly Foucauldian sense) embodied in these developments means that reductionist interpretations of the apartheid landscape must be abandoned along with our tendency to seek out caricatures of historical subjects.

In the case study below, where a small number of local native administrators form one part of the story concerning the growing regulation of urban space in Port Elizabeth, the ambiguities of both the position and the identities of these administrators disrupt a stable, dualistic account, and invite us to question the histories we have been writing. In Chapter 7 I suggest that it is at least partly our position in the (negotiated) present which enables us to challenge dualistic histories written out of a time of struggle.

The case study traces the history of the African township in Port Elizabeth (New Brighton) from its origins at the turn of the century until 1971, when the administration of African urban areas was transferred from local councils to the central state. It will enable us to ground some of the more general claims concerning state power and urban space and will also provide a rich source of historical material through which we can explore the complex ways in which the various interests and rationalities discussed in this and the previous chapter worked themselves out in one particular locality.

Notes

1   Alan Mabin (1991) and Sue Parnell are currently working on these themes.
2   Report of the Interdepartmental Committee on the Native Pass Laws 1920. 1922. Cape Town: Government Printers. UG. 41–1922. p.11.
3   Report of the Native Affairs Commission for the year 1921. 1923. Cape Town: Government Printers. UG. 36–1923. p. 28.
4   Report of the Interdepartmental Committee on the Native Pass Laws, 1920. 1922. Cape Town: Government Printers. UG. 41–1922. p. 8.
5   Ibid. p. 11.
6   Ibid. p. 9.

7   If South African political liberalism failed to challenge the perva-
    sive twentieth century ideology of segregation and lacked a strong
    political base from which to pursue its programmes, activists left a
    legacy of segregationist practices which have shaped the urban
    policy of successive governments in important ways (Rich, 1980b;
    1984). The mid nineteenth century assimilationist policy in the
    Cape – a *laissez-faire* colour blindness which did not challenge white
    supremacy (Fredrickson, 1981: 188) – was influenced in the last
    decades of the century by the international currency of eugenecist
    and social Darwinist ideas (Schreuder, 1976). Reinforced by the
    mining revolution in South Africa and by the concomitant labour
    requirements (Rich, 1984: 2), the ideology of segregation emerged
    as a dominant political discourse in the first decade of the twenti-
    eth century (Cell, 1982). But an early liberal consensus with the
    ideas and practices of segregation (largely referring to territor-
    ial/regional-scale segregation) fractured in the late 1920s as white
    politicians hardened in the face of rising black political activity
    (Bradford, 1984; Dubow, 1989: 45–50). A conservative brand of
    liberalism persisted in parliamentary politics – symbolized by G.H.
    Nicholls' concept of 'trusteeship' – while other more radical liber-
    als (such as E. Brookes and McMillan) broke with the ideology of
    segregation. But whilst the national political policy of segregation
    was the focus of much controversy, the incipient practice of urban
    segregation remained an area of relative consensus. The location
    and the location superintendent, together with a complex set of
    location regulations (much the same as those passed for the 1902
    Cape Native Reserve Location Act), were to secure order over the
    bulk of the African population in urban areas. This strategic state
    policy, which was at the centre of every urban 'native' policy
    proposed since the turn of the century, was intended to achieve the
    defusion of the perceived political threat of African proletarianiza-
    tion (Dubow, 1989).

8   The case of liberal involvement in the elaboration of the location
    strategy is instructive in reminding us, following Foucault, that
    power is usually productive (of both subjects and truth) but also
    that efforts to liberate and improve people's lives are frequently
    enmeshed in prevailing discourses or could themselves have
    impacts which are not so much emancipatory, but simply transform
    (and enhance?) existing power relations. In seeking to improve the
    location as a place for African people to live, liberal activists
    reinforced the location strategy, and refined its potential as a
    surveillance mechanism – at the same time as insisting that the
    welfare of those living in locations should be the concern of the
    authorities.

9   University of the Witwatersrand Cullinan Library, South African Institute of Race Relations Archives (UW SAIRR), AD 843, 27.1.1. Notes on Conference on Native Affairs 30-10-1924 to 1-11-1924, Johannesburg.

10   Editorial, *Bantu*, 1954: 11.

11   Interview with S.B. Bourquin on 8-9-1980 by Iain Edwards, housed in the Oral History Project, Killie Campbell Africana Library, University of Natal, Durban.

12   Ibid.

13   It would seem that, given the outcomes of recent negotiations and following Pateman's (1988) allegorical reconstruction of the myth of the fraternal contract, with the son's overthrowing of the rule of the father, the struggle of women for access to citizenship and the state remains an important political goal in South Africa.

14   La Hausse's (1993) study of what he terms the 'picaresque' in African political identity is interesting here. This notion has close similarities to the more indigenous 'trickster' of folk tales, and La Hausse presents to us, in rich and grounded historical detail, the outline of a post-colonial subject: hybrid, stitching together complex fragments of identities, slipping between dominant and indigenous cultures, arguably duplicitous in relation to both. La Hausse describes a particular grouping of African politicians and petty bourgeoisie, attempting to survive in the interstices of a world with decreasing opportunities for themselves, caught always between collaboration and their ability to live off their own communities. But perhaps it is not only the unfortunate and opportunistic petty-bourgeois politicians of La Hausse's period whose subjectivities were so complex as to be labelled devious. If, instead of relegating to the 'outside' those aspects of our 'characters' which undermine the structure of our historical tales, we accept the profound ambivalence and duplicity of most/all historical subjects; if we abandon the entire, well-constructed (sutured) subjects which usually people our stories, and allow the inexplicable to become a part of the tale; then indeed the trickster, in a whole variety of guises, becomes a useful metaphor way beyond La Hausse's particular case study.

4

Government by enlightened neglect: progressive policies and location administration in Port Elizabeth, 1923–1935

Port Elizabeth has always been a second-tier urban centre. Competing for a time with Cape Town in the nineteenth century, and despite stout efforts on the part of the local elite to promote the growth of the town, it has been overshadowed by the three main urban conglomerations in the country, Johannesburg' Durban and Cape Town. This has been mirrored in the historians, neglect of the town in favour of the other metropolitan areas, despite its important history of African political organization (Lodge, 1983). But, as with many localities around the world, the local elite in Port Elizabeth have at various times asserted their claims to distinctiveness and have been eager to take the credit for initiatives which put the town ahead of others in some or other field. During a large part of the period under review in this case study (1923–72), the local council laid claim to superiority in the realms of housing and native policies. They asserted that their locations or townships were a 'model' for the rest of the Union. They also set great store by their efforts to prevent the implementation of harsh central state legislation designed to control the movements of African people. They felt that they had developed an alternative form of urban governance from that promoted by the central state.

In fact, there were a lot of similarities between the two systems of urban control and, as the following chapters will make quite plain, it was not always because of their altruistic, liberal perspective that the authorities in Port Elizabeth opposed certain aspects of the central state's urban policies. While there certainly was something distinctive about the history of urban policy in Port Elizabeth, the case study demonstrates that the protestations of uniqueness were more than a little overstated. Influx control may have been implemented later than in any other town in the country, but the council was as reluctant as the next municipality to finance African housing, and as eager to ensure that strategies to control 'their' natives were effective.

But this history was shaped as much by those the policies were designed to hold in their place as it was by the inclinations of the elite. For over time the population of Port Elizabeth's locations organized themselves to oppose aspects of the council's policies, making the council somewhat hesitant in their implementation of some measures. This was especially true in respect of influx control and beer brewing – both areas in which Port Elizabeth could claim some distinctiveness. And from the mid 1940s, these opposition movements became more coherent and more radical. The council's neat side-stepping of their culpabilities in the political domination of the African population of the town became fully exposed when, during a tense time of political protest in 1952, a serious 'riot' erupted in New Brighton, triggered by a tin of paint (see Chapter 6).

There are important aspects of the particularity of Port Elizabeth's political history which I do not in any way wish to diminish. But even as I hope I have paid sufficient attention to these, I trust that the case study which follows also points to some of the continuities in urban policy which I have been discussing so far. The discourses of native administration, as well as those of public health, planning and policing, were all important in shaping the trajectory of local 'native' policy. And the location strategy, we will see, played a central part in the local council's efforts to secure both political domination and urban order throughout the period under discussion.

At the beginning of the period covered by this case study (1923), the local council had only very incompletely implemented African segregation in the town. This was not because the local state had no interest in controlling the African population or no appreciation of the value of the location strategy in securing political control. Rather, as Maylam (1982) has pointed out, the local state was 'hamstrung with contradictions', unwilling to expend money on location development, yet wishing to achieve control over the African population. In Port Elizabeth two further place-specific contradictions emerged. Firstly, a vigorous place entrepreneurialism on the part of the local council added to other factors which undermined the effective implementation of the location strategy. Indeed, the council's professed liberalism was closely allied to the drive for local economic development and it was often more concerned with achieving urban control at minimal cost than with defending African rights. Secondly, a politically vocal African community co-ordinated popular resistance to high rents which resulted from the council's unwillingness to fund developments in the location. To the council this threatened to increase the financial burden of implementing appropriate strategies for better urban management. Resistance was at least partially defused by the paternalist and clientist administrator, but the location administration also faced opposition to many of its routine controls, especially from women in the township.

Before moving on to consider the particular role and form of the location in Port Elizabeth during the middle decades of this century, several aspects of the earlier history of the town will help us to understand later events. We turn, then, to review the origins of the relatively disordered racial geography of 1920s Port Elizabeth.

The beginnings of urban native administration in Port Elizabeth

Port Elizabeth's foundation and early development was directly associated with colonial conquest. The first white settlement in the area of Port Elizabeth took the form of dispersed farmers. This was followed by the establishment of Fort Frederick in 1799 to defend both the coastline and the scattered white farmers. Unsurprisingly, they had come into conflict with the indigenous people whose grazing and hunting rights in the area had been threatened. Port Elizabeth's role was not confined to colonial defence, though, and with time the town came to play an important part in the economic development of the hinterland as a port and a marketing centre. The population grew from the small garrison force and surrounding settlement of not more than a few hundred people when the town was laid out in 1815, to a settlement of some 4,793 people in total when the first census was taken in 1855 (Christopher, 1987; Cherry, 1988).

From its inception Port Elizabeth's urban geography was racially patterned. Within the town itself there is some evidence that the racial stratification of the population into different economic 'niches' generated a certain amount of racial segregation (Christopher, 1987). And for various reasons, distinct African settlements first arose on the outskirts of the town and near the docks (Baines, 1988; Redgrave, 1947). Mission settlements, primarily for 'Coloured' (Khoi-khoi) people, at the London Mission Society sites in the town and at Bethelsdorp, just outside Port Elizabeth, complete this early racial geography.

The first initiatives to house Africans living in Port Elizabeth in a formal location arose out of an 1847 colonial government regulation, which – alongside its provision for rural locations – permitted 'native' locations to be established 'within one or two miles of the centre of towns or villages' (Baines, 1988: 16). The rules governing these

TABLE 4.1 *Population distribution in Port Elizabeth, 1865*

	Municipality	Fingoe location	Hottentot location	Gubb's location
Whites	6,886	20	25	9
Khoi	338	61	82	–
Africans	696	394	26	600
Coloureds (including Malay)	780	705	151	–
Total	8,700	1,180	284	609

Source: Baines, 1988: 14

locations were much the same as those which applied to rural locations elsewhere in the colony. However, legal problems arose and the colonial government did not approve Port Elizabeth's first application for a location, and the effort duly floundered. A later attempt, stimulated by a grant of land made by the Governor of the time and intended specifically for an African location, proved more successful and in 1855 the 'Native Strangers' (Fingoe) location' was founded. Baines (1988) sees this as having occurred in response to the increasing influx of Africans to the town and the subsequent desire on the part of the dominant classes to control and to regulate African residence in town. This desire was heightened by the rapid influx of Xhosa people to Port Elizabeth after the cattle killings of 1856–7, which caused the Strangers' location to become overcrowded very quickly. New private locations, such as Gubb's location, were also founded around this time (Appel, 1984). Table 4.1 shows the population distribution in Port Elizabeth in 1865 (see also Figure 4.1).

With the growth of the town and the controversial conditions in the Strangers' location some efforts were made to remove Africans to new and more distant locations. One of the reasons behind the efforts to remove the Native Strangers' location was an interest amongst the white elite (especially the propertied classes) in the now-valuable land on which the location was situated (Baines, 1989). But this attempt and a later effort in the 1880s were also inspired by 'white fear' as the number of black 'faction fights' reportedly increased, probably due to increasing competition between in-migrants and previously settled Mfengu people over employment in the town (Baines, 1987; Kirk, 1987). Segregation on ethnic grounds occurred within the location, possibly because of this competition, but separation along class lines did not generally occur (Kirk, 1987). Successful African opposition forestalled the removal of these locations until the 'plague' removal of 1902 (Swanson, 1977; Kirk, 1987), but even then African resistance undermined the government's efforts at segregation and control.

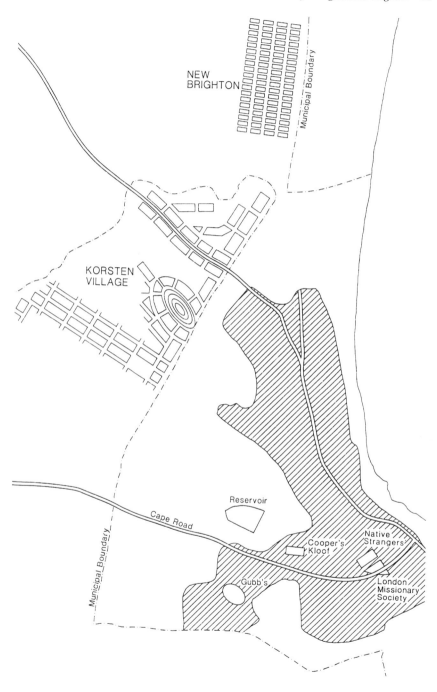

Figure 4.1 Nineteenth and early twentieth century areas of African residence in Port Elizabeth

Soon after the turn of the century, the old locations scattered about the town were razed to the ground and in a concerted police campaign the inhabitants were removed to a new, more regimented and distant location, New Brighton, some eight miles out of town (see Figure 4.1). The location was established by the Cape colonial government under the 1902 Native Reserve Location Act, which specified that all non-exempt Africans in urban areas of the Cape Colony were required to live in a demarcated location. The foundation of New Brighton, as with Ndabeni in Cape Town (Saunders, 1978), was in many respects a direct consequence of the 1902 outbreak of plague (Swanson, 1976; Christopher, 1987; Kirk, 1987). But it was also the result of a long-standing concern amongst the authorities for health and sanitation and for proper control of African people in South African towns.

Removals were of course influenced by several motives (such as the desire amongst white people for the prime residential and retail land upon which black people had come to be living), but running through the official concerns was the perceived need to create an orderly environment appropriate for the black population who were to be housed and governed there (Swanson, 1976). The Senior Government Plague Officer, David Chas Rees, considered the earlier municipal locations to be responsible for the poor health and the 'bad social condition' of Africans in the area and expressed the view that 'proper housing' in a new location had become imperative. Unlike in the earlier locations, where Africans had been permitted to build their own homes in what seems to have been a relatively haphazard fashion, the new location was to be laid out 'in the form of a township' with parallel streets and ready-built corrugated iron and wood dwellings. Efforts to limit expenses and to increase the speed of construction dictated that these inferior materials and not brick or concrete were used. In fact, many of the barrack-like houses were inherited from an army concentration camp[1] (see Figure 4.2), further contributing to a regular and regimented environment.

Resistance to living in the new formal location resulted in a large settlement of Africans and others at Korsten Village, just outside the town border (see Figure 4.1). Here some African people acquired land (many purchasing it on an instalment basis) and houses of varying quality were erected. This development evoked considerable controversy over government control and regulation of the area and the Port Elizabeth city council did consider extending its boundaries to include Korsten soon after the founding of New Brighton (Appel, 1984; Baines, 1994: 49). Kirk (1987: 230–1) has interpreted this resistance among African people to moving to New Brighton as being especially important in explaining the relative freedom experienced by African people in Port Elizabeth in later years since, as a result of their efforts to

Figure 4.2 Original houses in Red Location, New Brighton, *c.* 1988

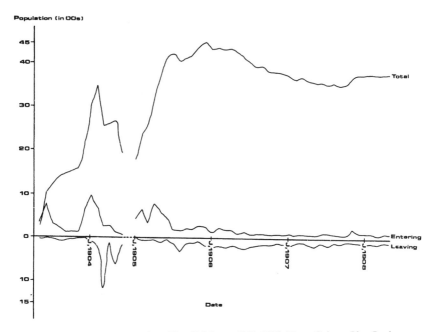

Figure 4.3 Population returns from New Brighton, 1903–1908 (Cape Colony, Blue Books on Native Affairs)

protect their right to freehold land and self-government in Korsten, African people preserved an alternative to forced residence in the location.[2] But they did not do so without considerable struggle. The city council and the Cape government ensured that legislation was amended to make the Native Reserve Location Act applicable to areas within five miles of the city boundaries. Thus while the initial population in New Brighton was extremely low, efforts to implement this legislation and to force all African people in the town to live in the location led to an increase in the location population (Baines, 1994: 49–51) (see Figure 4.3).

Overcrowding and housing shortages soon became the norm in New Brighton. Together with a generally ineffective machinery for enforcing residence in the location and the existence of exemptions from such legislation for voters and others, this housing situation resulted in a relatively large black population residing within the municipal area itself – this despite the fact that at Union Port Elizabeth was one of the most highly segregated towns (Christopher, 1987; 1988; Baines, 1994; see Table 4.2). It was these groups of people – those who remained in the town and those in Korsten – who were to become the object of state concern and slum clearance policies over the years.

TABLE 4.2 *Population distribution in Port Elizabeth, 1911*

Area	Whites	Blacks	Coloureds	Total
South End	3,654	440	4,162	8,256
Central	8,922	700	3,194	12,816
North End	5,653	524	3,439	9,616
Korsten	510	2,352	1,660	4,522
New Brighton	52	3,414	184	3,650
Walmer	1,086	221	285	1,592
Other urban	350	66	396	812
Total	20,227	7,717	13,320	41,264

Source: Christopher, 1987: 14

Within the location itself the attempt to create a sanitary and orderly environment was accompanied by an effort to impose an effective administrative order, which at this time was the responsibility of the colonial and then (after 1910) the central state's Native Affairs Department. The 'native reserve location' of New Brighton was run along much the same lines as the rural locations in the Cape Colony, apart from the absence of tribal chiefs (Beinart and Bundy, 1987). They were replaced by an advisory body, part elected and part appointed (Baines, 1990). Location regulations, gazetted in 1902, provided for the supervision and surveillance of the population within the area of the location, which was undertaken by a resident magistrate, a superintendent and an assistant superintendent, a gaoler and several 'native constables'.

The administration of New Brighton location did not impose itself upon the population in a smooth and unproblematic fashion, though. Not only were the residents 'difficult to control' from the point of view of the authorities, but the administrative staff themselves were not necessarily a compliant instrument in the hands of the state. Even the local state, presumably more able than the distant colonial government to supervise its staff, had experienced problems with effecting proper control in its municipal locations by means of a superintendent. Indeed, Mr Newcombe, superintendent of the municipal locations at the time of the plague, was accused of 'gross dereliction of duty' and forced to resign for failing to appear at council meetings or to carry out his appointed tasks[3].

The central government had similar difficulties with the superintendent that they appointed. Faced at the close of 1904 with a large number of people unable to afford the relatively high rents in the location, Mr Quirk, the 'inspector of natives', proceeded to prosecute and to jail large numbers of residents, and was only restricted in his efforts by the size of the local jail.[4] Of course people fled the location, resulting not only in a rapid decrease in the population but also in a reduced likelihood of ever reclaiming the arrears rents involved. The central Department of Native Affairs (DNA) office was alarmed by the information contained in the weekly returns that they were receiving.[5] The population had already decreased considerably in the first few years after the location was founded: as the medical officer of health (MOH) explained, 'natives appear to find it cheaper and more to their liking to reside in Korsten'.[6] In his efforts to stop this absconding, though,[7] Mr Quirk exacerbated rather than relieved the problem. He was suspended for a 'want of tact and unfriendly conduct generally towards residents in the discharge of his official duties'.[8] He was also found wanting in terms of his efficiency and general supervisory abilities.[9]

Native administration in the towns, as in the rural areas, was very much dependent upon the individuals who held these jobs. This was not only because rules require people to implement them but because at this early stage of location development and with relatively weak state capacity in urban areas, the basis of administration of Africans rested upon the individual relationship between the administrator and the population. During the 1920s the administration of the location was described as very much a 'one-man show', not only as a matter of expediency because of the small staff[10] and the relatively small population, but also as a matter of principle. As Evelyn Grattan put it, having single control vested in one man 'gives the Natives a definite Head to whom they have a right to apply in regard to every matter affecting their interests'.[11] According to Mr Grattan, not only did this conform to a 'native conception of government' (by chiefly rule) but it also made certain that all matters concerning the location inhabitants were 'dealt with by a man who knows the native and is known by them'.[12] The superintendent was thus responsible for everything which occurred in the location. This reinforced the personal nature of the administration and the superintendent used this not only to the supposed benefit of the residents (by being available for personal interviews and by extending sympathetic treatment to those with whom he was acquainted) but also as a means for improving the effectiveness of his control of the location. As Grattan wrote:

> the system of having one head to whom they can and do look for everything, has here resulted, on several occasions, in serious labour troubles being averted (among other good results).[13]

Consultation, persuasion and promises (false or otherwise) contained many potentially explosive situations, but nonetheless some problems did develop as, for example, in the 1920 shootings when several Africans were killed in their attempt to free an imprisoned union leader (Bloch, 1981; Baines, 1988).

Grattan's successor, Mr Bellairs, also had clear principles upon which he based his administration of the location. These, he commented, were founded upon 'the greater part of a lifetime spent among them with unusual opportunities of observation'.[14] He saw the 'native races' as having emerged from barbarism to comparative civilization under the 'long period of peace' which 'sympathetic and paternal' colonial and then Union government had ensured. The problem in his view, though, was that these changes had occurred in a relatively short period of time – especially in the case of urbanized Africans – and in this regard he noted that it was

> such a comparatively sudden change from a more or less spacious life at their kraals to the confinement in urban locations that invites our consideration of a policy which will to some extent ameliorate the conditions under which they at present live in such areas'.[15]

To the superintendent this 'sudden' change in the living conditions of African people meant that guidance, education and supervision were necessary if orderly, healthy and civilized locations were to be created. He continued by outlining some of the aspects of the location in Port Elizabeth which required considerable attention if these ambitions were to be achieved. He acknowledged the considerable congestion which existed and advocated that more houses be constructed and that gardens and trees be cultivated. He also discussed the need to control the production and consumption of liquor in the location, although he felt that the traditional African beer was a food of sorts and was useful in combating certain diseases.

Both Grattan and Bellairs therefore reflected the general ideology which prevailed amongst Cape native administrators of the time, especially in terms of their paternalistic mode of operation. But their expressed concern for the welfare of the 'natives' was supplemented by their desire to retain order and some measure of control, discipline and decency. This less altruistic edge to location administration, even in these times of relatively weak administrative and state capacity, is evident in both the routine and the more overtly political practices of Port Elizabeth's location superintendents. In their efforts to control the location, superintendents in Port Elizabeth and elsewhere enlisted the assistance of a number of African 'headmen' or 'wardsmen' who were each assigned responsibilities in specified areas in the location. Apart from their routine administrative tasks, these headmen acted as a vital source of information for the superintendent. Grattan observed that, as compared to general police in the town, headsmen and police in the location

> are of a much more intimate nature and affect the domestic life of the community in a very marked degree. Location police are in a position to gather information – and I may add gossip – which is of great use to the Superintendent'.[16]

These informers[17] offered regular insights into the daily lives and homes of the location residents and while cases of corruption and petty intrigue did often emerge amongst the headmen, and were even brought to the notice of the white city council,[18] relations of dependence and friendship frequently developed between the superintendent and these employees.[19] And with the formation of native advisory boards (part elected, part nominated) in the location, the possibilities for extending these clientist relations further into the community were expanded (Baines, 1994: 180).

Routinely, though, systematic house raids in search of offenders as well as the general implementation of location regulations formed the basis of the supervisor's artillery of control. In addition, in an effort to instil respect for the administration in the general populace, the superintendents attempted to maintain an air of superiority, power and prestige about their activities and those of their employees. They complained, for example, that the accommodation available for administration offices did not in any way enhance their 'standing' in the community, and neither did the fact that headmen were expected to undertake menial tasks such as the delivery of letters in the location.[20]

In a wide variety of ways the location administration impinged upon and circumscribed the lives of those who chose or were compelled to reside there. Registration cards and rent payments provided routine and bureaucratic means of supervision, but the administration also took it upon itself to regulate in detail the social lives of the inhabitants – for 'their' benefit, of course. An extreme example of this attitude is found in the restrictions which were imposed upon gatherings: no social occasions were allowed (except in public halls, schools or churches, and then only with prior permission) after 10 p.m. Monday to Friday, after 11 p.m. on Saturday and at all on Sunday. The superintendent explained this restriction by commenting that:

> It enables the Superintendent to see that people who have to go to work and those who like a quiet night are not kept awake by the jollifications of their neighbours'.[21]

Any manner of regulations were possible under this system,[22] and no doubt many people found them irksome and left the location if they could.[23]

In August 1923 the municipality acquired control of New Brighton as the unified central state sought to standardize 'native administration' throughout the Union. This brought Port Elizabeth more into line with other urban centres in the Union, and with the government policy of administering Africans in urban areas through what Rich (1980b) has termed an 'alliance' with the municipalities. In other towns this was largely because it was the municipality that had the infrastructure and the experience of governing the African urban population (see Maylam, 1982; Edwards 1987), but in Port Elizabeth such experience had ended with the founding of New Brighton under state control and the removal of inner-city African locations.

The location superintendent who was working in New Brighton for the Native Affairs Department refused a transfer to the municipality, stating that he 'wished to remain in government service'.[24] Mr Evelyn Grattan was then replaced by a Mr Bellairs, who had retired from his position as a magistrate in East London. This was not an unusual appointment, since for most of this century much of the work of the NAD was performed by employees of the Department of Justice (that is, by local magistrates). As we have seen, and like their counterparts in rural areas (Schreuder, 1976), the superintendents of Port Elizabeth's locations were heir to a fairly coherent set of ideas which informed their day-to-day relationships with the populations that they ruled and which also determined their longer-term views of what was often their life's work.

But the location administration was now responsible to the local city council and on this body an air of complacency and general neglect of the African population of New Brighton prevailed. For the council at this time 'control' consisted of formally employing the superintendent (whose wages were in any case paid out of the separate native revenue account, into which little or nothing was contributed by the general rate fund), and also in placing matters which required council attention on the already full agenda of the Finance and General Purposes Committee, for whom problems of the African location were a very low priority. But they were soon challenged over the state of the location that they had inherited as well as over the competence of the superintendent that they had employed.

At a series of meetings of the newly formed Rotary Club of South Africa,[25] the focus of attention fell upon the New Brighton location. Both the superintendent and two local priests addressed themselves to the several physical and social problems which location life and administration entailed.[26] Unfortunately for the superintendent, Bellairs, who became a scapegoat for the council's neglect and was fired, the issue received press coverage which spurred the council into some reforms of their 'native administration'.[27] Efforts were made to police more strictly the brewing of traditional beer in the location and some 188 new houses and a single men's hostel were built in 1928 and 1929 (see Figure 4.4). In addition, a separate standing committee of the council was established to deal with 'native affairs'.[28] But the council's general neglect of African concerns continued, and many of the problems raised in this liberal controversy continued to greet city councillors for many years: overcrowding, beer brewing, lack of facilities, unclean surroundings and

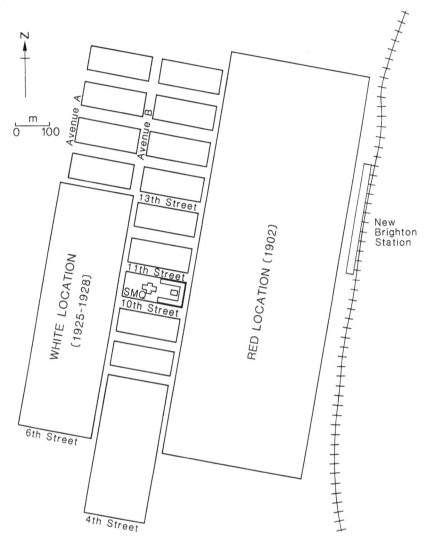

Figure 4.4 Plan of New Brighton showing new developments, *c*. 1930

a general air of decay and disorder about the location. The council's only strategy for control of African people in the town – the location and its administrator – suffered in the efficiency of its operation from a lack of financial investment in both housing and services. This was characteristic of all white councils of the time, whose predominantly white electorates had interests far removed from those of their actual and potential employees and servants living in locations.

Some attention was paid to the council's responsibilities in this area when either the African inhabitants or, more influentially at this stage, self-styled 'friends of the native'[29] pressed the spectre of disorder or scandal upon the city's elected officials. As long as the African population remained largely out of sight and out of the newspaper reports,[30] the council tended to rest easy – even when the inhabitants themselves constantly complained about the conditions under which they were forced to live. In the case of the 1925 controversy, neither the denunciations of the city's Medical Officer of Health[31] nor the complaints of the residents themselves had moved the council. Rather, the liberal interests, with which the council was personally and socially connected, spurred them to some meagre action.

On the one hand, then, the city council acknowledged the importance of the superintendent and of the location to its control of the African population within the town. On the other hand, neither this control nor its extension to those outside the location were considered worth much expense or effort. Two prevailing characteristics of the local council were at the root of this contradictory attitude. A strong 'place entrepreneurialism' together with a liberal majority on the council underpinned the 'enlightened neglect' – involving a combination of parsimony and paternalism – which characterized the local mode of political regulation until the 1950s.

'Progressive Port Elizabeth': industrial policy and liberal politics

One of the most enduring attributes of the local elite in Port Elizabeth has been a place entrepreneurialism which has actively attempted to promote local industrial growth since the 1920s. From its colonial origins Port Elizabeth grew to be an important national centre for international trade and finance. Wool and ostrich feathers and, prior to the construction of the railroad from Cape Town to Kimberley, diamonds were the chief products traded through Port Elizabeth (Appel, 1984; Mabin, 1986b). The town's merchants were active in their attempts to influence both local and colonial state policy as well as foreign and local banking interests. Some success in these efforts, together with the productivity of the wool regions which formed its hinterland, led to Port Elizabeth exceeding Cape Town in trade and other economic terms for much of the latter part of the nineteenth century (Mabin, 1986b; Inggs, 1986). Its demise came because of the vulnerability of its harbour operations to strikes and the unfortunate timing and routes of railway construction. This led to an increasingly disadvantageous differential in the costs of transporting certain products to Port Elizabeth, as opposed to other harbours. The failure on the part of Port Elizabeth's merchants to gain a more favourable position *vis-à-vis* Cape Town after the recession of the early 1880s contributed to her economic decline. However, the competition between Cape Town and Port Elizabeth outlasted the late nineteenth century reversal in their relative importance in the colonial economy and this encouraged the growth of a powerful local business lobby in Port Elizabeth. The local state was harnessed by both merchants and the local elite in their efforts to transform Port Elizabeth from a run-down and poorly serviced colonial town into a suitable place for capitalist expansion.

The revival was certainly not achieved in a smooth fashion: one account suggests that the working classes of Port Elizabeth were not at all supportive of the formation of a municipality, and were certainly opposed to the principle of local taxation, the proceeds of which they felt would only go to benefit the wealthy (Redgrave, 1947: 371–391). Despite this resistance, the council did embark upon infrastructural developments such as roads, sewerage works and water supply, and joined in the pressure being put upon the central state to improve the town's harbour facilities (Inggs, 1986). From early in the municipality's existence (founded in 1847) individual businessmen sat on the local council, no doubt displaying their 'strong sense of civic and national responsibility' (Parker in Leigh, 1966) but also their desire to effect the collective investment necessary for the pursuance of their economic interests. Merchants and traders tended to dominate the city council but in the 1920s their horizons shifted from promoting local conditions facilitative of their own activities to the active encouragement of industrial investment in the town. This new policy initiative was obviously also in the merchants' own interests because import and export trade would certainly increase with industrial growth, as would local demand for goods and services.

A world-wide industrial boom in the early 1920s saw South Africa as a whole as well as individual localities such as Port Elizabeth competing for their share in the growth of industry and trade.[32] Most conventional texts on South African economic development mark off 1925 as a turning point for South African industry. This was the year in which the Pact government introduced protective measures for industry encouraging local manufacturing, or import substitution (De Kiewiet, 1941; Hobart Houghton, 1973; Kaplan, 1976; Nattrass, 1981). Major sectors influenced by this legislation included the motor assembly and (later on) motor production sector as well as the clothing and footwear industries (Hobart Houghton, 1973). All of these sectors became important in Port Elizabeth from this time on (Adler, 1993).

Accompanying this industrial protectionism was a period of state intervention in racial employment practices which attempted to deal

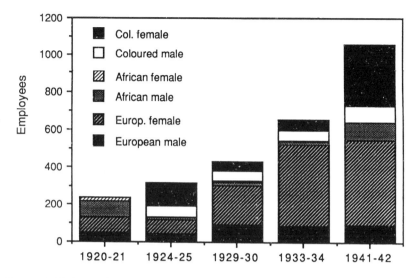

Figure 4.5 Clothing industry employment in Port Elizabeth, 1920–1942 (South African Industrial Censuses)

with the political crises of urban poverty and unemployment amongst 'poor whites' (Davies, 1971; Yudelman, 1983). Port Elizabeth was a centre for the migration of poor rural whites from the farming areas of the Cape midlands. Concern for the welfare and employment of these 'poor whites' constituted an important influence upon council policy at the time. The employment practices of local industry were also significantly affected. The newly formed General Motors factory, for example, boasted on the front pages of the local daily newspaper that their vehicles were built with 100% white labour.[33] The new 'growth' industries represented employment opportunities predominantly for whites, although over time the race composition of the overall workforce shifted towards either 'Coloured' (in the cases of clothing and boots) or African labour (in the case of motor vehicles) (See Figures 4.5 and 4.6). The preference for white labour in general, and especially on the part of the railway authorities, occasioned much hardship for Port Elizabeth's African population.[34]

In this context the municipality became involved in a great deal of activity aimed at attracting industrial development to its area, and frequently extolled the virtues of their efforts and of the economic progress being made by the town in general.[35] An industrial review in the local paper at the beginning of 1925 dwelt upon the extent of local industrial development as well as on the nation-wide promotion of South African production and the need for protective tariffs to sustain

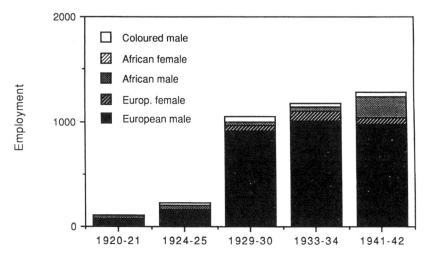

Figure 4.6 Motor vehicle industry employment in Port Elizabeth, 1920–1942 (South African Industrial Censuses)

economic growth. But it was also observed that if Port Elizabeth was to receive new industrial investments, there would have to be substantial publicity given to the town and its potential. In addition a 'strong invitation' would have to be issued to capital to locate in Port Elizabeth.[36] While the writer acknowledged that business would have to play its part in this, he felt that the municipality had primary responsibility for promoting the town. He noted that Pretoria had recently provided assistance to a cotton ginnery which chose to locate in that town, and suggested that the Port Elizabeth town council and well-meaning citizens who often exhorted 'that we must not allow such and such a town "to put it across us" in various spheres of activity, should now act upon these sentiments'.[37]

The president and members of the chambers of commerce and industry in the region included past, present and future town councillors – Millard, Young, Mangold, White – and this fact no doubt encouraged the council to take up these demands. Local industry and commerce did make efforts to promote economic activity in the area, publicizing themselves, advocating the development of the harbour and railways and, amongst other things, encouraging both cotton growing and processing in the region.[38] But the city council alone was in a position to co-ordinate campaigns based on the attractiveness of the locality to industry. It could also provide discounts on various facilities such as electricity and gas and engineer land availability.

But while the local newspaper regularly asserted that Port Elizabeth was 'on a wave of definite and commanding progress' during the

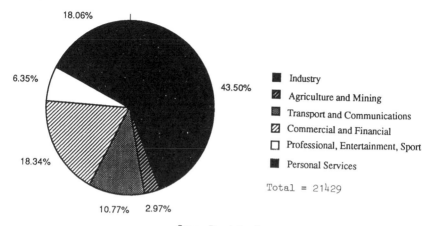

18.06%

6.35%

43.50%

18.34%

10.77%   2.97%

■ Industry
▨ Agriculture and Mining
▦ Transport and Communications
▨ Commercial and Financial
□ Professional, Entertainment, Sport
■ Personal Services

Total = 21429

Source: Population Census, 1936 UG 11-42.

Figure 4.7 Employment by economic sector in Port Elizabeth, *c.* 1936

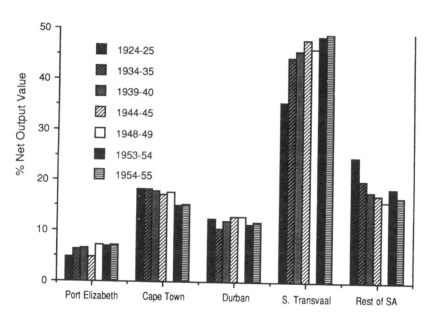

Figure 4.8 Regional distribution of industries, 1924–1955 (Hobart Houghton, 1973: 138)

1920s,[39] it is sobering to recall the actual extent of these advances. Port Elizabeth was then a small town and even by 1936 less than half of its employed population was involved in manufacturing – 17,010 in total (see Figure 4.7). In addition, the town contained less than 10% of the nation's industrial activity (see Figure 4.8). Much was made of small achievements, though, and even one new industry in the town attracted extensive comment both in the newspapers and in the council's debates. Journalists praised the grand architecture of the new factories and the cleanliness and spaciousness of the surrounds in which workers were to operate.[40] Their faith in modernism and manufacturing was evident in the proud claim that Port Elizabeth 'looks like a bit of Detroit in the North End'.[41] Port Elizabeth's ruling political and economic elite clearly had great faith in the town's ability to capture a share of the growing prosperity of South Africa during the late 1920s. As the Chamber of Industries asserted, 'Port Elizabeth, because of its geographical position and its unrivalled climate, is destined to become one of the greatest industrial centres of the Union of South Africa'.[42] The council contributed to this image of Port Elizabeth by advertising (see Figure 4.9) in 'suitable places', including railway stations, the *Rand Daily Mail* and the *Cape Times*. The Mayor also wrote to 'several leading firms in England' 'advancing the claims of Port Elizabeth as the premier manufacturing centre of the Union', inviting them to locate a branch in the town.[43]

Port Elizabeth's claims to locational superiority over other port towns and the Witwatersrand were well founded until after the Second World War. Then the growth in local primary industrial production undermined its key role in distributing imported goods from a point at the centre of the major markets of Cape Town, Durban and Johannesburg. By the mid 1950s the council was increasingly concerned about the slow-down in industrial development and even the removal of some industries from the town.[44] Since then, the place entrepreneurialism of the council and local business groups has become a desperate search for ways of preserving the local economy, but to no avail as the economic crisis in Port Elizabeth has simply deepened.

However, these decades of 'progressive' industrial policy left an important legacy in terms of land use, employment and housing in the town. The prioritizing of industrial development meant that much of the best land was set aside for industrial use, including land which might have been more suitable for housing. Indeed, much of the land which came to be used for industrial purposes had previously been occupied by the poor. Moreover, the subsidization of industrial land sales and services diverted funds from other much needed housing and social facilities, especially for the poor. But growing industrial employment also provided an opportunity for the African community to consolidate their opposition to repressive local and national policies (see Chapter 6).

The second major characteristic of the local council which significantly influenced these processes was its claim to a 'liberal' political

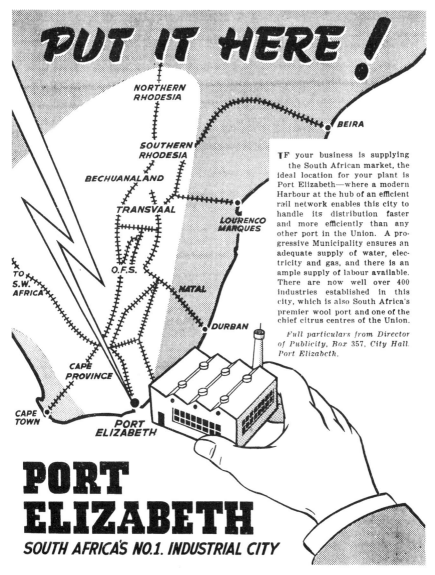

Figure 4.9 'Put it here': advertising Port Elizabeth (PE Publicity Association, 1937)

persuasion. Several of the councillors were involved in local liberal organizations, and soon after the first joint council of Europeans and Natives was established in Johannesburg the Port Elizabeth town council enquired after its activities and expressed an interest in the formation of such a body in the town.[45] This occurred only in 1931, though, and the

society was forged out of an earlier philanthropic organization, the
Native Welfare Society.[46] During its more active years the PE Joint
Council, as with the earlier Native Welfare Society, brought together a
collection of individuals concerned for African well-being and 'better-
ment', including town councillors (such as Mr T.C. White and Mr
Archibald Linton[47]), religious ministers (including Cowan and Newell,
who instigated the 1925 controversy), concerned citizens, the location
superintendent and his wife, African ministers and 'educated' people
such as Mr P.J. Nikiwe, Rev. Molefe, Mr Zwide and Mr J.M. Dippa (all of
whom were involved in township politics, some serving on the Native
Advisory Board[48]). At its initiation the Joint Council in Port Elizabeth
comprised 34 European and 36 Bantu members, a small body of people
which declined in numbers over time. After several years of inactivity
the council was closed down in 1946.[49] During the years of its existence
this organization attempted to promote contact between black and
white people, initiated some welfare work and held regular meetings
and discussions.[50] Other societies, such as the Bantu Improvement
Association and the Child Welfare Society, attracted a similar group of
liberal-minded whites and largely petty-bourgeois African people,[51] and
attempted to promote both African welfare and the 'physical and social
uplift of the natives'.[52] Yet, whilst these projects and organizations
played a part in influencing council attitudes or in supplementing the
(absence of) welfare provisions, they were by no means popularly
supported by the local African population. As one participant, Mr
Tshangana, a member of the Native Welfare Society, noted:

> we educated class of natives are being suspected by the native to be co-operat-
> ing with the Europeans.[53]

And another member of the Joint Council and the Native Advisory
Board in the New Brighton location pointed out that many Africans say
to those involved in these organizations,

> What is the good of you, we suffer; we sit side-by-side in the joint council and
> native welfare societies; but what is the good of it all, we suffer.[54]

A lack of popular support amongst the African people was therefore a
limiting factor on the ability of liberal organizations to realize their
aims and objectives. But their efforts were also obstructed by the white
community. This nucleus of concerned Europeans and aspirant petty-
bourgeois Africans operated within the broader framework of a
predominantly white local electorate which was not very interested in
African needs, and they had to make representation to a council whose
personal and political links with business were (as shown above), at
least as strong as those with organizations of a liberal persuasion.

The economic project and *laissez-faire* attitude of the council undermined their ability to govern and to control African people in the town since it contributed to a growing urban and territorial disorder. This contradiction became clearer as the population of the town rose substantially in the 1930s and as the local housing crisis reached alarming proportions. The council's response was to reproduce and to extend the prevailing, partial system of African government – the location.

New Brighton location: a model?

After the 1925 controversy the council had initiated several developments in the New Brighton location: in total 310 houses were built between 1926 and 1930 as well as a single men's quarters and various ancillary improvements such as a post office, latrines, an electric light connection and new administrative offices. Nevertheless, by 1930 the location was still overcrowded and many of the houses were considered by the Medical Officer of Health to be 'far from desirable'.[55] The new developments had also generated considerable resistance from the residents in the location, who could not afford the high rents being charged for the new dwellings. Discontented people moved out to Korsten, where unpaid rents and unpleasant interventions from the superintendent could both be avoided.[56] But the superintendent's assessment of life in the location was always most favourable – little crime or 'misbehaviour' and few incidents even of drunkenness. On the whole he considered the residents of New Brighton to be orderly and well behaved. In practice the location population was vociferous in its criticism of municipal policy, though, and one of the important tasks of the location superintendent was to defuse and contain such popular opposition.

In 1926 Mr. J.P. (Paddy) McNamee was appointed as the new location superintendent in whom the council placed their hopes after having dispensed with the services of the elderly Mr Bellairs. He was probably in his early 40s at the time, with a young family, and had previously worked at Tyantyi location in Grahamstown. His nickname in New Brighton came to be 'the one who kicks over barrels', or *Gilifatye*, suggesting his vigour in combating illegal beer brewing.[57] One of his sons, also known as Paddy, followed in his father's footsteps, later working as a location superintendent in nearby Uitenhage and then in Port Elizabeth. The younger Paddy McNamee's memories of a childhood spent in New Brighton location are full of friends and happy, caring interactions with people he perceived to be trustworthy neighbours and playmates.[58] The McNamee family lived in the superintendent's house, a 'sprawling classically colonial building'[59] situated in the

'European enclave' of the location where other location staff and the Jewish traders who operated in the area also had their homes. By his own account the McNamees were concerned white people who felt closely attached to those with whom they lived and worked[60] – albeit that their work was in fact to 'rule' the population from the enclave and from the administrative offices. No doubt the rule of Paddy McNamee (senior) was infused with his personal values of fairness and compassion (Baines, 1990b), but he also created an administration which depended upon favouritism and clientist relations with staff and the Native Advisory Board. McNamee, like many other superintendents around the country, found himself in a complex and deeply ambivalent position in relation to the people whose lives he was employed to regulate (Baines, 1994: 84–5).

The ambivalences of his administration emerge quite clearly in his handling of the controversies which surrounded the construction in 1929 of the new hostel for single males (the single men's quarters, SMQ) and the new town houses for families. Prior to the construction of the hostel single men had jointly rented rooms, many in special differentiated blocks, and others had been lodgers in the same houses as families or lived with other men and women in similar circumstances. Lodgers paid a set fee to the municipality in order to live legally in the location, and for much of the time this was 3s per month.[61] Single men occupying houses prior to the SMQ being constructed therefore paid 3s each to the municipality, which meant that – whereas a comparable dwelling rented by a family fetched between 6s and 9s per month – one occupied by ten single men fetched 30s per month. The total rents received from the location thus regularly exceeded that due on the housing stock *per se*.[62]

However, the new single men's quarters were not received very favourably by those for whom they were intended and the authorities experienced great difficulty in persuading the men to occupy them. Apart from a long list of complaints about the building's defective structure, the lack of privacy, the height of the beds and so on, the fees charged were three times the cost of previous accommodation for single men. But, in response to resistance from the single men, the administration attempted to force the men to move out of their less regulated and sexually mixed existence to the SMQ by raising the fees for single men living anywhere in the location from 3s to 9s per month, which was calculated to be the 'economic' rent for the SMQ.

The superintendent reported in September of 1929 that the numbers of single men in the location had been 'considerably reduced' as men moved out to cheaper accommodation in Korsten where they grouped together to hire rooms jointly.[63] Not only did the men 'vote with their feet' but their dissatisfaction was aired at a large public meeting which was held after the superintendent attempted to force single men to move into the SMQ by prosecuting those who were residing elsewhere in the location.[64] More people fled to Korsten, and one member of the Native Advisory Board, James Dippa, commented after the public meeting that it was only McNamee's 'fatherly spirit' which saved a potentially ugly situation from developing.[65] The Council agreed to reduce the rent to 5s per month (still a large sum for a casual labourer at the time, who earned about 3s per day when he worked), and in fact the dispute led to some efforts on the part of the native commissioner (also playing his 'paternal' role) to attain a city-wide wage increase for these workers.[66] The rent reduction did not solve the problem, though: by 1934 only 93 out of 240 places were reported to be occupied[67] and the local wage agreement was not adhered to by most employers.[68]

The new 'family' houses were similarly a source of considerable controversy. Compared to the old houses in the location, which were (even then) in very poor condition and were rented relatively cheaply (6s to 9s per month), the new brick houses were rented at the exorbitant sum of 20s to 30s per month.[69] Arrears rents on these buildings accumulated rapidly,[70] and were probably responsible for the rising deficit on the native revenue account, which the council eventually wrote off from the general rate fund at the rate of £500 p.a. some years later.[71] The council and the Native Advisory Board received numerous complaints and deputations regarding these rents,[72] and the residents of the 'new town' tried to get the council to equalize the rents by raising those of the older houses whilst reducing their own. Needless to say, these vast differences in cost engendered disputes and internal bickering, with the new town residents suggesting that, if the Advisory Board would not take up the matter, 'will it please leave it to us and we may appeal to the Council, that is what we think and there should be no Board but the Committee (which they had constituted) to hold its office'.[73] There were other such suggestions, numerous public meetings and many residents asking to move back to the old houses.[74] The council's response was always unsympathetic – offering only to reduce services provided in order to decrease the total rent charged (an offer that the Advisory Board refused),[75] and maintaining insistence upon charging an economic rent.

The superintendent's role in all of this was conciliatory and sympathetic to the residents. He pointed out to the council that no native housing scheme could be a success

> if tenanted by a people made discontented through having to pay a rate of rent higher than their earnings allowed.[76]

His advice in the area of housing development, though, was largely confined to commending the founding of a 'native village' where the 'better class native' could build his own house. Only 'deserving natives' would be considered for the scheme and McNamee expected that 'the result would be a better citizen and a greater asset to the city'.[77] This idea of a scheme for land ownership was well supported by the predominantly petty-bourgeois Advisory Board,[78] who also made use of the concept of 'citizenship' in advancing their claims upon the state. For example, in their 1929 report the board considered that the peacefulness of the location was tribute to their sense of responsibility, which made them 'valuable citizens of the state'.[79] McNamee felt that a native village would stabilize part of the workforce, encourage thrift, and make the residents better citizens of the town as well as more law-abiding. However, in his view even this place of residence for 'advanced natives' would have to be overseen and regulated in order to prevent deterioration 'along the lines of Korsten'.[80] But the village was never built, and instead all of the African landowners in the city were eventually dispossessed of their land and forced into the expanding location (Cherry, 1988; see Chapters 5 and 6).

The Advisory Board was dominated by and largely represented the ambivalent interests of the petty bourgeoisie, pressing for better housing, trading rights and land ownership, but they also interacted with the demands of the working and popular classes. Many of the Native Advisory Board members in the 1920s had been leaders of various popular organizations, including James Dippa (who was secretary of the New Brighton Vigilance Committee, as well as ICU secretary for a time), A.F. Pendla (who was chairman of the New Brighton Vigilance Committee as well as executive member of the PE Native Welfare Society) and F. Mokwena (who belonged to the South African Native Congress). Their formal jobs included positions as attorney's clerks and newspaper reporters. According to Bradford (1984), this class of African was personally pressured by declining real wages and employment opportunities[81] as well as by the ambivalence of their position as popular political leaders. The members of the Native Advisory Board certainly quarrelled amongst themselves and held different shades of political opinion.[82] But in general they sought to advance both the cause of the 'civilized' native and their own personal interests,[83] although during the late 1920s and 1930s they did continue to seek amelioration for the poorer and 'less educated' location inhabitants. Members themselves occasionally circumvented the Advisory Board's role as location representative and directly approached the city council at the head of various deputations. The more radical members such as Dippa and Pendla persistently attempted to advance the cause of the ordinary location resident in matters of rent, housing, sanitation, beer brewing rights and so on. On occasion, though, broader and more challenging demands were made, such as those for adequate wages, compulsory education and national political rights.[84] Council appointees, the chairman (superintendent) and other more moderate members took a more deferential approach to the city council whilst still supporting some of these popular demands. This meant that distrust and disapproval of the Advisory Board was not an uncommon attitude in the location.[85] But Baines (1990b: 22) concludes his consideration of the Advisory Board with the observation that it 'had provided some sort of testing ground for political mobilization of a constituency around everyday issues before 1952 in spite of the problem of the Board's legitimacy'. The board thus contributed in some measure to the formation of a strong popular political movement in New Brighton (see Chapter 6; and see Baines, 1994: Chapter 8 for details of the Native Advisory Board in PE).

Popular resistance to administrative control occurred on a number of fronts. Studies of other regions of South Africa have shown that beer brewing was the source of a great deal of conflict in many areas, especially between women and the authorities (La Hausse, 1982; Bradford, 1987a). For women who settled in the town the potential for earning a living was very limited. Employment of black people was extremely sex-selective and an important source of income for women came from provisioning other members of the location with, amongst other things, traditional African beer. In most towns the authorities followed the innovation of the Durban municipality (Maylam, 1982), though, and declared a monopoly on beer brewing in an effort to fund township administration and development without recourse to their general rate funds.

While beer brewing was certainly a contentious issue in Port Elizabeth, the outcome was very different. Firstly, since the time when New Brighton was founded in terms of the Native Reserve Location Act and administered by the central government within an administrative structure largely responsible for rural areas, home beer brewing had been permitted subject to certain restrictions on quantities. These restrictions were further complicated by the residents themselves, some of whom – apparently churchgoers[86] – did not wish to have beer brewing in their area. Thus, a very complicated rotation system emerged, in which one half of the location was never allowed to brew beer and the other half was divided into three wards whose residents were permitted to brew beer in rotation for six days at a time.[87] Strictly speaking, there were no legislative grounds for this regime of beer brewing,[88] but its enforcement by the location and South African police caused considerable grievance, especially as a result of house-to-house searches and fines.[89] The women protested at the strict regulations[90] and created informal networks for avoiding conviction.[91] Partly as a result of these protests the superintendent commented that he considered the 'Native woman of today' (1930) to be a 'totally different person from what she was 10 years ago', in that 'they were now much more independent than before'.[92]

In the face of these determined and increasingly militant women, whose survival frequently depended upon beer brewing and other informal activities, the municipality – as the superintendent put it – 'tended to tread very warily'. Apart from their unwillingness to expend funds on new ventures such as a Council monopoly of beer brewing,[93] the municipality originally 'had great hesitation about interfering with this delicate problem',[94] and the superintendent frequently advised the council against changing the brewing system for fear of strong resistance. So, although the idea of municipal brewing was raised occasionally as a means for funding the application of the Urban Areas Act to New Brighton, it was shelved until the late 1960s.[95] But this delay exacerbated the financial problems which all location administrations in the country faced and led to several politically significant rent protests in the 1940s and 1950s (see Chapter 6).

The location administration system – with its regulations, headmen, personal supervision and pacifying political role, and despite the financial contradictions that it generated – offered the local and the central state an efficient and relatively effective method of urban government. Locations were also housing estates, though, and it is to the further development of New Brighton location as a mechanism for addressing both a severe local housing crisis (especially in Korsten) and the persistent problem of governing the African population, that we now turn.

Notes

1   Port Elizabeth Intermediate Archives (PEIA) Administration Board (AB) File BN1. A.P. McNamee to Bantu Administration Department 16.9.1970. Also CA M1/3373. Plan of New Brighton Reserve Location. Proposed conversion of huts dd 28.07.1903. A label on the plan reads: 'Plan of Military Hut converted into Class "C" hut'. See also Baines (1994: 45).

2   This analysis is certainly appropriate, but the chapters to follow suggest that the absence of pass legislation was more significant in securing the relative freedom of which she speaks. In addition, the Korsten population during the twentieth century was far less politically organized than people living in the formal township: thus residential freedom does not necessarily explain political strength in the town.

3   Cape Archives (CA) 3/PEZ 1/3/1/2/1 Minutes of Meeting of Health and Location Committee 23.4.1903.

4 CA NA 656 Quirk to ARM New Brighton Location 23.8.1905.
5 CA NA 656 `Return of Population' Returned to ARM New Brighton from NA Office Cape Town 31.6.1904.
6 CA NA 656 D. Rees (Senior Government Plague Medical Officer) to MOH for Cape Colony 30.7.1904.
7 CA NA 656 Office of the Inspector of Native Locations to ARM New Brighton Location 2.4.1904.
8 CA NA 656 ARM New Brighton Location to Secretary to NA Office Cape Town 21.9.1904.
9 CA NA 656 Office of the Inspector of Native Locations to ARM New Brighton Location 2.4.1904.
10 CA 3/PEZ 1/3/2/15/1 Memo from Superintendent 5.9.22, NAC Agenda 8.4.27. Location Staffing in 1927 was as follows: superintendent, second grade European clerk assistant, clerk interpreter, carpenter, foreman, nurse, 4 native clerk interpreters, 1 native nurse, 15 labourers, 1 hospital cook, 1 office cleaner, 1 charwoman, 16 native constables (6 wardsmen included).
11 Ibid.
12 Letter from E. Grattan, printed in Saunders (1920).
13 Ibid.
14 *Eastern Province Herald* (EPH) 17.6.25.
15 Ibid.
16 CA 3/PEZ 1/3/2/15/1 8.4.1927 Location Superintendent, Memo No. 2 Police Organization – New Brighton Location under Municipal Control, 5.9.1922.
17 African police and informers played an important role more generally in colonial government. See Gann and Duignan (1978: Chapter 7).
18 CA 3/PEZ 1/3/2/15/58 NAC Agenda 30.11.1934.
19 CA 3/PEZ 1/1489 (Native Advisory Board) Minutes 27.3.1926.
20 CA 3/PEZ 1/3/2/15/1 NAC Agendas 9.9.1927 Superintendent's Report.
21 Letter from E. Grattan, printed in Saunders (1920).
22 Ibid. For example in King William's Town apparently no washing was permitted, and no visitors were allowed at all except that they were reported to the superintendent.
23 Kirk (1987) discusses this for the period to 1910.
24 CA 3/PEZ 1/3/2/15/1 Letter to the Town Clerk, 23.8.1922, NAC Agenda 8.4.1927.
25 In 1925, the Rotary Club of South Africa was founded, and a branch was opened in Port Elizabeth in May of the same year with a member of the city council as its chair, a Mr T.C. White. Amongst its members the Port Elizabeth branch boasted four city councillors and the chairman of the local school board as well as the president

of the Federated Chamber of Industries in the area. This (white) club was dedicated to 'serving' its community and only those who had demonstrated suitable service were admitted to its ranks. EPH 9.2.1925; 17.7.1925; 5.2.1926; 15.2.1925.

26 The Revs J.J. Cowan and C.E. Newell, claimed, along with Bellairs, to have 'intimate and thorough knowledge of the location and of the homes and lives of the people in it', resulting from long-standing personal observation. EPH 8.5.1925; 17,6,1925; 1.10.1925.

27 The location was described as being severely overcrowded, the population underpaid and undernourished, and the administration manifestly unable to control the burgeoning and socially destructive brewing of traditional beer. While their criticisms were as damning of the city council as they were of the superintendent, it was the superintendent, Bellairs, who became the scapegoat in this particular 'controversy'. The mayor demanded an account of these claims from Bellairs who, after listing details about rents and facilities, tried to argue that, in his experience, New Brighton compared 'more than favourably' with locations elsewhere and that after improvements which were at that time being planned by the Finance and General Purposes Committee, the location in his view would 'bid fair to be a model one'. Overcrowding he blamed on the central government's failure to improve conditions during the course of its administration before 1923. EPH 28.8.1925; CA 3/PEZ 1/1275 Bellairs to Town Clerk 22.9.1925; 6.10.1925; Mayor to C. Newell 17.10.1925; EPH 1.10.1925 Letter to the Editor, from J.Cowan.

28 CA 3/PEZ 1/1275. Millard Report to Native Affairs Committee (NAC), 3.12.1925; 3.12.1925 Report of the sub-committee appointed by the PE Rotary Club to investigate the conditions of native life in the city.

29 This term was used widely to refer to those who saw themselves as liberals, protecting the interests of the African people, although they frequently were responsible for policies which were very damaging to African interests. Rich (1984) provides one of the most comprehensive accounts of liberal activities this century.

30 Newspaper reports generally failed to cover African-related issues except in times of crisis. See McCarthy and Friedman (1983) on this issue.

31 Mayor's Minutes (MM) 1924. Medical Officer of Health (MOH) Report.

32 For example, the publication Union of South Africa (1924) was intended 'for those considering investment outside Europe whose supply of raw materials is satisfactory and whose geographical position and labour conditions are suitable' (1924: 1–2).

33 EPH 28.8.1925.
34 National Archives, Transvaal, Pretoria (TA) K26 Vol. 7 Native Economic Commission Evidence 18.3.1931 to 10.4.1931, Port Elizabeth, Evidence, Dippa, p. 5874; Tshangana, p. 5989. CA 3/PEZ 1/3/2/15/1 NAC Agendas, NABd minutes 24.3.1927. See also Cherry (1992) for extensive details concerning industrial employment in Port Elizabeth.
35 *Evening Post Industrial Supplement* 30.7.1960 'The Mayor who Sold the City to Industry', p. 7., referring to J.S. Young.
36 EPH 7.1.1925.
37 EPH 9.2.1925.
38 EPH 7.1.1927; 6.1.1926; 27.4.1927; 9.11.1925.
39 EPH 26.2.1927.
40 EPH 15.4.1927; 15.6.1927; 11.6.1927.
41 EPH 27.6.1925.
42 EPH 15.4.1927.
43 EPH 7.1.1927.
44 *Evening Post Industrial Supplement* 30.7.1960, p. 11, the Mayor of Port Elizabeth Alfred Markman.
45 Archives of the Church of the Province of South Africa (AC) Cullinan Library, University of the Witwatersrand. AD 1433/Cp5.1 11.9.1924. Town Clerk of PE to Johannesburg Joint Council.
46 AC AD 1433/Cp5.4.1 Vol. 1 21.4.1931 Minutes of the PE and District Native Welfare Society. Cp5.1 15.10.1946, Letter from V.F. Coulridge to Secretary of Race Relations.
47 EPH 31.7.1926 Editorial; 6.5.1927.
48 AC AD 1433/Cp5.4.1 Minutes of PE and District Native Welfare Society. Cp5.3 Report of the Joint Council of Europeans and Bantu 1934–1935. TA K26 Vol. 7 Evidence, H. M'belle. See Baines (1990b) for a fuller account of Native Advisory Board activities during this time.
49 AC AD 1433/Cp5.4.1 Vol. 1 21.4.1931 Minutes of the PE and District Native Welfare Society. Cp5.1 15.10.1946, Letter From V.F. Coulridge to Secretary of Race Relations.
50 AC AD 1433/Cp5.1 L.F. Addis-Smith to J.D. Reinallt-Jones. 11. 10.1931; AC AD 1433/Cp5.3 Report of the Joint Council of Europeans and Bantu 1934–1935, Third Annual Report; Annual Report, October 1939; Annual Reports, 1938–1944.
51 EPH 27.7.1925; 27.11.1926; see Bradford (1984).
52 AC AD843/B26.5.1 Constitution of the Bantu Improvement Association of PE; AD 1433/Cp5.6.4 Third Annual Report of the Bantu Improvement Association of PE.
53 TA K26 Vol. 7 Evidence, Tshangana, p. 5992.
54 Ibid., Pendla, p. 6013.

55 TA K26 Vol. 7 Native Economic Commission Evidence 18.3.1931 to 10.4.1931, Port Elizabeth, Evidence, D.L. Ferguson.
56 CA 3/PEZ 1/3/2/6/9 NAC Agendas Superintendent's Report to NAC 16.4.1940.
57 Interview with Mr Ivan Peters 14.4.1988.
58 McNamee, A.P. Unpublished Manuscript, p.13. He comments: 'I wonder if my friends of other days, Jewish, Black and Christian, become sad and smile as I do' when thinking of rising segregation in all spheres of South African life.
59 Ibid.
60 EPH 28.8.1925.
61 Thus rents which were payable by inhabitants exceeded that due on the housing stock *per se* by £182 12s 0d per month in 1926, CA 3/PEZ 1/1275. Superintendent's Report, 25.1.1926. In their criticism of location administration the Revs Newell and Cowan insisted that the rents should be reduced if such a profit was being shown, EPH 28.8.1925.
62 EPH 28.8.1925.
63 CA 3/PEZ 1/1276. 19.9.1929 Superintendent's Report.
64 CA 3/PEZ 1/1277. 19.9.1929 Native Advisory Board Report for 1929.
65 CA 3/PEZ 1/1276. 17.10.1929 NABd Minutes.
66 The municipality, the central government's native commissioner for PE, the location superintendent and representatives of commerce and industry met in the city hall, where it was represented to employers that 'the Natives were in a very bad way'. Moved by these accounts, employers agreed that 5s per day was an economic wage for Native labourers, and McNamee records that he 'went away feeling very, very optimistic about the future and I thought that PE was making history in South Africa in regard to the matter of relations between employers and employees'. However, the agreement progressively broke down, ostensibly under pressure of the declining economy and at the next meeting it was agreed to increase wages to 3s 6d per day by 1 December 1929 and then to 4s per day by 1 June 1930. Many employers failed to meet these standards, leaving Africans in an even worse position during the bad years of the depression. TA K26 Vol. 7 McNamee, Harraway; MM 1932 Location Superintendent's Report, MM 1934 City Treasurer's Report.
67 3/PEZ 1/3/2/15/8 NAC Agendas, 19.10.1934, Superintendent's Report, 17.10.1934.
68 TA K26 Vol. 7 Harraway and Freger, Chamber of Commerce representatives.
69 MM 1929, Location Superintendent's Report.

70 In December 1927 already half of outstanding rents were due to the 111 new huts, out of a total of 3,137 dwellings.
71 MM 1934, Treasurer's Report.
72 For example, CA 3/PEZ 1/1275. 31.8.1926 NABd Minutes, 19.9.1926 Superintendent's report to NAC; 3/PEZ 1/1276. 13.6.1929 Letter to NABd from 'dwellers of the New Town', 3/PEZ 1/1277. 14.4.1928 Special meeting of NABd with residents' delegation.
73 This is probably a reference to the Vigilance Committee.
74 CA 3/PEZ 1/1278. 30.1.1930 Petition from Residents of New Town to NABd.
75 CA 3/PEZ 1/1278. 15.2.1927 Minutes of NABd Meeting with NAC; 22.2.1927 Minutes NABd Meeting.
76 CA 3/PEZ 1/3/2/15/1 NAC Agendas 2.12.1927 Superintendent's Report.
77 CA 3/PEZ 1/3/2/15/1 NAC Agendas 31.1.1927 Superintendent's Report.
78 CA 3/PEZ 1/1275. 27.3.1926 Minutes NABd Meeting. 3/PEZ 1/1277 New Brighton Departmental 16.9.1929 Minutes NABd Meeting.
79 CA 3/PEZ 1/1277. NABd Annual Report for 1929.
80 TA K26 Vol. 7 Native Economic Commission Evidence 18.3.1931 to 10.4.1931, Port Elizabeth, Evidence, McNamee, p. 5933.
81 CA 3/PEZ 1/3/2/15/1 NAC Agendas 8.4.1927 Advisory Board Meeting, 24.3.1927, Cllr Gqamlana requested that more Africans be employed by the location administration since other avenues were increasingly being closed to them.
82 See their evidence before the Native Economic Commission, TA K26 Vol. 7.
83 CA 3/PEZ 1/1277. Various applications for eating houses, double houses, trading facilities etc. from the NABd members.
84 CA 3/PEZ 1/1275. Council Minutes 10.3.1926 Deputation of New Brighton Natives.
85 Grattan reported in 1920 that many in the location distrusted the Advisory Board, and this feeling emerges frequently, even in the Advisory Board's own minutes: for example, 3/PEZ 1/3/2/15/1 Native Affairs Committee Agenda 7.10.1927, Advisory Board Minutes of 20.9.1927.
86 TA K26 Vol. 7 Pendla.
87 CA 3/PEZ 1/1277. 12.9.1929 Minutes, NABd Meeting; 3/PEZ 1/3/2/15/8 NAC Agendas 15.3.1934.
88 CA 3/PEZ 1/1277. 14.11.1929 Superintendent's Report.
89 CA 3/PEZ 1/1277. 12.9.1929 Minutes NABd Meeting.
90 CA 3/PEZ 1/1277. 29.11.1928 Minutes NABd Meeting.
91 CA 3/PEZ 1/3/2/15/8 NAC Agendas 30.11.1934. A headman who was dismissed reported or fabricated tales of corrupt practices

amongst headmen involving protection of certain women, bribes etc.

92 TA K26 Vol. 7 McNamee, p. 5937.
93 At first they tried to sub-contract the monopoly rather than begin their own brewing establishment, CA 3/PEZ 1/3/2/15/1 NAC Agendas 20.7.1927; 29.7.1927 Letter to Town Clerk from the Secretary for Native Affairs (SNA).
94 TA K26 Vol. 7 McNamee, p. 5935.
95 MM 1928; CA 3/PEZ 1/3/2/15/1 NAC Agendas 5.5.1927 T.C. White and J.P. McNamee to Town Clerk 30.4.1927; 1/3/2/15/8 NAC Agendas 16.3.1934 Location Superintendent's Report.

5

An example to the whole Union?
State power and liberal policy in the
making of McNamee Village,
1935–1945

Between 1926 and 1936 the population of the Port Elizabeth metropolitan area more than doubled. A large proportion of this growth was as a result of the incorporation of densely populated surrounding areas (including Korsten) within the municipal boundaries in 1931. Both the rapid population growth and the character of the incorporated areas compounded problems of urban administration and government for the local state. Similar circumstances confronted all of the larger urban areas in the country at the time, and during the mid 1930s the central state introduced improved legislation permitting the clearance of slums and subsidizing the construction of public housing. Within this general context of urban renewal, African people were once more forced into a location where, as we have seen, the state sought to secure routine administrative control and political domination. During this period the location strategy was articulated through a liberal ideology, epitomized in the planning and design of the location extension, McNamee Village. Again, both the administration of the location and the detailed organization of space within the township contributed to its effective operation as a mechanism of domination.

Thus, liberal ideology and parsimony aside, the local state in Port Elizabeth showed an interest in remaking the urban environment along lines appropriate to effective government and administration. But the fragmented character of the state and its interests is also most apparent as we document the process whereby the urban landscape of Port Elizabeth was reorganized during the course of the 1930s. Not only were a number of different professions – health, policing, administration, planning – involved in determining the particular form of state intervention in the town, but the interests of the local state, rooted in the locality and fiscally dependent upon white ratepayers, made the co-ordination of state intervention even more problematic. The central state had to rely upon local government to implement urban policies. Within this context the local state was able to impose, at least partially, its own vision of urban political order upon the landscape. But this should not obscure the considerable area of overlap in the interests of local and central state executives concerning both the ideology and the practice of racial domination. The key area of conflict was over the question of limiting African migration to the town, and even here the council displayed considerable ambivalence (Baines, 1994: 34–6). But until the 1950s they argued that in the location strategy they had found a means for securing urban control and containing the influx of African people to the town without implementing unpopular influx control legislation.

Moreover, in South African cities during the 1930s, any concern about securing political control over African people was strongly shaped by a crisis of urban order in general. A severe shortage of housing, especially for the poorer classes, exercised the minds of state officials around the country and gave cause for a wide variety of state employees to develop and implement their visions of urban order. Most often, these visions allied themselves to the extension of the native location as a solution to a wide variety of urban problems.

This was especially true of Port Elizabeth in the late 1920s and early 1930s where the local council confronted an urban crisis of mounting proportions. Central state commissions had regularly singled Port Elizabeth out as having some of the worst examples of slum housing in the country (South Africa, 1913, 1921, 1922). But with the central government's growing concern over African urbanization and proletarianization, the congregation of Africans – 'uncontrolled' – on the city's borders came to represent a problem of some enormity. In addition, the health risks of these areas, as well as the prevalence of slum houses throughout the city centre, occasioned repeated outbursts from both the local Medical Officer of Health and the Union Health Department.[1] Some employers also showed an interest in securing better living conditions for their labourers. They assisted in developing the North End Girls' Hostel, built in 1930 for young white women newly arrived in the town, for example, and one firm requested land on which to establish a 'model village' for their African workers.[2] On the whole, though, the living conditions of labour and of the poor had long been neglected by both employers and the state. Mr Kemp, Port Elizabeth's chief sanitary inspector (later Medical Officer of Health) from the turn of the century until around 1925, had been very critical of the council's disregard for the housing needs of the poor,[3] and the report of the

Union Housing Committee of 1920 also severely reprimanded Port Elizabeth for its insanitary living conditions. They concluded their description of the town with the scathing observation that:

> a measure of control and direction in regard to expenditure of money on the part of the local authority is much needed. Whilst energy is displayed in catering for the comfort of visitors to the town and in providing great public buildings, there is not the least attempt made to improve the sanitary conditions of the town.[4]

Housing conditions in the town were by all accounts appalling (although this was the case more generally in the country), and the rapid growth in population was by no means matched by the construction of housing, which proceeded at a very slow pace. The population grew by 32% (or some 11,766 people) between 1921 and 1926 – a rate at least 5% higher than that experienced by any other large town in South Africa – and by some 104% between 1926 and 1936 (although a large proportion of this was due to the incorporation of Korsten into the municipal area).[5] But, from the passing of the Housing Act in 1920 until 1929, the municipality built only 409 (economic) houses for European and Eurafrican people, 72 houses for Europeans under the assisted housing scheme, and 310 new houses for Africans in the location.[6] In 1925 the Medical Officer of Health considered that 'relatively little progress had been made', and in 1928 he observed that the housing situation for the poorest Europeans had certainly deteriorated[7] and that the position for other races was even worse.[8] The housing shortage was exacerbated by the continual displacement of people from residential areas which occurred as industry expanded into land suitable to their requirements, especially in the North End, and as people were evicted from houses under the Slums Act.[9]

While the poor housing conditions were concentrated in the older, racially mixed parts of town, new developments took place either in racially segregated municipal schemes (Nel, 1989) or in private townships which generally inserted racially restrictive clauses into the deeds (Christopher, 1988). Systematic inspections of the town led to some houses being declared 'unfit for human habitation', but in the absence of any alternative accommodation the city council was frequently unable to proceed with either evictions or demolitions. The housing crisis within the municipal area during the 1920s and 1930s was vastly overshadowed by that prevailing in surrounding districts where the population overflow found shelter of varying but usually very poor quality. Korsten grew into one of the largest urban slum areas in the country, and although, as we have seen, houses in the formal location were overcrowded and the provision of services was inadequate, those in Korsten were reported to be even worse and they evoked considerable outcry from the authorities themselves.

Prior to Korsten's incorporation into the municipality this outcry took the form of vague accusations that Korsten posed a 'health threat' to Port Elizabeth. Later, after Korsten had been included within the municipal boundaries in 1931, it was declared to be a slum area – the 'worst slum in the world', according to the visiting Minister of Health, Sir Edward Thornton. But the attempt by the council to remove African people living in Korsten to the location between 1936 and 1942 was the result of a variety of concerns and motivations, and in the following section we will discuss three of these: health, policing and administration. On all of these counts, though, the authorities looked to the formal location as the 'model' for a solution to the physical and social problems which they perceived to exist in the town.

The problem of Korsten: motivations for municipal intervention

Korsten, originally laid out as a village in 1853, was first occupied by African people after their houses and the municipal locations were demolished in 1902 as part of the government's response to the spread of the plague into the eastern Cape (Swanson, 1976; Christopher, 1987; Cherry, 1988: 30). Kirk (1987) describes how, despite the relatively poor sanitary facilities and housing in Korsten, African people much preferred the relative freedom of this area to the restrictions and supervision of New Brighton location. Struggles over the rights of African people to remain in Korsten and to govern themselves resulted in a victory for the African people and their representation on the Korsten Village Management Board. Some twenty years later, though, renewed assaults were made upon the independence of the Korsten Africans along much the same lines as these earlier struggles.

In 1903–5 Korsten was perceived by the white authorities to be insanitary, lacking in any infrastructure and inhabited by drunken, lawless 'natives'. Apart from the significant growth in population in the area, the authorities' view of Korsten had not changed much when the influenza epidemic of 1917–1918 brought it back into public focus. The Housing Committee, for example, made this comment in their 1920 report:

> On the boundary of the municipal area but just outside, is the village of Korsten – a large collection of wood and iron houses and shanties, more or less regularly planned, on a very fine site. There is no road or street making attempted, no sanitation, light or water supply. When the inhabitants run short of rain or well water they purchase from the municipality at so much a gallon. The population is about 6,000. It is said that about half are natives, the remainder being poor whites and coloured people. Most of these people work in PE and it appears to us that the place should be controlled by the municipality of that town.[10].

Much of the apparent motivation for state action, then, lay in the insanitary conditions in Korsten (although these were at least partly a result of government neglect). But other concerns were not far below the surface. Running through and perhaps intrinsic to public health concerns were concepts of order, control and daily hygiene, even discipline. For example, the Port Elizabeth medical officer of health wrote in his report in 1928 that:

> From a health point of view, Natives should, so far as possible, be confined to the location where they are under observation and the sanitary conditions are under the direct control of the local authority.[11]

Medical power thus played an important and independent role in the remaking of South Africa's cities. In her study of the removal of African people from Korsten to New Brighton in 1936, Janet Cherry (1988) highlights the role of medical authorities. To ordinary people these were known as the 'plague removals', since on the basis of the plague – which took 19 lives in all throughout the city – the entire population of Korsten was subjected to medical terror. By popular accounts, any report of illness led to the destruction of a person's house and goods, and their removal to the lazaretto or plague camp and thence to New Brighton. The programme to combat the plague was in fact very rigorous, and since the medical authorities considered the squalid slums of Korsten to be the site of most cases – and because they believed that the majority of victims were 'blacks who had come to the city in search of work' – it was the residents of Korsten who bore the brunt of ruthless anti-plague measures. Anyone suspected of contact with a plague victim was isolated and disinfected with cyanide and their homes were gassed. Eventually these homes were demolished and the people were rehoused in slum clearance schemes.[12]

At the same time the council's progressive industrial growth lobby was casting its eyes around for land for further industrial development. The city engineer had noted in 1927 that land for residential and industrial development was becoming very scarce.[13] When the Korsten removal was going ahead, the Industries Committee was still seeking out further areas for the development of new industries, and they noted that the 'fine site' on which Korsten was located was in their view 'admirably suited in every way for industrial purposes'.[14] The council had originally (1927) sought to incorporate Korsten, amongst other reasons, for the benefits of the extra land and its potential use within their scheme of progressive industrial development.[15] But the incorporation had proved problematic to effect and took several years to come to fruition. Even by 1951 the municipality's plans from 1927 had not yet been fulfilled (see Figure 5.1) because Walmer, a neighbouring white municipality, refused incorporation.[16] Korsten residents had also been

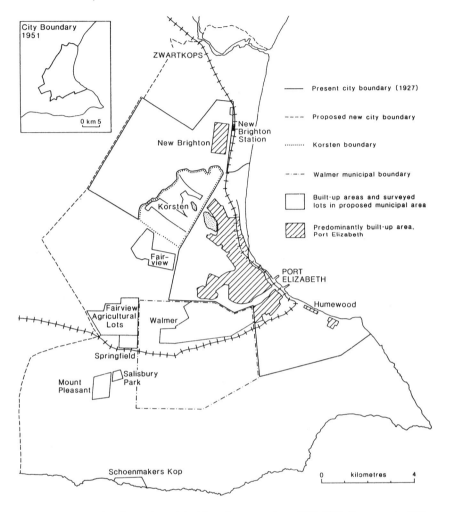

Figure 5.1 Proposed and actual municipal boundary extensions, 1927–1951 (Annexure to MM 1927)

firmly opposed to being placed under the jurisdiction of the Port Elizabeth municipality.[17] In 1926, when the idea of amalgamating adjacent local authorities was first mooted, the Secretary of the PE and District Vigilance Committee in Korsten wrote to the newspaper stating emphatically that their inclusion in Port Elizabeth would 'only be disadvantageous for them'. He observed that:

> The ignominious removal of the old locations – Russell Road, Strangers, Coopers' Kloof and Reservoir – is still fresh in the minds of the survivors of that gruelling time. The torturing methods for their removal will never be forgotten...

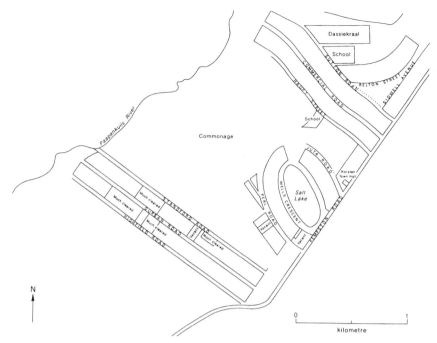

Figure 5.2 Layout Map of Korsten showing areas subject to slum clearance, *c.* 1939 (Air Photographs Job 141, 1939)

> In plain words the people of Korsten do not in the light of past experience trust the Municipality.[18]

But, although an arrangement satisfactory to the residents (or the Village Management Board) was purportedly agreed upon,[19] subsequent events proved the suspicions of Korsten residents to have been well founded. Two further brutal removals followed (in 1936 and 1956) and African landowners were eventually stripped of their land by the council (see Cherry, 1988). Partly this was the inevitable end result of one of the other motivations which lay behind the incorporation and later the removal of Korsten: namely, the 'problem' of African people living outside any 'control' whatsoever. Just as the location was perceived to offer the opportunity for medical supervision, its possibilities for improving both policing and administration were equally apparent to officials.

From its inception, Korsten had been a difficult area to police. Kirk (1987) provides evidence from 1903–4 that police were frequently prevented from interfering in people's lives: arrests were physically thwarted and residents refused to assist police officers. This had not changed by 1925 when, for example, an incident was reported which involved four men freeing a woman who was in the process of being arrested. All of those involved were eventually arrested, though, and the reporter concluded that this 'should act as a warning to many natives in Korsten and elsewhere who have resorted to interfering with the police when the latter are carrying out their duties'.[20] While to some extent such 'lawlessness' represented a measure of resistance and independence from the white municipal authorities, it was also at times a source of concern to some people living in the area. In July 1933 ratepayers of Korsten expressed distress at the rising lawlessness and the serious assaults which were being made on the 'law abiding residents of Korsten', and representations to the council and the police resulted in some deliberations as to the nature of the problem and the best possible solutions.[21] It was agreed that the police force was inadequate to the task, but the commandant questioned whether more police were going to solve the matter. One of the ratepayers pointed out that it was not the whole of Korsten which was a problem and that most of the complaints came from the Hills Kraal, Francis Street, Perl Road and Durban Road vicinity (see Figure 5.2). Perhaps police efforts could be concentrated in these areas? Another expressed the opinion that it was the 'kraal natives' who were causing the trouble, and that they should be sent away to their own people. This was disputed, however,[22] and the possibilities of declaring one part of Korsten a location were discussed but rejected because there were 'Coloured' people living there too. The idea of dividing the area into blocks with their own appointed headmen, 'as was done in the location', was also rejected for this reason. The meeting ended somewhat inconclusively, with the police pointing out that much of the trouble would be solved if the council ordered a curfew – but in its liberal tradition this was not a course of action that it would consider.[23] Despite having been incorporated into the municipality, then, Korsten continued to exist 'without any municipal control'.[24]

The district commandant firmly denied that the problem rested in inadequate policing. Instead he insisted that rising influx and the concentration of about 12,000 natives, many of a 'very undesirable class', in overcrowded, uncontrolled and insanitary conditions was to blame. As he commented, 'the harbouring of thousands of Natives together under the conditions existing is bound to cause lawlessness and trouble'.[25] He substantiated his claim by referring to New Brighton where, in his view, several thousand natives were congregated together in such a way that they were 'properly housed and controlled'. As a result of this, he argued, the area was comparatively free from serious crime and there was a total absence of the lawlessness complained of in Korsten.[26] These complaints reinforced the persistent pleas of the

Medical Officer of Health for action on slum housing in the town and its environs and the council ordered a preparatory survey of Korsten. The preparation of proposals for rehousing residents followed. However, before exploring the nature of the solutions which were offered in response to this problem of 'chaos and disorder', there is one last strand to be drawn out in this explanation of Port Elizabeth's urban transformation.

Although New Brighton had been incorporated into the municipality on 1 August 1923, it had continued to be administered under the 1902 Native Reserve Location Act, as amended, and not under the 1923 Natives (Urban Areas) Act. There were a number of reasons for this. Some difficulties had been encountered with the ownership of the land on which the location was situated,[27] and there was some concern over the problems which might be experienced in implementing the municipal monopoly of beer production which the financial obligations of the Urban Areas Act made attractive to local authorities.[28] Apart from the opposition which it was expected such a move would evoke from the population (especially from a number of women who made a living from the sale of traditional beer), a complicated, but strictly speaking illegal, system of permits for brewing beer had evolved in the location. The implementation of the Urban Areas Act would have exposed this.[29] However, these were only obstacles along the way and it was generally agreed by the council that the exclusion of New Brighton from the working of the Act was only temporary. The rest of the town had been included within its ambit from the Act's inception, and it was felt to be inappropriate that the location was administered under 'out of date' legislation.[30] Not long after his arrival in Port Elizabeth, the new superintendent, Mr McNamee, had expressed the opinion that the Urban Areas Act would provide a much better basis for administration than the old location regulations.

McNamee also felt favourably inclined towards the extension of 'government interference' in location administration, which the Urban Areas Act entailed. This he preferred to call 'supervision', and he saw the Act as having contributed to a great improvement in the condition and administration of locations in the country generally,[31] as well as having promoted a welcome unification of policy 'instead of ... each Municipality seemingly being a law unto itself'. After some delays caused by the beer brewing issue and the insistence on the part of the central Native Affairs Department that new location regulations be framed in terms of the Act, the location was eventually included under the Urban Areas Act on 1 January 1933.[32]

One of the effects (and a cause) of this legislative change was an extension of the specific responsibilities of both the Native Administration Department and the Native Affairs Committee beyond the confines of the location.[33] In 1930, for example, McNamee replied to a question from the Native Economic Commission regarding conditions in Port Elizabeth outside of New Brighton:

> I have no knowledge of it. You see I live at New Brighton and my time there is fully taken up.[34]

But his exposure to various nation-wide trends in native administration through conferences, visits to other areas and contact with other organizations,[35] as well as the possibility of the application of influx control legislation to the town (Baines, 1994: 35–7), had instilled in him a vision of what a more efficient and city-wide administration might entail. This included 'assisting the native in his transition from tribal life to urban existence' and ensuring that 'they develop along the right lines'. The municipal Native Affairs Department, he felt, should replace the tribal chief in the realm of traditional law and government, and also take an active interest in the welfare and the control of Africans throughout the town. But in addition to these the superintendent felt that there was a need to regulate the influx of Africans to the town so that their numbers did not exceed the town's requirement and so that the wages of local Africans were not undercut. He insisted that,

> no aspect of native life or any Native in the city should be beyond the scope of the Native Administration Department.[36]

The idea of extending the range of the Native Administration Department stimulated a rethink of the spatial organization of the administration, and some discussion was held over whether to locate the superintendent's office centrally in the town in order to facilitate overall control. It was also expected that locations might be built in a number of different areas of the city. In that case a superintendent would have to be appointed in each location in order to continue the strategy of administrative control then in operation.[37] This widening of the scope of location administration hence added to the existing pressures on the council to act on both the housing situation and the 'problem' of thousands of Africans living outside any control. The council had enacted the provisions of the Urban Areas Act enabling the regulation of African influx to the city soon after the Act was applied (1934), but had to do so again four years later since its application had been prevented by the inadequacies of the available administrative apparatus. Only in New Brighton was this possible, and even so the council was circumspect as to the wisdom of implementing this contentious legislation. In 1940 they resolved to defer consideration of influx control *sine die* – ambivalence and lack of capacity turning them back upon the location strategy as their key means for maintaining control over African people in the town (Baines, 1994: 35–7).

A variety of different motivations therefore existed for local state intervention in the urban environment at this time – all of which centred on the location strategy as a solution. The passage of national legislation also affected the local decision-makers and, together with the slow cycle of bureaucratic decision-making, influenced both the timing and the form of intervention. The council finally addressed the serious problems of the poorest sectors of the population in the post-depression years when central government legislation and pressure (especially from the Health Department) provided sufficient encouragement and incentive for action. The council had no desire to spend any of the ratepayers' money on the African population, and so this national-level 'encouragement' was decisive in ensuring that the local state's intervention was of a sufficient scale. Inputs from the central state during this period were largely consonant with the local state's own purposes, except in financial terms. The advisory role of the central state was also very important in planning the specific housing developments which were undertaken by the council. The contingent interaction between the 'location strategy' and the liberal policy and ideology prevailing at the time shaped the particular form of housing provided for African people in Port Elizabeth. The landscape of control which resulted in the late 1930s was marked with liberal ameliorations.

A complicated planning process preceded the construction of McNamee Village, the 1930s extension to New Brighton, and the forces at play in these bureaucratic moments reveal much about the intentions and ambitions of the state in initiating this development. The 'location strategy' was to take a new guise, however, as a 'model' of urban African local government and housing.

The new model location: McNamee Village and remaking Port Elizabeth

The various pressures which were being brought to bear upon the local state to take some action regarding the poor housing conditions and the perceived dangers of slum areas received a major spur when the central government made sub-economic loans available for low-income housing.[38] Nevertheless, the council at first resisted these funds since they entailed an equal loss on the part of the local state and the central state (a total loss of 2.5%) which, in terms of 'native policy', would have entailed a new principle for Port Elizabeth in that the council would then be subsidizing African housing from ratepayers' funds.[39] Despite repeated efforts to alter this 'burden' for the local council, they were eventually obliged to proceed under the constraint of 0.75% loans with

TABLE 5.1 *Estimates of the population in Korsten, 1911–1936*

Date	Area	Estimated population	Data source
1911	Korsten	2,344 (African)	1911 Census
1921	Korsten	3,876 (African)	1921 Census
1925	Population living outside but working in Port Elizabeth	14,560 (total)	MOH 1925[1]
1930	Korsten	8,500 (total)	MOH 1930[2]
1931	Added areas (mostly Korsten)	15,000 ('non-European')	MOH 1931[3]
1932	Korsten	9,500 (African)	MOH 1932[4]
1934	Korsten	12,400 (African) 24,000 (total)	Municipal Survey[5]
1936	All urban except New Brighton	21,270 (African)	1936 Census

Sources: [1] EPH 15–8–1925; [2] Mayor's Minutes 1930; [3] Mayor's Minutes 1931; [4] Mayor's Minutes 1932; [5] 3/PEZ 1/3/2/6/68 Housing and Slum Elimination Committee Agenda 8–4–1936

the loss shared between the central and local governments at a ratio of 2:1 in favour of the municipality. Although a decision had been made to 'do something' about the accumulated problems of housing in the town, exactly what and how much was to be done constituted the next hurdle.

Estimates of how many people lived in Korsten were subject to considerable uncertainty. Even those very familiar with the area itself (such as the local police, residents and landowners) differed in their estimates of the African population which they suggested was somewhere between 10,000 and 12,000 in 1934. These estimates were acknowledged to be only approximate, though, because the extent of sub-letting of housing and the proliferation of shacks made it exceptionally difficult to count the population. Table 5.1 shows the varying population estimates of the Medical Officer of Health and the census returns over time, illustrating this uncertainty.

The population was obviously growing very rapidly and, although it was difficult for the authorities to know exactly how many people were living there, more exact information regarding the number of slum dwellings and the size of the population was required before action could be taken. The council therefore ordered that a population survey be conducted by the Medical Officer of Health.[40] Such a survey was also required by the Department of Health if an application was to be made for a central government subsidy for housing schemes.[41] The survey revealed a total population of 24,000 living in Korsten, compared with the 1932 estimate of 21,000. The racial breakdowns of these estimates are shown in Table 5.2.

The Slums Act of 1934 gave the council enhanced powers to deal with buildings declared unfit for human habitation. Action had been

TABLE 5.2 *Results of survey of Korsten population, 1932 and 1934*

	1932[1]	1934[2]
European	4,000	5,200
Eurafrican		6,000
Asian	} 7,500	400
African	9,500	12,400
Total	21,000	24,000

Sources: [1] Mayor's Minutes 1932; [2] Mayor's Minutes 1935

TABLE 5.3 *Distribution of people in dwellings declared unfit for human habitation, 1930 and 1935*

1930

District	European	Coloured	African	Total
North End	255	811	116	1,182
Central	85	243	67	395
South End	80	678	70	728
Total	420	1,732	253	2,305

1935

District	European	Coloured	African	Asiatic	Total
Korsten	85	1,600	11,456	–	13,141
North End	100	341	60	10	511
Central	24	38	2	8	62
South End	17	551	94	16	678
Newton Park	37	13	10	–	60
New Brighton	19	–	–	–	19
Total	282	2,553	11,622	34	14,491

Sources: Mayor's Minutes 1930; 1935

proceeding in a slow and piecemeal fashion on this front for some time, and the major obstacle which had been encountered was the lack of available alternative housing for those who would be displaced. But the new housing schemes would soon change that. The Medical Officer of Health was aware that the problem was enormous and would require 'a careful, firm, well-balanced and considered policy if it were to be successful'.[42] The solution available in the form of the Slums Act guided the action taken, and dwellings declared unfit for human habitation were the focus of attention. The distribution of such identified dwellings through the town in 1930 and 1935 is shown in Table 5.3. Korsten had the greatest concentration of slum dwellings in the city, and the magnitude of the population in the area as well as its composition (largely African) encouraged the council and officials to think that a 'separate solution' was required for this area as distinct from the rest of the town.[43] The council, though, was reluctant to adopt any sort of solution at all if it was to cost them money, especially as regards houses for Africans.

The council and the town treasurer were both adamant that the 'ratepayer' should not be called upon to finance or to subsidize the housing of the African population. This, they noticed, would set an entirely new precedent which they, and most certainly the ratepayers, were most reluctant to do.[44] Rejecting the idea of a sub-economic housing scheme because of the costs it entailed for them, the council attempted to explore cheaper alternatives. First among these was a 'native village' – a proposal which had been discussed a few years previously, but which had been shelved because of legal difficulties in declaring freehold land within the location area. This idea was revived in an effort to solve the housing crisis at no cost to the council.[45] It was fated from the beginning because, as one councillor pointed out, it would not provide for the 'ordinary native' but only for those in permanent (and reasonably well-paid) employment. In addition, given that freehold land ownership was not permitted in the location and that leasehold would not be popular where alternatives (such as ownership outside the location) were still available, the scheme would also be unlikely to attract many people.[46]

The Native Advisory Board members continued to stress the problems presented by high rents in New Brighton and the need for cheaper accommodation, as did the superintendent.[47] This was not only because of the very low wages paid to Africans, which together with the extent of unemployment reduced their ability to pay, but also because of the practice of charging the location residents on an economic (and often profitable) basis for all their services. In the location the total monthly charge for services per household was 8s 6d (see Table 5.4), which – on the superintendent's estimate of a 'reasonable' total charge being 12s 6d per month (making with transport 17s 6d per month, or 25% of an average African man's earnings) – left only 4s for an economic rent. In the superintendent's view people could only afford this with difficulty anyway. Clearly an economic (i.e. non-subsidized) housing scheme would only generate further problems of this sort.[48] McNamee's solution to the dilemma was to use cheap, unskilled (black) labour in the construction of the houses – but in terms of the government's civilized (white) labour policy, this was impossible.

The council, realizing that larger and cheaper schemes were necessary, approached the Central Housing Board to waive the council's share of the loss that they were meant to bear on the sub-economic loan for African housing. This was refused,[49] but similar resistance from other local authorities to footing this bill lead to a change in the legislation

TABLE 5.4 *Breakdown of monthly service costs per house in New Brighton location, 1936*

Description of service	s	d
Administration	1	2
Contributions to other municipal departments		5
Medical services	1	0
Sanitation and rubbish removal	2	1
Water		11
Repairs and building maintenance	1	1
Rent collecting, headmen's salaries		7
Reserve for bad debts		5
Miscellaneous (road repairs, grants)		5
Capital charges		5
Total	8	6

Sources: 3/PEZ 1/3/2/6/8 Housing and Slum Elimination Committee Agenda, 18–9–1936, Superintendent's Report 7–9–1936

(Parnell, 1987), which required local councils to bear only half of the amount of the loss carried by the central government instead of an equal share. This effectively meant that the council was receiving large loans to house labourers, improve their town, increase the rateable value of land cleared of 'slums', and free large areas for potentially lucrative development at a subsidized interest rate of only 0.75%.[50] Nevertheless, by the time the matter had been under consideration for two years the council's proposals for African sub-economic housing stood at only 500 houses, and they were constantly trying to reduce the cost which even this small development would entail. But Korsten had been named in the Central Housing Board reports as one of the most appalling slum areas in the country, and the patience of the Minister for Public Health was wearing thin. In October 1936 the Secretary for Public Health wrote that in the light of the reduction in the cost of sub-economic loans to the council,

> the Minister does not consider that the question of dealing with the Korsten slums and the rehousing of its inhabitants can be left in abeyance any longer.[51]

Increasingly aware of the benefits of proceeding with the slum clearance – such as releasing further industrial land,[52] a rising rateable value[53] and a brief flirtation with the possibility of making a more direct gain from the land that they would acquire – the council was moved along from a scheme of 500 houses for Africans in New Brighton to one involving 3,000 dwellings for Africans and 5,000 sub-economic houses in total. The possibility of siting the housing for Africans at Korsten had been briefly debated, but was rejected almost immediately in response to the argument that building houses there would have meant, in addition to other disadvantages such as having to build on an already occupied and potentially valuable site, 'the duplication of the whole of the administrative side'.[54] This point is instructive for our purposes, since it highlights the strong interconnections which existed between the location as the 'ideal' place for Africans and the essential role which the administration was seen to play in realizing this ideal. The strategic function of the location administration and the costs of reproducing this elsewhere were thus appreciated by the council.

The principles for planning the new 'model location' , however, were somewhat different from those used in planning earlier locations. Port Elizabeth's new development – to be called McNamee Village after its superintendent – came to embody the particular liberal vision dominant at the time. Although the detailed plans for McNamee Village were as influenced by questions of economy as were the negotiations over financing, the planning exercise was, especially in retrospect, surrounded by a self-consciously noble, liberal, and even religious rhetoric. An observer who visited the new township in 1941 enthusiastically described the authorities as possessing

> not merely professional pride and thoroughness but a real spirit of goodwill and friendliness – the human touch too often lacking in organised social service – toward those for whom they were planning and working.[55]

To this commentator the authorities in New Brighton were amongst those 'building the Kingdom of God on earth'. The city council itself claimed a lot of credit for their 'progressive housing policy', which justifiably or not was cited as a model throughout the Union and beyond.[56] Many municipalities requested information concerning McNamee Village, as did the treasurer of Pietermaritzburg in Natal, who wrote that:

> owing to the various bouquets which are being handed to your city in respect of your sub-economic Housing Schemes, we are naturally 'sitting up and taking notice' and I have been requested ... to obtain details.[57]

Councillors – especially Councillor Schauder, who was an ardent supporter of the housing scheme[58] – applauded their own endeavours in housing the growing population both in terms of the size of the scheme (some 5,000 houses) and with respect to the form which the scheme took. They felt that the plans and the houses conformed to their generally 'fair and just' treatment of the African population in that, to their minds, a 'model' or 'garden' village had been created: one which enhanced both the environmental and the social living conditions of the population. This was despite the fact that the council had to be vigorously persuaded to take on financial responsibility for a housing scheme at all, let alone one of a size and cost reasonably appropriate to the population in need of accommodation. They were also very much indebted to outside actors for the vision of a garden village, most notably to F. Walton Jameson of the Central Housing Board (see Chapter 3).

The first plans for the African township were drawn up by the city engineer in October 1936 when negotiations with the central government were just beginning. He proposed a uniform, repetitive plan of regular plots 35 feet by 50 feet.[59] The Central Housing Board criticized this on the grounds that the plots were too small and the houses inadequate in design terms.[60] Walton Jameson, then chairperson of the Central Housing Board, forwarded to the council a paper that he had written on the matter of 'native' housing (it appeared later in the *Race Relations Journal* in 1937), commenting that since he received so many requests for information concerning the planning of housing schemes he had decided to 'write it all down on paper' and circulate this document to interested parties instead.[61] If the Port Elizabeth case is any indication, then this paper and Walton Jameson himself were certainly influential in the housing schemes developed around the country at this time.[62] In Port Elizabeth both the city engineer and the location superintendent considered the paper to be 'most valuable', and they duly took detailed note of the recommendations.[63] But since the initial plans failed to satisfy the Central Housing Board, Walton Jameson himself travelled to Port Elizabeth and spent a week assisting the engineer in drawing up more appropriate detailed plans.[64] McNamee township, then, is certainly a 'model village' in the sense that it reflected the dominant vision of key figures in the housing field at the time that it was built.

The site chosen for McNamee Village was part of the land granted to the municipality by the government in 1923 for African residential use. This comprised several hundred hectares around the New Brighton location but, apart from its availability, there were other considerations involved in the selection of this site, such as the transport facilities which were acknowledged to be of great importance. The pre-existing railway link to New Brighton was definitely an advantage, as was the possibility of diverting the line through to the proposed location extension and then on to the city centre via Korsten.[65] Narrow and insubstantial roads were built in McNamee on the basis of this plan, but the railway extension never materialized, leading to considerable transport difficulties and excessive wear on the inadequate roads.

The layout and housing design reflected Walton Jameson's compromise between economy and 'social upliftment'. The scheme was planned along the lines of a 'garden city', with a central open space and roads radiating out from this (see Figure 5.3). The houses were to be situated on numerous culs-de-sac which were intended to provide privacy, variation in appearance and safe playing areas for children.

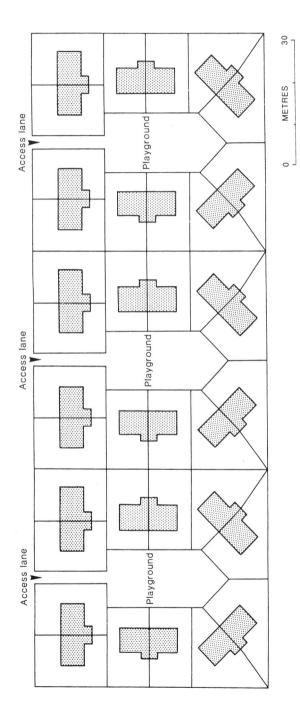

Figure 5.3 Layout plan of McNamee Village

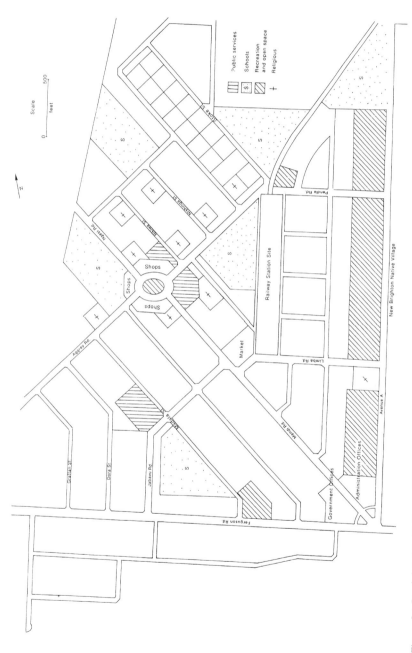

Figure 5.4 Road detail in McNamee Village

This layout scheme was designed in order to reduce the costs of service provision (water, sewerage, electricity) by cutting down the road frontage (see Figure 5.4). Specific local factors were considered in matters such as the floor covering, but another detailed aspect of house design was the effort to ensure some variation on the standard houses constructed. As Walton Jameson commented, in a manner reflective of his religious inspiration:

> shall it not be that from these first fruits of design there will emerge other pleasing types, yet all of the same family though the likeness of individual members of the family will vary![66]

Each house was to have a garden, which was a central feature of Walton Jameson's intention to create a 'homely' environment, and hedges were planted around each house in an effort to achieve this (see Figure 5.5). The council's Garden Department spent many years on this project.[67] Basic services such as house lighting (which was unusual at the time and even today is a mark of distinction between McNamee and the rest of the sprawling African township in Port Elizabeth) were provided. These contributed to the council's perception that they were 'improving' and 'uplifting' the African population. Although the internal design of the houses included some basic facilities (concrete shelves, cooker), and even though these houses were amongst the most heavily subsidized ever built in the country, the question of economy kept them very small. The largest houses had dimensions of 13 feet by 21 feet, and consisted of only two bedrooms and a living/kitchen room, which in the opinion of a later commentator:

> shows complete disregard of planning for family living. No real seclusion is offered to sleeping rooms, there were no internal doors and walls did not reach to the roof and ... the living and cooking functions are combined. (Calderwood, 1953: 19–20).

The interaction between the vision of social upliftment and the constraints of economy was generally problematic for authorities planning housing developments, and they resolved these difficulties in a number of different ways. In Johannesburg's 'white' slum clearances, for example, a selection process ensured that those moving into council houses were able to afford the rents. But, in fact, this meant that those most in need of housing and – from the authority's point of view – rehabilitation, could not receive it (Parnell, 1987). However, in Port Elizabeth, there was no selection process since this was thought to be incompatible with the authorities' basic ambition, which was to clear the entire slum area of Korsten. One of the strategies employed in both Johannesburg and Port Elizabeth (and elsewhere) in an effort to achieve social rehabilitation was the appointment of women housing

Figure 5.5 Houses in McNamee Village, 1988

supervisors, known as Octavia Hill managers, whose role was to collect rents but also to oversee the process of rehabilitating the slum dweller. They were to do this by means of regular visits to the tenant, encouraging him [*sic*] 'to adapt himself to his new environment and help him not to slip back into old habits'. Tenants could be evicted, it was suggested, 'who are a nuisance to their neighbours or extremely dirty or who keep a disorderly house, or carry on an illegal trade'.[68] In Port Elizabeth (and elsewhere) these managers were deployed in the white and Coloured housing estates, providing an interesting feminine contrast with the masculinity of African location administration which was, as we have seen, just as concerned with the project of rehabilitating the slum dweller.

This ambition of rehabilitation was linked to a wider council policy of promoting what they termed 'harmonious progress' in the town. But we have to place this generally noble-sounding motivation against the background of inequality, unemployment and the extremely inferior access to state resources which black people in the town experienced as compared to their white neighbours. And the council had not lost sight of the role of its housing developments in ensuring social and political order in the town.

Addressing the Annual Congress of the Native Advisory Boards of the Union of South Africa in 1949, Councillor Alf Schauder, who was by then a member of the National Housing and Planning Commission, began by outlining the connections which he felt existed between housing and 'native policy'. Without adequate housing and associated 'civilized' lifestyles, he argued, a suitable 'native policy' was not really feasible. He considered that Port Elizabeth was an exception to the generally poor relations which existed between 'European' and 'non-European' sections elsewhere in the country. This he ascribed to the town's progressive housing policy, but also to its refusal to implement the pass regulations which applied in most other major towns in the country.[69] Both of these distinctions contributed, in his view, to Port Elizabeth's 'fair and reasonable treatment' of the African population. As evidence of their success he discussed the new residents in McNamee Village, who had successfully turned to housekeeping and gardening in their new homes, and he also cited the allegedly low level of 'native crime' in Port Elizabeth.[70] Along with many people who were involved in housing and official policy developments at the time, Port Elizabeth's councillors felt that a new environment – 'gay little gardens and clean houses' as opposed to the 'disorder and filth' of Korsten[71] – was able to transform the dissident slum dweller.[72]

The local state's support for the location strategy was not entirely motivated by the philanthropy evident in their public pronouncements. Providing housing in the location was also meant to achieve a measure of political control and domination which slum areas did not allow. The control functions of the location were one of the main arguments employed by the council in its resistance to the central government's influx control policy. The location regulations provided for the registration of all location residents, and laid down rules requiring visitors to report their presence in the area to the superintendent. Residents were obliged to produce residence certificates when required. Thus, the council argued, such provisions together with the exercise of administrative discretion in allowing admission to the location had the potential to control influx, so long as alternative areas of urban residence were eliminated.

However, rapid population growth and the excessive costs to both the council and the African population of providing formal housing were to undermine the effectiveness of this mode of regulation. Low wages, the parsimony of the white ratepayers, relatively high rents and resultant African resistance, in addition to the continuing rapid expansion of the urban population, all made reliance solely upon the location strategy increasingly difficult. Slum areas began to spring up yet again despite the removals associated with the development of McNamee Village. In its place, the Port Elizabeth council was pressured to apply central state legislation (influx control) to prevent the growth of the African population in the town. But, although the policy context shifted substantially during the 1950s, the location strategy itself remained of central importance to the implementation of state power in the town.

Notes

1   MM 1926, p. 4.
2   EPH 28.2.1925; CA 3/PEZ 1/1730 Housing New Brighton. E.H. Walton and Co. to Town Clerk 8.11.1935.
3   EPH 15.8.1925.
4   Union of South Africa, 1920, p. 17.
5   Fourth Census of the Population of South Africa 1926 UG 32–1927.
6   MM, 1929, MOH Report. Port Elizabeth, then, was somewhat different from the cases of Cradock (Butler, 1985) and Johannesburg (Parnell, 1987) where African and European housing were respectively prioritized during this period, since housing for both did receive at least some attention.
7   MM 1928, MOH Report.
8   MM 1929, MOH Report.
9   CA 3/PEZ 1/3/2/15/1 NAC Agenda, Superintendent's Report, 5.5.1927; EPH 19.11.1925.
10 Report of the Housing Committee, UG. 4–1920.
11 MM 1928, MOH Report, p. 81.
12 Ferguson (1981: 26–7).
13 Annexure to MM 1927, Report of the Port Elizabeth Municipal Boundaries Extension and Re-distribution of Wards Commission.

14 CA 3/PEZ 1/2/15/1 Minutes Industries Committee 2.3.1936; CA 3/PEZ 1/3/2/3/1 Industries Committee Agendas 2.6.1936, City Engineer's Report 25.10.1935.
15 MM 1927; the medical officer of health noted for example, that the boundaries were extended 'principally for health reasons' (Ferguson, 1981: 25).
16 MM 1928, p.18; 1929.
17 EPH 3.7.1926.
18 EPH 12.7.1926 Letter to the Editor, F.H.M. Zwide. See also Pendla in NABd meeting with NAC, 7.4.1935, where he explained the lack of enthusiasm for the location by reference to peoples' memories of Strangers' Location, when they were 'driven out like dogs'.
19 MM 1931.
20 EPH 10.1.1925. Also 20.1.1925; 19.11.1925; 4.6.1927.
21 CA 3/PEZ 1/3/2/15/8 Native Affairs Committee Agenda 22.4.1934, Minutes of Meeting of NAC and Ward 7 Electors' Association with District Commandant 13.2.1934.
22 Ibid. Cllr Relton commented 'there were a number of undesirable people in Korsten' who had been in Korsten all their lives.
23 Some white residents also complained, CA 3/PEZ 1/3/2/15/8 NAC Agendas 18.5.1934 Letter from Electors' Association of Wards 5 and 6.
24 CA 3/PEZ 1/3/2/15/8 NAC Agendas 27.4.1934 District Commandant to Town Clerk 21.3.1934.
25 Ibid.
26 Ibid. The commandant advocated relocating the troublemakers to the location, but at this suggestion the superintendent and the NABd expressed some horror, CA 3/PEZ 1/3/2/15/8 NAC Agendas 29.6.1934 Town Clerk's Memo.
27 CA 3/PEZ 1/3/2/15/8 NAC Agenda 5.6.1934, Town Clerk's Memo.
28 MM 1926.
29 CA 3/PEZ 1/1277 23.4.1929 Town Clerk's Memo for NAC Agenda.
30 MM 1927, p. 8.
31 CA 3/PEZ 1/3/2/15/1 NAC Agendas 27.1.1927 Superintendent's Memo on the Urban Areas Act.
32 MM 1930, p. 14.
33 CA 3/PEZ 1/1275 3.12.1925 PE Rotary Club Report to City Council NAC.
34 TA K26 Vol. 7 McNamee.
35 The superintendent attended several of these and always reported on them with great enthusiasm. CA 3/PEZ 1/3/2/15/8. NAC Agenda 16.3.1934.
36 CA 3/PEZ 1/3/2/15/8 NAC Agendas 16.5.1934 Town Clerk's Memo, Superintendent's Report 18.3.1932.

37 Ibid.
38 CA 3/PEZ 1/3/2/15/8 NAC Agendas 20.4.1934 Letter from Secretary for Public Health to Town Clerk.
39 Until then all housing costs had been charged to the native revenue account and recouped in the form of economic rents.
40 CA 3/PEZ 1/3/2/6/9 HSlEl Agendas 10.8.1937 MOH Report.
41 CHB Annual Report, UG. 18–1936.
42 MM 1934, MOH Report, p. 53.
43 CA 3/PEZ 1/3/2/6/8 HSlEl Agendas 9.6.1936 Extract from CHB Report quoted in Town Clerk's Memo.
44 CA 3/PEZ 1/2/1/47 Minutes of Proceedings of the Joint Meeting of NAC and Health and Market Committees, 26.6.1934.
45 CA 3/PEZ 1/2/1/47 NAC Agendas 5.6.1934 Town Clerk's Memo.
46 CA 3/PEZ 1/1730 7.11.1935 Minutes of Meeting of NABd with NAC.
47 CA 3/PEZ 1/1730 NAC Agenda 16.9.1935, Superintendent's Report 5.6.1935.
48 Ibid. 18.9.1936 Superintendent's Memo on Native Housing 7.9.1936.
49 Ibid. 29.7.1936 MOH Report 6.7.1936, Acting Secretary for Public Health to Town Clerk 7.7.1936; CHB Report 1936 UG 18–1936.
50 CA 3/PEZ 1/3/2/6/8 8.4.1936 MOH Report.
51 Ibid. 28.10.1936 Secretary for Public Health to Town Clerk 23.10.1936.
52 Ibid. 10.6.1936 Reference from Industries Committee meeting of 2.6.1936 requesting the area around Korsten Lake for industrial usage.
53 CA 3/PEZ 1/3/2/6/8 8.4.1936 MOH Report.
54 CA 3/PEZ 1/1730 New Brighton Location Departmental 16.9.1935 Minutes of Proceedings of Joint Native Affairs and Health and Abattoir Committee and Board of Works.
55 Anonymous, 'Impressions of the McNamee Township at New Brighton' *SA Outlook*, 1.3.41, p. 48.
56 CA 3/PEZ 4/2/1/1/360. Letters of enquiry about housing were received by the City Council from Springs, Cape Town, Uitenhage, Grahamstown, Kimberley, Durban, Cradock, East London, Pietermaritzburg, Pretoria, Graaf Reineit, Kroonstad, Johannesburg, Stellenbosch, Krugersdorp, Germiston, Boksburgr, from the Department of Trade and Commerce in Canada, from Kenya and from Salisbury, Bulawayo and Livingstone in what was then Rhodesia.
57 CA 3/PEZ 4/2/1/1/360 City Treasurer Corporation of Pietermaritzburg to City Treasurer Port Elizabeth 31.12.1938.
58 His absence from a deputation to the Central Housing Board was

noted and the comment passed that the housing scheme 'had been his baby', that he had 'more or less "lived" with the scheme of slum clearance'. CA 3/PEZ 1/3/2/6/9 6.7.1937. Minutes of Proceedings of Meeting of Deputation with members of the Central Housing Board 14.6.1937.

59   CA 3/PEZ 1/3/2/6/8 Agenda 28.10.1936, City Engineer's Report 10.10.1936.

60   CA 3/PEZ 1/3/2/6/9 Agenda 6.7.1937 Secretary CHB to Town Clerk 16.6.1937.

61   CA 3/PEZ 1/3/2 Agenda 28.10.1936, F. Walton Jameson to PE Town Clerk 31.8.1936: as he said, 'so many people appeal to me for help that I have decided this is the best way to help in an informative way'.

62   He was described by the city engineer of Cape Town as 'a dear old chap and one of the biggest enthusiasts I have met for a long time', 'who very nearly made me giddy with his lengthy discussions on the housing problems generally' (CA 3/PEZ 4/2/1/1/360 T.P. Fox to G. Begg 8.12.1936). In a letter to Reinallt-Jones, Walton Jameson himself remarked: 'I cannot tell you the days on end I spend in these small towns persuading, guiding and pleading for the native and in his name. It is an uphill task and often most exhausting... You can't force these little towns to do things. They are too poor – and they can be awfully troublesome by inspanning their local MP and MPC' (CA SAIRR AD 843 26.8.3, F. Walton Jameson to J.D. Reinallt-Jones 4.8.1937).

63   CA 3/PEZ 1/3/2/6/8 Agenda 28.10.1936, City Engineer's Report, 22.10.1936. Also Superintendent's Report 26.10.1936.

64   At the suggestion of the CHB and the Department of Health: CA 3/PEZ 1/3/2/6/8 Agenda 10.6.1936 Secretary Central Housing Board to Town Clerk 5.5.1936.

65   CA 3/PEZ 1/3/2/6/9 Agenda 18.1.1937, Report by F. Walton Jameson 15.1.1937. Davies (1971) points out that by 1971 this plan still had not been implemented, and in 1989 the idea of a suburban commuter rail along this route was still being debated.

66   CA 3/PEZ 1/3/2/6/9 Agenda 18.1.1937, Report by F. Walton Jameson 15.1.1937, p. 2.

67   For example, MM 1940.

68   CA 3/PEZ 1/3/2/6/9 Agenda 26.5.1937 Town Clerk's Memo; MM 1939, Report of the Chief Housing Officer, Mr W. T. Jarman: Miss N.M. Deverell, a trained Octavia Hill worker from the UK was appointed as woman housing supervisor in April 1939.

69   A. Schauder, 1949. A Social and Housing Policy for the Urban Bantu. Paper Delivered to Annual Congress of Native Advisory Boards of the Union of South Africa. Port Elizabeth, December

1949. Indeed, as Baines (1994: 36) has shown, there was considerably more ambivalence about the question of influx control than popular representations such as that of Schauder suggest.

70 Baines (1994: 208–13) offers substantial evidence that this was most definitely not the case after the Second World War, and expresses some scepticism as to its validity prior to this date as well.

71 Mrs Holland, City Councillor, quoted in *SA Outlook* 1.5.1941, 'Urban Native Administration Examined', p. 93.

72 Mayor's Minutes 1939 Chief Housing Supervisor's Report p. 104. Examples of this idea abound in the sources.

6

Riots, removals and regulations: forging a new mode of control, 1945–1955

In Port Elizabeth, as elsewhere in the country, the state could not easily impose its authority on the population. Many of the strategies employed by the state in its efforts to build power and to ensure domination in the town were vigorously contested by the people living there. Port Elizabeth's town council was confronted with one of the most organized and politically coherent African communities in the country, and during the 1940s and 1950s this community posed a significant challenge to the prevailing local liberal ideology, which was exposed for its complicity in racial domination. The growth of political tensions during the course of the ANC's 'Defiance of Unjust Laws Campaign' will be documented. These tensions ultimately sparked off a 'riot' in the location, in which several people were killed. In concert with this incident, the changing political composition of the white population and an urban crisis far in excess of that which occasioned the first Korsten removals induced the local council to shift their policies to accord with those of the central state. The detailed public and private debates which informed this decision will be explored below. But the old location strategy was at the centre of efforts to secure order and control in the town, and was itself crucial to the implementation of the new legislation. All African people from Korsten (and elsewhere in the town) were removed to the vast extension of New Brighton, KwaZakele. Once again, state capacity and territoriality were mutually dependent. Large state resources and careful strategizing were necessary in order to implement the location strategy, but this territorial arrangement was also essential if new legislation which substantially improved state capacity was to be successfully enforced.

Throughout this period, though, the strength of local African political organization was a major consideration in all state deliberations.

African political organization: challenging local ideology

Port Elizabeth's African community has a long tradition of political organization. For a time this was spearheaded by an emerging local petty bourgeoisie, but in the 1940s some important developments occurred which consolidated opposition into a coherent mass political force. Firstly, Communist Party activists stimulated trade union organization amongst the growing African industrial workforce, and – together with the relatively small size of the African professional and petty-bourgeois element in the town at this stage – the strength of union activity encouraged both the emergence of a distinctive working-class leadership within popular organizations and the co-ordination of community and work-place opposition.[1] In other parts of the country the ANC and Communist Party leadership was drawn predominantly from the petty-bourgeois and professional classes (Lodge, 1983: 50–1). An additional factor which contributed to the relative strength of African working-class organization in Port Elizabeth was the freedom to organise which the absence of pass laws offered.

The first legislation governing trade unions and industrial conciliation (the 1924 Industrial Conciliation Act) excluded 'pass bearing' Africans (those whose contracts were governed under the Masters and Servants Act) from the definition of employee, thus preventing most African men from participating in trade union activities. Although later legislation tightened the definition of employee to exclude those whose employment was governed by certain clauses of the Urban Areas Act (as amended), in the very few places where these laws were not applied African men could still participate in registered unions. Women were not excluded by any of this legislation, but the number of African women in the industrial workforce was very small. As long as the registration of service contracts and the enforcement of Section 10 of the Urban Areas Act were delayed, the workforce in Port Elizabeth enjoyed a relative freedom. Furthermore, the presence of a large Coloured labour force in Port Elizabeth and Cape Town meant that 'non-European' union activities were relatively strong in both areas. This strength came to an end with the Native Labour (Settlement of Disputes) Act No. 48 of 1953 which 'deprived African unions of any recognized role' (Simons and Simons, 1983: 560).[2]

Another factor contributing to the strength of local African political opposition was an 'unintended consequence' of the location strategy. One of the ambitions of this strategy had been to place African people

TABLE 6.1 *African gender division of labour in Port Elizabeth, 1946 and 1960*

1946

	Male	Female
Agriculture and mining	12	15
Industry	8,236	235
Transport and communication	2,716	18
Commercial and financial	154	30
Professional, entertainment, sport	393	123
Personal service	1,899	6,627
Other and undefined	2,442	1,521
Independent	168	173
Total estimated workforce	15,020	8,744
Total African population	23,982	23,437

1960

	Male	Female
Agriculture, forestry, fishing	207	6
Mining and quarrying	175	8
Manufacturing	10,652	717
Construction	2,604	9
Electricity, gas and water	957	1
Commerce and finance	5,663	301
Transport, storage and communication	3,437	12
Government, personal services, business	4,942	10,291
(domestic service)	1,085	8,618
Unemployed and unspecified	4,806	5,031
Total estimated workforce	33,443	16,376
Total African population	59,174	64,088

Source: Population Census, 1946 and 1960

under close surveillance. However, the centralized administration together with the common hardships experienced by those living in the area combined to provide a clear focus for township-wide protests and complaints.[3] The location regulations themselves encouraged mass village-wide meetings to deal with various township issues, and ever since New Brighton's foundation people had frequently gathered together to confront a large number of different problems. Many of these were of particular concern to women – rents, living costs, health and sanitation conditions. As we mentioned above in Chapter 4, in the 1920s and 1930s the location administrators considered the women of New Brighton to be especially vocal and determined. This persisted and assumed an increasingly organized form, until by the late 1940s and 1950s the location superintendent was receiving frequent and ever larger deputations from women demanding council action on a number

TABLE 6.2 *Port Elizabeth municipal loans, 1954*

Fund	Amounts sanctioned (£)	
	Revenue producing	Non-revenue producing
General rate fund:		
Public recreation and		
town attractions	318,325	37,603
Roads	23,570	2,224,377
Sewers	–	1,607,581
Stormwater drainage	–	713,369
Miscellaneous	539,706	533,348
Housing fund:		
Economic housing	335,201	750
Assisted housing	195,480	–
Native administration fund	79,300	4,532
Abbattoir fund	38,558	–
Electric light fund	5,279,563	120,601
Gas fund	556,616	13,290
Markets fund	31,498	112
Waterworks fund	5,015,617	53,167

Source: Mayor's Minutes 1954, p. 209

of social and physical problems experienced in the township.[4] Although the women's protests were organized with the knowledge and support of the ANC executive, it is nonetheless instructive to reflect upon the influence which the stark gender division of labour in the town (see Table 6.1) had in dividing political organization between men (in trade unions and national campaigns) and women, who dominated township politics to the extent that one ex-administrator considered the ANC in Port Elizabeth to have been managed entirely by women.[5] Despite their constant representations to the authorities, though, the council's response was seldom favourable. This was also true in terms of the issue of township rents which was both central to the contradictions inherent in the Council's pre-apartheid mode of domination of the African population and an important focal point for political organization in the township.

The rent issue had been bubbling through township politics from the very foundation of New Brighton, and had been the cause of numerous popular meetings, petitions and complaints to the superintendent, the Native Advisory Board and the council. But not long after the completion of the McNamee scheme, the council began to show some concern over the costs which they were incurring as a result of this development. Despite the fact that in general they felt their financial position to be healthy, such that they were embarking upon numerous capital investment projects to improve the town (and even that the mayor could report in 1944 that they were 'coping well with the housing losses'[6]), the city treasurer warned that the losses were going to increase, especially with the extra development of 100 houses in 1943.[7] Certainly the cost of these houses was greater than those in the main scheme, but the total loss to the council of all sub-economic housing was only £43,000 per annum compared, for example, with the £500,000 that they were preparing to spend on a land reclamation scheme to extend the CBD at the time (see Table 6.2).[8] Nevertheless, the councillors proposed a rent increase to 'limit the ratepayers' liability for Native housing' and tried to justify this by referring to post-war increases in African wages.[9]

Not surprisingly, this occasioned a very angry response from the African population. The superintendent pointed out that 'the people were very discontented at the idea of paying a higher rental... the council could ask for a higher rental but could not force the tenants to pay for it'.[10] The residents' strong protest reduced the proposed rents on the 100 new houses in McNamee from 5s per week and £1 1s 8d per month to £1 per month[11] (as was the case with some of the earlier McNamee houses), but the council persisted in its efforts to raise the rents on the entire McNamee scheme. At every turn the residents expressed their clear opposition to the rent increases. One such protest, a peaceful and orderly march, was held on 27 January 1945 and was supported by several thousand African people and others. It created much controversy amongst the members of the city council and the Communist Party councillors who organized it were eventually fined in court for contravening local regulations.[12]

Both sides in this issue mobilized the local liberal ideology in their defence. The more conservative councillors saw the protest march and the conflict over rents as ultimately damaging to the interests of the African people, since such actions were seen to be 'destroying the goodwill of the European people of Port Elizabeth'.[13] The African people, on the other hand, used the argument that by pursuing the rent increases and other harmful policies (such as restricting Africans from buying land in Korsten) the council was going back on its traditional liberal treatment of the population, of which it was publicly so proud[14]. That the opposition leaders made use of the proclaimed liberality of the council in their arguments against various Council policies did not, however, imply that they endorsed the Council as being either concerned or philanthropic. The local policies were subject to strong popular criticism and, as the records have demonstrated, such criticism was quite justified. In a letter to the local newspaper, one correspondent observed that 'we Native people are not impressed by the claim of City Councillors that Port Elizabeth is the "most liberal municipality". It definitely was in the past, but is not today.' This was in response to the council's proposal to expropriate African freehold land in Korsten and Dassiekraal. And another letter writer quite specifically commented that 'those in New Brighton who have faith in the leadership of Mr. Schauder are heading for an abyss. Our fight is not racial, but it is a fight for justice'.[15]

This local ideology was now clearly under some pressure. Although Schauder and other councillors continued for some time to claim that Port Elizabeth's African population was contented and peaceful, behind the scenes the majority of councillors and officials were clearly disturbed by these obvious and public displays of discontent.[16] Schauder commented after the January march that the procession

> has caused bitterness and resentment among the many friends of the Native people who have worked for years to make Port Elizabeth a model of liberalism in the Union; and it has strengthened greatly the hands of reactionaries who would like to bring to Port Elizabeth the policy of repression which is so evident in some other parts of the Union.[17]

This was in stark contrast to his mayoral report for the previous year which had claimed that:

> Concerted rioting, disturbances and strikes such as have occurred in various parts of the country have been unknown in Port Elizabeth and this speaks volumes for our policy of sympathetic administration and control.[18]

To him and to others,[19] the residents' complaints about the rent increases were of less concern than the problem which their protests presented for the efforts of the ruling elite: to maintain the fragile balance which the council had achieved in the area of native policy. But clearly the residents felt otherwise. High living costs, the increased demands placed on income by the move to McNamee[20] and the high costs of basic foods following post-war shortages all mitigated against the effects of the formal wage increases that the council and the local press dwelt upon at some length in response to the rent protest. However, even formally determined wages were relatively low,[21] and the reported high male employment rate in the formal township was matched by extremely limited opportunities for women.[22] On top of both the 1947 rent increase and generally rising costs came an unannounced bus fare increase in April 1949. This provoked a boycott of the buses which resulted in the South African Railways terminating this service to New Brighton (Lodge, 1983: 52–4). The residents also protested vociferously against a further proposed rent increase in 1951, which was eventually implemented (in 1953) despite the strong objections raised (see Table 6.3) .[23] All of the evidence suggests that the community in New Brighton became increasingly organized and militant from the mid 1940s onwards.

Political activity in New Brighton and elsewhere in Port Elizabeth was not limited to local grievances, though, and national campaigns

TABLE 6.3 *Rent increases in McNamee Village, 1945–1953*

No. of dwellings	Rent per week (s/d) 1945	1947	1953
2,698	3/8 and 4/7	4/8	8/9
784	3/3	4/2	6/6
24	6/6	7/4	12/6
6	4/8	4/8	4/8

Sources: Mayor's Minutes 1946; 1947; 1954

promoted by the Congress organizations received an overwhelming response in the town. Chief amongst these was the 'Defiance of Unjust Laws Campaign'. In 1952 this took off in Port Elizabeth with 'religious fervour' (Lodge, 1983: 43) and over 2,000 people were arrested, mostly between June and October of that year, for their 'defiance of unjust laws'. Large mass meetings were held regularly in New Brighton and Korsten to organize this campaign (even in the driving rain), and between 2,000 and 15,000 people attended at various times, participating in prayers and hymns as well as planning the various defiance events. Donations for those arrested and charged during defiance activities were also received.[24] The campaign began on 26 June 1952 when the newspaper reported that 'the scene chosen was New Brighton, a Native urban township with a reputation for good behaviour.' At the first light of dawn 30 defiers walked in three files to the railway station and entered through the European entrance.[25] Defiers were arrested, jailed and, after periods of up to a month in custody, charged with contravening the railway regulations. Fines increased as the campaign continued and as the number of defiers rose. The first 'batch' were sentenced to 2 months imprisonment or £10 fine, and some of the later volunteers received 90 days or £15.[26] Most of the arrests occurred at railway stations in the town, and the police response to the campaign became increasingly severe.

By August, less than two months after the protests had begun, the police descended upon the Eastern Cape en masse in an effort to 'deal with the defiance campaign'.[27] They were also called upon to 'defend' industrialists, some of whom had been firing employees who were jailed for defying unjust laws and were therefore unable to attend at work. The strong unionization of the local workforce led to a number of strikes in support of those fired in this manner,[28] and the police were called in to the factory gates supposedly to control the crowds. The newspaper reporters were insistent that both the defiers and the strikers had behaved in a quiet and disciplined fashion, though, and that it was only the large police contingents who were provocative in support of the scab labour brought in to replace those who had been fired. The police (CID) also raided the homes of activists, seeking evidence against them in terms of various new pieces of security legislation which had been introduced.[29]

Although political tension had been mounting considerably, and despite the fact that the council had welcomed the increased police presence in the town with enthusiasm,[30] none of these heated campaigns managed to undo the council's public commitment to their 'liberal' policies. In their efforts to establish urban order and control without invoking certain aspects of national legislation they remained opposed to pass laws, curfews and service contracts, even as they sought to give effect to the Group Areas Act and agreed to establish a voluntary Labour Bureau.[31] The council continued in the belief that good housing and no passes had produced a 'very law-abiding African community' and a 'very happy relationship' between the council and the inhabitants of New Brighton. By now they were willing to concede that this relationship was not perfect, but in their view this was due to a small minority of people (political leaders) who were 'creating trouble'.[32] Practically overnight, though, this adherence to a local ideology which had been under strain for some time was to vanish. The cause? A tin of paint.

'White Port Elizabeth shakes in fear': the 'paint riot' and its consequences

On Saturday afternoon, 18 October 1952, after a crowded train had returned to New Brighton station from the centre of town, railway police accused two men of stealing a tin of paint. After a short scuffle the men apparently fell onto the railway line, and 'in front of scores of bystanders a constable [drew] his revolver and [shot one of] the man'.[33] The crowd responded very angrily and threw stones, whilst a number of people 'rampaged' through the township assaulting whites and attacking and burning buildings and vehicles associated with white people (including the Rio cinema, the post office, the trading stores and the administration offices). Four white people and at least seven black people were killed and 25 people were injured.[34] The police response was immediate and heavy-handed. Armed police completely cordoned off New Brighton, refusing entry or exit to all but 'authorized persons', and armed patrols were mounted in European areas.

During the course of the defiance campaign there had been many encounters with the railway police over newly segregated station facilities. In their closed meetings even the city councillors acknowledged that railway apartheid had much to do with the events of 18 October. Although the 'riot' occurred in the context of an emotive and vigorous campaign against racial discrimination, it was the direct result of the generally aggressive and unpleasant behaviour of railway officials who had given the residents of New Brighton cause for complaint over several decades. Baines (1994: 229) has also pointed out that contrary to the council's claims that New Brighton was virtually crime-free, crime and gangsterism (tsotsism) had been on the rise since before the Second World War. He notes that most of those arrested and tried as a result of the riot were young and unemployed. However, the response of the authorities was particularly insensitive to both the general and the immediate causes of the 'riot', and was certainly out of all proportion to the events involved.

The central government lost no time in blaming the ANC and the council's liberal approach to native administration for the disturbances.[35] And although members of the local council were well aware that both the immediate and the more fundamental causes of the violence were complex and not unconnected to the indefensible actions of the railway police and the rise of increasingly discriminatory legislation, as a body they maintained a deceptive silence on these matters. Instead they used the opportunity to blame the incident upon 'agitators' who were conveniently held to be the political leadership in the township.[36] And, despite the ANC's credible dissociation of itself from the incident in tandem with its strong condemnations of the violence, the council responded by taking actions which were aimed at hampering black political organization.[37] They also set out to reconsider their 'native policy' and to implement various defence measures in New Brighton.

The council's first response was to call in the police and to request assistance from the army. They made speedy arrangements for guards of council property in New Brighton to be armed and for the bulldozing of a new road to permit easier police access in the region of the railway line.[38] In addition, the mayor was authorized to request the Minister of Justice to impose curfew regulations as soon as possible. From a policing point of view, then, the council's actions were every bit as repressive as those of the central government. Verwoerd and his department saw this event as an opportunity to pressurize the Port Elizabeth city council into implementing recent legislation applicable to blacks in urban areas, but the council continued to provide some obstacles to this. Their motivations were complex, and the appeal to a morally superior 'liberal tradition in native policy' was by now very thin and was eventually completely overturned.

Partly as a consequence of the strong political organization amongst Africans and partly because of the fear generated by the paint riot and the council's alarmist response to this event, the city council's liberal ideology was replaced by a whole new set of legislative and administrative arrangements which substantially changed the local balance of political power. These altered circumstances of political control remained dependent upon the racial-territorial ordering of the town and, contrary to the local mythology surrounding the history of Port Elizabeth (and of other 'liberal' centres), the new legislation was not imposed entirely under central government duress. There are a number of explanations which could be offered for the shift in council policy which occurred in the early 1950s, only one being the impact of and local response to the October 1952 'riot'. As recorded by one regular commentator, Christopher Gell, who had links with important local black activists, the council had displayed a 'panicky attitude to Native administration since the 'tragic events of October 18, 1952', and throwing overboard the traditions of a century they not only had imposed restrictions against the African community but seemed to be hastening to embrace the prevailing official ideology of their own free will, 'unrepentant, unashamed and unexplained'.[39] But, as was already evident immediately after the first Korsten removals, there were many local incentives for implementing a 'harsher' policy towards Africans in the town, including the imperatives of urban management and administration and also the particular interests of different state apparatuses. The changing social and geographic composition of the local electorate was also a significant factor here. In the following section I will set out the material conditions within which the changing technology of control took shape, and then move on to discuss some pertinent themes in the second Korsten removal and the planning of KwaZakele, both of which were the practical spatial outcomes of state policy at the time.

Defending 'a square deal'? Choice and constraint in the implementation of government policy

At the same time that African political organization in Port Elizabeth was being consolidated and strengthened, the composition of the white population was changing with important consequences for the political character of the local council. Although at the beginning of our period (1925) the council was dominated by merchants and a few industrialists, by the mid 1940s the balance had swung in favour of professional people (doctors, accountants, lawyers). Old stalwarts and merchants such as Schauder, Young and McLean remained, as did the more philanthropically minded Holland and Gelvan (two liberal women) and a handful of local businessmen. For a short time two Communist Party members, M.M. Desai and E.T. Dietrich,[40] made up the complement. Business representatives on the council preserved its entrepreneurial role which had been forged many years previously and persisted in their

TABLE 6.4 *Home languages of whites in Port Elizabeth, 1936–1960*

Year	English and Afrikaans (%)	English (%)	Afrikaans (%)
1936	4.1	65.3	30.6
1946	1.8	59.5	38.7
1951	2.3	56.3	41.4
1960	2.1	55.6	42.3

Source: Population Census

efforts to attract local industry to the town.[41] The group representing the local 'liberal ideology' continued to hold the balance of power in 'native affairs' but a new voice was now to be heard, that of local pro-Nationalist Party Afrikaans-speaking councillors.

The business of the council was conducted entirely in English until well into the 1960s, and correspondence in Afrikaans was translated prior to circulation or response. But the composition of the local white population in terms of official languages was changing long before this (see Table 6.4), and the distribution of poorer Afrikaans-speaking people in council housing (located in Korsten, Sidwell, Algoa Park, South End and North End) would have overstated their electoral influence in certain wards.[42] The decline in the African and Coloured population in Korsten and South End during the 1950s and 1960s diminished their influence long before the 1972 removal of Coloured and exempt African voters from the local electoral roll. And in the meantime, the conversion of tenancies in Coloured council housing from a monthly to a weekly basis deprived these residents of a vote even during the 1940s.[43] Although local council elections received relatively low polls, the available evidence suggests that the changing social geography of the town influenced the political composition of the council. The first post-war assault on the council's policy against influx control and labour registration was launched by three men representing this new Afrikaner influence, but for the moment at least they were soundly defeated. Before we dwell upon the process whereby the legislation that they were advocating eventually came to be implemented, we will sketch the various material pressures compelling the local state apparatus to take action to control African urbanization.

Two of the most powerful professional and administrative centres in the local state apparatus were the first to press for influx control. After the first Korsten removals and as a result of large-scale urban migration immediately after the Second World War, authorities concerned with health and housing urged the council to adopt regulations governing the right of black people to remain in the town. For the Medical Officer of Health and the Town Clerk, the solution to many of the

TABLE 6.5 *Port Elizabeth city council African housing losses,*
1938–1957 (£.s.d)

Year	McNamee Village	Total
1938	–	500.00.00
1939	4,216.15.00	4,802.15.00
1940	9,733.00.00	10,233.00.00
1941	10,791.15.00	11,404.17.07
1942	17,553.04.04	18,260.00.10
1943	27,014.11.02	28,950.04.03
1944	26,411.08.04	26,635.04.09
1945	30,959.10.05	31,378.14.09
1946	39,644.14.09	40,051.07.10
1947	25,399.00.09	25,827.07.00
1948	29,490.11.07	35,303.02.06
1949	23,140.18.03	31,803.12.11
1950	25,285.05.07	28,586.05.02
1951	31,392.00.00	37,533.07.04
1952	39,774.04.01	48,080.13.01
1953	31,217.05.03	36,197.18.08
1954	7,652.13.00	7,652.13.00
1955	6,091.06.05	6,091.06.05
1956	5,782.00.00	5,782.00.00
1957	–	–

Sources: native revenue account, Mayor's Minutes, various years

problems that they faced in their respective spheres of professional responsibility lay in restricting the numbers of Africans allowed into the town. A desire for general political and routine administrative control over black people in the town was also important (especially for the police and the manager of native affairs), but for a long time there were other overriding considerations.

Amongst these we can place concerns about the anticipated cost of implementing this procedure. For a money-conscious council the fear that the anticipated income from the influx control scheme would prove insufficient to cover the expenses was enough reason to reject the legislation. In terms of the location strategy the council was concerned about the housing losses they were being called upon to bear, and over time they had decreased these losses to zero (see Table 6.5). In addition, the council was unwilling to alter the labour market situation in the town[44] which had been an important aspect of Port Elizabeth's supposed attractiveness as a site for industry. As a fundamental reason for the council's refusal to implement either influx control or labour registration, this was only spelt out when the liberal consensus was under serious threat. But even this basic strategy of an entrepreneurial local state was not without some controversy. Local capital, in whose interests the defence of the labour market was conducted, displayed a growing ambivalence to the anti-influx and registration stance of the council. This was partly a result of the strongly organized workforce which they faced, as well as the labour consequences of political struggle which were highlighted during the defiance campaign.

The strong political force which the people who made up the local 'labour pool' had become was also a major constraint on the council itself. Fear of African resistance and violence in the face of pass laws was very high. Ironically, though, it was just such a feared event, the 'paint riot', which enabled the council to implement more severe police and military controls over black people, ultimately creating the conditions which allowed this repressive legislation to be implemented. During the first post-war council debate on the issue of registration, the possibility of sparking off resistance and 'disturbances' was high on the list of motivations against implementing this legislation. Anti-pass movements elsewhere in the country during 1944 and 1945 provided evidence to substantiate this concern (Hindson, 1987: 56), and Councillor Young expressed the majority feeling on the council when he commented that 'if Natives rebelled against measures like registration they could not be blamed'.[45] With very little evidence, the liberal councillors asserted that there was a shortage of African labour in the town, and thus no need for any controls on influx. But the strongest appeal was made to 'undying principles', the need to protect African freedoms and to ensure that they 'received a square deal instead of being shackled'.[46] One or two cautionary notes were sounded. Mr Adcock, for example, felt that 'there should be some control of the natives', although he was definitely opposed to the implementation of the legislation in question. But on the whole the debate was a self-congratulatory reflection on the council's beneficence or, as the editor of the *Eastern Province Herald* put it, the 'enlightened guardianship' of the council's native policies.[47]

This public face had its Janus-like opposite in the administrative memoranda dealing with the subject. The Medical Officer of Health, having first advocated labour registration and influx control in the context of housing provision, also felt that it would provide the means for better control of patients suffering from infectious diseases. The movements and employment of African men would thus be subject to their having a clean bill of health,[48] and medical power could once again play its part in urban control. Control more generally was an issue which these officials stressed in connection with the 'excess labour and housing commitments' occasioned in the city by the 'continual influx of Natives from outside areas'.[49]

Immediately after the war the population in Port Elizabeth was growing at an extraordinarily rapid rate (see Table 6.6), and yet housing schemes for all race groups were being developed at a very slow pace owing to both financial and material supply constraints.[50] Shacks

TABLE 6.6 *African population increases in selected towns, 1951–1960 (%)*

Johannesburg	32.3
Cape Town	25.5
Durban	36.6
Pretoria	63.3
Port Elizabeth	75.8
Germiston	41.7
Bloemfontein	34.2
Springs	11.6
Benoni	27.4
Pietermaritzburg	53.5
East London	42.0

Source: Population Census 1960 (RP 62/1963)

began re-emerging in Korsten, many made out of the motor packing cases used for importing vehicles to local motor factories. Observing this, the council arranged to have these cases donated in order to provide emergency housing for Africans. The result was KwaFord, a settlement of 978 two- and three-roomed houses made out of packing case wood and asbestos roofs, built in 1948 with European labour.[51] An experimental austerity scheme – named Boastville – of 312 brick houses was also built soon after the war using African labour. This was an innovation sanctioned by the Nationalist government, who were trying hard to find ways of cutting the costs of African housing. Elundini was built in a similar fashion between 1952 and 1954 and comprised 2,502 houses which were used to accommodate people removed from Dassiekraal (near Sidwell) and also to relieve some of the overcrowding in New Brighton (see Figure 6.1).[52] But even these austere designs using free wood or hand-made blocks were too expensive for many potential residents, especially if they were to be rented on an economic basis. With the numbers in Korsten and elsewhere growing so fast, the city seemed to face what appeared to its managers to be an insoluble problem: how to maintain their reputation as the 'most progressive city in the Union as far as housing is concerned', whilst still meeting the constraints of both extremely low-income black tenants and predominantly white ratepayers who were unwilling to accept any financial burdens with respect to African housing.[53]

But, although providing housing carried considerable adverse financial consequences for the council, so potentially did the implementation of labour registration and influx control, even if this implementation would theoretically reduce the number of houses required. This was one of the arguments used by some of the city council's delegates at a meeting called by the local divisional council in January 1951. Along with the neighbouring local authorities, the divisional council (responsible for

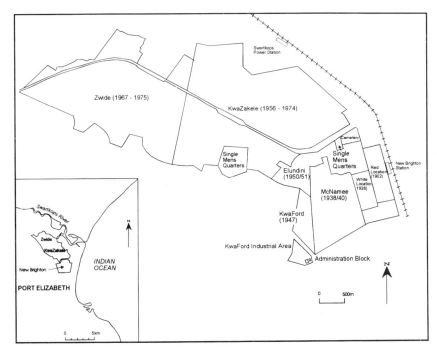

Figure 6.1 New Brighton township development, 1902–1970

surrounding rural and peri-urban areas) wished to implement this legislation in order to cope with, amongst other things, the growing housing
crisis. They quite rightly felt that without Port Elizabeth's co-operation
any combined local scheme would be unsuccessful. Only one of Port
Elizabeth's delegates to the meeting agreed with the divisional council
that positive benefits such as reduced overcrowding and unemployment,
higher wages and less crime would result from implementing the legislation. The other two council delegates (Holland and Gelvan) based their
disagreement upon the role which 'adequate' labour supplies had played
in the industrial development of Port Elizabeth. Influx control legislation, they argued, would increase the cost of labour and prevent the
expansion and progress of the city. Councillor Martin's hope that the new
legislation would ensure that 'the natives would be under control and it
would assist the police tremendously' did not yet sway the other Port
Elizabeth Councillors.[54] Neither did the arguments of central government representatives who, on another occasion, explained that they had
elaborated this new system of controls in an effort to achieve 'a proper
and expeditious distribution of such labour according to the needs of
each area', thereby 'localizing labour'.[55] But the central state was

hamstrung by its dependence at the time upon the local state's co-operation in achieving this ambition, and their arguments succeeded only in convincing the council to establish a voluntary Labour Bureau.[56] It was only after government pressure following the October 1952 riot that the council's decision of March 1951 to once again postpone the consideration of influx control *sine die* was overturned by a small majority.

There was fierce debate both within the council and between the council and the central DNA over what constituted an appropriate response to the October events. One area of consensus existed in their mutual concern to control the activities of 'agitators' and to prevent political meetings. This was partly achieved through a curfew and a ban on meetings. But while some councillors felt that influx control and registration laws might help with this, they observed that such controls were in practice inoperative, even in centres where they were legally in force. They were also aware of the generalized opposition amongst the African community (including those they deemed to be 'law-abiding') to these regulations. These councillors were also conscious (although they never said so publicly) that the 1952 'riot' had had much to do with the imposition of apartheid laws and repressive central government actions. But even those who thought that better control of African people in the town was necessary were concerned over the costs and practical problems of implementing new legislation. Most councillors felt that the immediate political crisis required urgent (military) measures, rather than longer-term legislative reforms. Councillor Dubb, for example, insisted that 'We are at war with the Natives.'[57]

Friendly persuasion having failed to produce a favourable response from the council,[58] and with Port Elizabeth definitely constituting an object of national concern (there had been considerable international coverage of the October event and a strong fall in gold shares had accompanied the news of violence),[59] the central government issued a strong directive to the council to implement the applicable legislation.[60] At first the council refused on the grounds of the 'existing unsettled conditions',[61] but the minister insisted that the council was obliged to implement these provisions since they were now *de jure* applicable to the town (and had been since 27 June 1952). He indicated that 'in view of the recent happenings at Port Elizabeth, he could not now support an application to the Governor-General for an exemption from the obligation' to enforce the legislation.[62] The central government was now determined to impose its own version of urban control in Port Elizabeth, convinced that the earlier local model ('experiment') had failed and that in order for strict political control to be exercised national legislation had to be implemented.[63]

An important influence here was the experience of those council officials and the police who were trying to control African political organization. Mass meetings had resumed in the township despite the ban, and the police found it 'impossible to take proper action unless control measures were enforced'. The arbitrary powers of arrest which influx legislation provided and the machinery for rapidly processing people accused of being 'undesirable or idle' were thought to be sorely needed if they were to enforce political control.[64]

Finally, in a special meeting on 15 January 1953, the council voted to apply influx control to the town by twelve votes to seven. But compulsory registration of employees (under Section 23 of the Urban Areas Act) was still not enforced owing to the expected high administrative costs and the potentially adverse consequences it was thought to hold for industry.[65] It was only by June 1953 that urban areas permits and the Labour Bureau were introduced. But even this partial legislation gave police the authority to demand proof of an African person's right to be in the area. However, the officials encountered many serious difficulties in actually implementing this legislation – difficulties which persisted for many years (see Chapter 7). In the face of strong resistance, then, the shared interest of both central and local state in routine government and also in racial political domination overcame the local state's specific concerns for local economic development and for the local fiscal consequences of new housing and legislative arrangements.

Despite these conflicts, the new legislative conditions were important to both the central and the local state if either were to succeed in achieving their interrelated tasks of national and urban political order. The national state had an interest in implementing pass legislation throughout the country because the pass books would theoretically place the Department of Bantu Administration in a position to 'trace at all times a native who had been issued with such a document'.[66] The first National Commission (1920) to discuss native affairs had emphasized the need to gather basic information about African residents in the country, and yet by the 1950s the national state still lacked the most basic tools of government with respect to much of the black population. For the purposes of social engineering on the scale envisaged by the Nationalist Party, superior and more centralized information and surveillance mechanisms were obviously required. The local state had a reasonable system of surveillance in the location, but outside these areas, most notably in the 'slums', even rudimentary control was all but impossible. And yet, as we will see below, the implementation of influx control and labour registration – which were meant to solve these problems for the local and central states – depended upon the creation of ordered, clearly demarcated and specifically administered locations.

It is at the level of the local case study, then, that we can identify the coincidence of local and national state interests in a segregated urban form, as well as discover the links between national state interests and the ideology and practice of segregating the urban African population. Without the basic state capabilities, provided by means of both territorial and administrative–legislative strategies, the best laid complex plans for labour regulation, canalization or reproduction – not to mention political control – would have been impossible. As it was, such policies were implemented with great difficulty and were eventually defeated by their own contradictions (Posel, 1987; Greenberg, 1987). Port Elizabeth was no exception, as the rest of this chapter, as well as the following one, will demonstrate.

'Treading very warily': the second Korsten removals

There is no doubt that part of the authorities' motivation for clearing the settlement at Korsten was to enable them to oversee the population more effectively. It has been a common theme with regard to shack areas throughout the country (and the world) that they make it very difficult for authorities to perform a wide variety of tasks, from service provision to policing and political control. And in South Africa, where detailed supervision of black people was considered the norm, shack settlements were a positive hindrance. As one of the more conservative members of the Port Elizabeth city council had occasion to comment: 'have you ever considered the difficulty of applying curfew and registration in an area such as the Korsten slums? Take the roads in that area and a mixed population living in shacks and slums. How can you possibly apply curfew regulations in that area?'. He was reassured by the central government representative that 'they were shortly going to zone the towns', and that he was sure 'things will eventually sort themselves out'.[67]

But it was exactly these attributes of such areas which made this 'sorting out' process a fairly mammoth undertaking for the local government. Unwilling to see their efforts undermined by the rebuilding of shacks such as had occurred after the McNamee removals and the Second World War, the local officials and councillors in Port Elizabeth were determined to effect a total destruction of Korsten with no residue and no opportunity for a resurgence of shacks. A vigorous marshalling of administrative and technical resources was what was needed if they were to succeed. But alongside this military-scale campaign a hint of caution prevailed as the authorities were only too well aware that Port Elizabeth's highly politicized black community was unlikely to succumb without resistance. In the event this combination together with the preoccupation of local political leadership with national issues allowed the authorities to realize their ambitions in relation to Korsten with very little opposition (Cherry, 1988), although going on to create a docile and submissive population presented them with quite a different challenge as we shall see in the following chapter.

Once again the authorities had to establish just how many people were living in Korsten – no mean task when the population was growing daily, according to witnesses.[68] As the Town Clerk observed, the census was the 'most important stage as without knowing the extent of the problem, no organization can be developed in order to solve it'.[69] Beginning on 14 March 1955 officials conducted a house-by-house survey of the Korsten area, but it was a survey with a difference. Not only were the people to be enumerated, but the officials were also instructed that it was essential to see Section 10 permits. Where these were not available the Labour Bureau would then be able to 'take immediate action to find out why the native is in Port Elizabeth when not entitled to be'.[70] Not surprisingly, these intrusions into an 'uncontrolled' settlement met with some resistance, and the inspectors reported that 'it was also necessary in the earlier days of the work to deal with considerable obstruction on the part of agitators and misunderstanding by the people'.[71] Nonetheless, some numbers were obtained. The results suggested that some 5,298 African families with 11,782 children as well as 1,082 single men and 71 single women were residing in Korsten at the time of the survey, and that together with people requiring rehousing from New Brighton a total of 9,500 African families and 2,100 single men required housing (single women were not to be included in the state's plans for African urban areas).[72] These numbers were to prove a serious underestimation, however, as the officials realized even as the survey was under way.[73]

The final scheme at KwaZakele was designed with 11,400 serviced sites and a large hostel for 8,000 single men,[74] but by the time this was half-full the Manager of Native Affairs estimated that there were still some 11,100 houses required. This was half as many again as had originally been planned (see Table 6.7 for breakdown).[75] The Town Clerk was alarmed, but his suggestion that the Manager 'may wish to reconsider his figures' could not take the housing problem away, albeit a housing problem severely magnified by the policy of urban segregation which removed many people from houses often no worse or any more overcrowded than those in the formal township to which they were relocated.[76] As this contradiction makes plain, though, the implementation of complete urban segregation had a rationale beyond resolving a housing crisis: it also aimed to improve state control.

Although from the perspective of the officials influx control was a handy tool for limiting the numbers to be rehoused, its implementation also presented considerable difficulties. As the Manager of Native Affairs stated emphatically before the removals began:

TABLE 6.7 *Estimated African housing requirements, 1958 and 1964*

January 1958

Origin	Estimated no. of families
Lodgers in New Brighton and waiting list (since 1949)	4,500
Divisional council area (work in Port Elizabeth)	1,000
Walmer	300
Korsten squatters	3,000
Korsten landowners	800
Central areas (estimated)	1,500
Total	11,100

March 1964

Origin	Estimated no. of families
Red location and KwaFord kitchens	900
Red location (affected by replanning)	2,239
McNamee and Elundini lodgers	1,070
Aloes, Woolhope, Kabega and Kragga Kama	51
KwaZakele waiting lists	950
Korsten occupiers	49
Uitenhage (working in Port Elizabeth)	100
Walmer	1,115
Veeplaas authorized shacks	247
Veeplaas (freehold lots)	1,237
Brickfields	50
Missionvale	110
Kleinskool	337
Bethelsdorp	147
Veeplaas	50
Total	8,652

Sources: PEIA A31 Vol. 2 Administration Census and Statistics 17–1–1958 Manager of Native Affairs to Town Clerk; PEIA, A 31. Vol. 5. Administration, Census and Statistics, 27-3-1964, Manager of Native Affairs to Town Clerk

> It is my considered opinion that influx control cannot be effectively carried out until the site and service scheme as envisaged by the Union Government is implemented...While it is impossible to control existing slum areas, unauthorized natives will present no serious task or problem when the 12000 sites are occupied by natives from the slum areas.[77]

Partly this was a problem of physical order which the government was determined to remedy by means of the new housing development. Despite the fact that the site-and-service scheme entailed the construction of temporary accommodation while building of permanent structures on the same sites was under way, the central DNA issued strict instructions that the site-and-service scheme was not to be regarded as a squatter camp with all its attendant evils, but as an 'embryo township'. In order to ensure this superintendents would need to maintain strict control, and would have to develop the area in an 'orderly and tidy manner' and 'ensure that the temporary rooms are erected neatly and methodically so that they are not facing in all directions or are indiscriminately jumbled together'.[78] But the effective control of the formal township and rigorous application of the new legislative measures were also to be achieved via the administration and regular surveillance effected by the location administration personnel. How (and whether) this was achieved in KwaZakele will be addressed in the following chapter, but first the council had to effect the removal of Korsten.

Many factors played on the mind of the Manager of Native Affairs as he came to plan his department's role in the Korsten removals. Resistance to resettlement in new housing schemes had recently formed the focus of serious challenges to the state's legitimacy, especially in the Transvaal, and Mr Boast was quite understandably afraid that similar events might mar the development of KwaZakele. He anticipated hostility to the removal, and commented that 'bearing in mind the highly developed political consciousness of the local native, a serious situation could develop'.[79] But he was also mindful of the fact that he did not really know anything about the Korsten population and the attitudes that they were likely to hold, although he expected that the previous absence of control in Korsten could prove problematic for a concerted propaganda campaign, given that this could provoke a 'shock effect'. For this reason he was wary of distributing leaflets, for example, and in addition he considered that

> the Xhosa is particularly conscious of any attempts to influence his free thought and the distribution of propaganda in the form of leaflets and literature in the early stages of the campaign could provoke hostility on a tremendous scale.[80]

In drawing up his plan of action Mr Boast had the example of Benoni to hand, where Mr Matthewson was directing the creation of the 'model township' of Daveyton. Matthewson had conducted a vigorous propaganda campaign whose fundamental aim had been 'to create and maintain in the minds of the Bantu people of the town the desire to live in the new township and to establish in each and every one of them an ambition to be a resident of Daveyton'.[81] To achieve this his administration had tried to build up a feeling of mutual trust, to keep up a flow of information about the new scheme, answer queries and assure people that this would be the last move that they would ever have to make. Still expecting 'counter-propaganda', though, the superintendents made an effort to keep a finger on the pulse of 'native public opinion' in order to resist adverse opinions by spying on political meetings and holding their own gatherings to counter opposition forces.

By contrast, the Port Elizabeth propaganda campaign was fairly low-key, but it involved some public meetings, the distribution of some copies of the government publication *Bantu* and also the circulation of information emphasizing the permanence of the new home, the idea of home ownership which was embodied in the scheme, as well as the improved services and privileges which would be provided. 'All the details' of the removal were supposedly circulated.[82] The Manager saw that the Port Elizabeth NAD had an important role to play in this removal by virtue of its 'special expertise which would combat the ever present danger of subversive activities upsetting all plans'. The department would ensure that the removals occurred smoothly by using propaganda, by exercising proper control and by virtue of the department's particular capacity to 'understand the native mind'.[83]

On the one hand, then, a strict application of new repressive and discriminatory legislation; on the other hand, a softly-softly approach to mustering support for the scheme, about which many people, even some on the council, had severe reservations. Presumably the campaign had some effect, but it is possible that the local officials underestimated the desperate nature of the housing situation, which meant that many people were living in very crowded conditions, paying fairly high rents and therefore reasonably willing to move, even to a relatively remote, poorly constructed and inadequately serviced housing scheme which at the time of removal was still incomplete (Cherry, 1988). In spite of this, though, the removal itself demanded harsh action from the authorities and a persistence which was matched only by the determination of some people not to move to KwaZakele. The council's ambition 'to get rid of all blacks living in shacks' was not easily achieved.[84]

Although much of the rhetoric surrounding the Korsten removals dealt with the necessity for swiftly eradicating the place along with its associated health and safety risks, in practice the removals were effected in two distinct stages. Both of these were associated with particular government efforts to control and to house defined population groups, first African and then 'Coloured' people. This disjuncture between the rhetoric and the actual removal proceedings reflected not only the timing of legislative provisions and housing developments which made the removal possible, but also the more sinister motivation of achieving a very specific form of state control over the people living in Korsten, a form of control in which the Group Areas Act and the more detailed organization of the physical fabric of the separate areas were deployed in an effort to achieve a number of government aims. One of these was the increase in the possibilities for routine surveillance. Another was to solve a politically dangerous housing crisis, but in a manner which served the state's interests. The first stage in this grand scheme involved clearing all African people from the Korsten area and removing them to the formal location.[85]

The central government under Verwoerd had introduced the idea of site-and-service schemes in response to several of the 'technical' problems which had beset earlier housing schemes. Particularly pertinent in this case was the fact that the speed of removal would not be governed by the speed at which houses could be built. A shack area could thus be cleared, the inhabitants either 'endorsed out' of the urban area in terms of influx control legislation, or moved to sites with rudimentary services (earth closets and one water tap per twenty plots) where temporary shelters had to suffice until more permanent structures could be built. The process was further speeded up since at first only half a house (two rooms) was built on each site, and later all of these half-houses were extended by a further two rooms. In some cases this took several years to achieve,[86] but from the authorities' perspective the slum areas had been cleared and proper control could now be exercised over black people in the area. As with several aspects of this scheme (down to the detailed furnishings of the single men's hostel), the central government dictated the plans and procedures to be used. In fact during the year prior to the removals there were several misunderstandings between the council and the DNA over details, and at one stage the city engineer had to confess that 'the conception which he [and the councillors] had had of site and service was at fault'.[87]

Some councillors were very critical of the scheme: Mrs Holland, in an address to the Port Elizabeth Women's Municipal Association in February 1955 complained that the central government had forced the city council to adopt the site-and-service scheme, refused to grant sub-economic loans and encouraged the development of one large township which would make travel to work very difficult. Those with no urban areas permits, she said, 'would be left high and dry' – a fate which sat uneasily with the consciences of some of the remaining liberal councillors.[88] But Councillor Schauder was as enthusiastic as ever about the 'biggest slum clearance ever made in Port Elizabeth'. He termed the proposed site-and-service scheme the 'finest possible solution' that 'we hope to make a model for the Union'.[89]

While the site-and-service scheme did offer a way forward in terms of effecting the speedy removal of Korsten,[90] a suitable legislative basis for ordering thousands of Africans to move to KwaZakele was required. At first the Slum Act was considered most suitable[91] – it had worked in the 1936–8 removals – but the medical officer of health soon complained that the process involved was far too complicated and lengthy and had been shown to be inappropriate during the recent removal of those living in Dassiekraal (Taylor, 1989). Instead, people were moved under the Urban Areas Act which made it an offence for

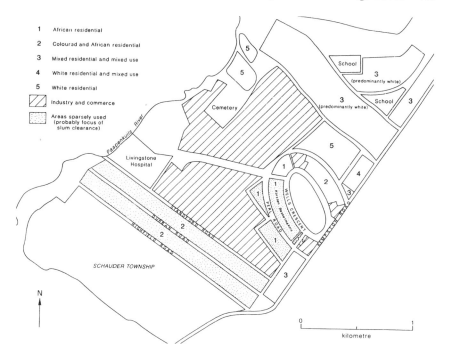

1   African residential

2   Coloured and African residential

3   Mixed residential and mixed use

4   White residential and mixed use

5   White residential

   Industry and commerce

   Areas sparsely used
   (probably focus of
   slum clearance)

Figure 6.2 Korsten layout map, *c.* 1959 (I.L. Griffiths, Manuscript, Cory Library, 1961; Dillon-Malone, 1978: 31; Air Photographs Job 422, 1958)

African people to live outside a formal location.[92] With this legislative support and with the added use of the influx control provisions to limit the numbers formally requiring housing, the council now had to embark upon the actual removal.

The first thrust of their strategy was to move those who voluntarily wished to do so. This was very successful, and was maybe testament to the urgent housing needs of many people in the town. By the end of 1955 the surveying of plots and the construction of water mains and roads had begun in KwaZakele. The first removals took place on 26 April 1956. Three months later 1,000 families had been accommodated;[93] by 31 December of that year 8,695 people had been moved; and by the end of 1957 a total of 6,772 families, 906 single persons or altogether 28,817 people had been relocated to KwaZakele. Obviously some were eager to move; but reports tended to describe only enthusiastic squatters 'joyously loading their belongings on to trucks',[94] despite the fact that many people continued to try to escape the authorities' net. As the officials turned from voluntary moves to the forced clearance of entire areas, people crowded into the remaining shacks. Forced (non-voluntary) removals were increasingly necessary, according to the

TABLE 6.8 *Population growth in Bethelsdorp area (including Kleinskool, Veeplaas, Missionvale), 1935–1960*

	1935[1]	1940[2]	1951[3]	1960[3]
Coloured	1,698	2,683	4,401	6,872
African	954	2,394	4,892	9,350
Asiatic	41	53	128	164
European	134	319	267	127

Sources: [1] 3/PEZ 1/1711 Report on Sanitary Inspection of Bethelsdorp 12–1–1936; [2] 1940 Census reported in 3/PEZ 1/1711 MOH to Town Clerk, June 1940; [3] 1960 Population Census

authorities, since for them it was 'difficult to control shack erection in scattered pockets [which remained] in cleared areas'.[95] Removals subsequently took place systematically from north to south , from the Livingstone Hospital towards the Perl Road area – the most notorious section of Korsten (see Figure 6.2).[96]

Even with this elaborate strategy, the council soon began to experience some difficulties in ensuring the effective removal of Africans from Korsten and in preventing a recurrence of the shack development. The 'problem' of Coloured shack dwellers living interspersed with Africans presented itself, and the authorities suspected that African people were crowding into the Coloured shacks which could not yet be demolished because no housing schemes were being developed at the time for Coloured people.[97] This was bound up with the delay experienced in declaring group areas in Port Elizabeth as well as the problems with acquiring adequate land for housing developments, specifically in finalizing the proposed incorporation of Bethelsdorp.

Further difficulties in achieving their ambitions with respect to Korsten were encountered in the form of a religious settlement of African people originally from Zimbabwe, known as the 'Korsten Basketmakers' (see Figure 6.2), and by a group of some 800 homeowners. Both of these groups were eventually removed under two different sets of legislation: that governing the presence of 'Foreign Natives' in the town, and the Group Areas Act which made African land ownership in areas reserved for other race groups illegal. But if the council was to create a situation in which all African people lived in the location, they would have to cast their net even more widely than Korsten. For a long time officials had been expressing concern over the growing African population in the Bethelsdorp area (see Table 6.8). But with the effort to clear Korsten under way and with evidence that former Korsten residents were moving to the Bethelsdorp/Veeplaas area, the council was concerned lest Bethelsdorp develop into another Korsten. Their belated concern (and their need for land) led to the incorporation of this area into the municipality in 1964.

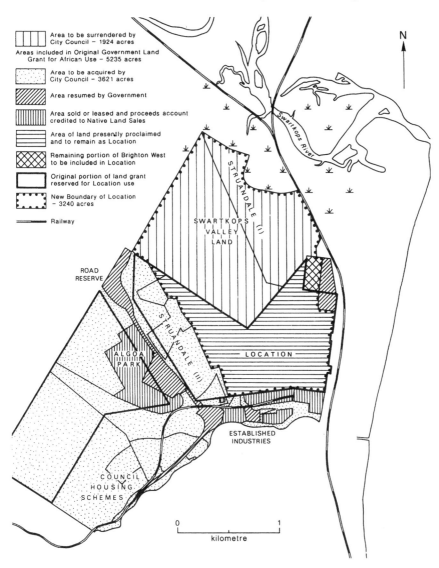

Figure 6.3 Details of land swap undertaken by the Port Elizabeth municipality and the Department of Native Affairs, 1955 (PEIA 25/391 No. 2)

Together with the removal of African people from all over the town under the Group Areas Act, the growth of the Bethelsdorp/Veeplaas settlement perpetuated the housing crisis and the crisis of control which the council had been facing since the early decades of the century. Their search for control was, however, severely hampered by shortages of housing and land – shortages which were partly of the council's own making. In terms of housing this was because many perfectly adequate dwellings were made illegal for African people under the Group Areas Act, and in terms of land it was because an exceptionally unfair land swap between the council and the location administration in 1955 left a relatively small, poor quality area of land for future African housing development (see Figure 6.3).

Further land acquisitions in the Veeplaas/Zwide area were slowed by the problems of negotiating their incorporation into the municipality and their subsequent zoning under the Group Areas Act. To this day, land availability remains a stumbling block to the provision of housing for the poor in Port Elizabeth.

During the late 1950s and 1960s the state persisted in its efforts to impose a spatial order in Port Elizabeth which they felt would facilitate domination and control. They also had to build administrative capacity if they were to secure these ambitions, though, and the following chapter explores both the growth of administrative capacity in Port Elizabeth over this period and the relationship between growing state capacity and the emerging spatial order in the town.

Notes

1   Baines (1994) notes, however, that there were significant differences and conflicts between union leaders and ANC and community structures. In addition, as Cherry (1992) has demonstrated, the union leadership was beset with problems of corruption and division. Nonetheless, the presence of these forces in Port Elizabeth was important in distinguishing it from other centres and in shaping the trajectory of conflicts with the local and central states.

2   In a Letter to the Town Clerk from the Eastern Province Trades Council, (Port Elizabeth dd 26.8.1945), it was noted that 'if the registration of natives is imposed by the Port Elizabeth City Council a further result will be that natives will be excluded from the definition of "Employee" under the Industrial Conciliation Act. It seems to us grossly unfair that natives should be deprived of these rights.'

3   Christopher Gell noted that 'the virtually complete segregation of the African community has given a tremendous impetus to black politics...this achievement was emphatically not intended by the Council and would hardly be regarded as "worthwhile".' Port Elizabeth Diary *Africa South* Vol. 1 No. 4 July–Sept. 1957, p. 67.

4   Interview with Mr John Poppleton, Former Deputy Manager, New Brighton Township, 23.5.1988.

5   Ibid. 'Interestingly enough, the ANC was managed entirely by women – there were no males involved in the ANC locally.'

6   MM 1944, p. 2.

7   MM 1944, City Treasurer's Report.

8   Ibid.

9   CA 3/PEZ 4/2/1/1/332 10.11.1943 Cllr J. Millard to Council; 13.10.1944 Notes of Interview between Native Affairs Committee and Native Advisory Board.

10 Ibid. 15.8.1944 Housing and Slum Elimination Committee Minutes.

11 Ibid. 8.9.1944 NAC Committee Minutes; 27.9.1944 Finance Committee; 27.9.1944 Council Minutes.

12 EPH 1.2.1945; 20.2.1945.

13 EPH 22.1.1945. Letter from Cllr Chaplin to Council for Non-European Trade Unions.

14 PEIA PEM 25/186 No. 9. 15.1.1945 Secretary APO (PE and District) to Town Clerk; 6.1.1945 Assistant Secretary Council of Non-European Trade Unions; EPH 29.1.1945.

15 EPH B.J. Mnyanda to the Editor 23.8.1952; EPH P.N. Ngvonga to the Editor 21.7.1952.

16 EPH Editorial 29.1.1945.

17 SA Outlook 1.3.1945, p. 36.

18 MM 1944, p. 4.

19 EPH 22.1.1945.

20 Stokes (1953) observed the effects of removals in Port Elizabeth around this time, and although her focus was upon the Schauder township, the effects of increased rents, travel and service costs on family budgets were of a similar (and probably more severe) nature in McNamee Village.

21 A survey conducted by the superintendent during the course of the debate about the affordability of the rents showed the majority of householders to be earning less than £6 per month, including the income of children. Only 481 men out of 2,452 households earned over £6 per month (EPH 25.1.1945).

22 In the Mayor's Minute of 1944 (p. 5) the council claimed that departmental surveys showed only 7.55% unemployment amongst the 'fit fixed' adult male population in New Brighton and a 9.27% unemployment rate amongst the 'floating' male population (i.e. migrant labourers).

23 During the course of the protests in 1951 the community organizers reminded the council of the rising cost of living, high levels of poverty and malnutrition in the town and also of the political and economic facts that Africans provided cheap labour and were not dependent upon the 'philanthropic charity' of the council, but rather 'paid their own way'. *Guardian* 18.10.1951; 29.11.1951. PEIA

PEM 25/100NB, Report by Town Clerk to Ad-Hoc Committee Dealing with Reorganisation of the Native Administration Department, 1955.

24 EPH 21.3.1953; 7.4.1952; 2.6.1952; 23.6.1952; 30.6.1952 (15,000 people were reported to have been at the 'defiance meeting' on 28 June); 7.7.1952.

25 EPH 27.6.1952.

26 EPH 11.7.1952; 13.9.1952.

27 EPH 13.8.1952.

28 EPH 29.7.1952; 30.7.1952; 31.7.1952; 2.8.1952; 8.8.1952; 9.8.1952.

29 EPH 31.7.1952. Raids were carried out in terms of the Suppression of Communism and Riotous Assemblies Acts.

30 EPH 13.8.1952. The mayor, Erasmus, conferred with a visiting police colonel over the police reinforcements being brought in and said that 'if necessary, even more police than at present would be brought to the city.' A photograph of the mayor welcoming the police was placed on the front page of the newspaper in an effort to ease the fears of the white population in the face of this unprecedented black political activity.

31 Guardian 15.3.1951; 22.3.1951.

32 Guardian 15.3.1951. PEIA PEM 25/383 No. 1 25.8.1952. Notes on an Informal Meeting of the City Council.

33 McNamee, in his unpublished memoirs, claims that his sister witnessed the event, and other sources agree that a man (or men) were accused of stealing a tin of paint and were attacked by railway police, and then the crowd came to the rescue. Baines (1994: Chapter 9) has a detailed account of the riot, which broadly corroborates the one I offer here.

34 EPH 20.10.1952; 21.10.1952.

35 EPH 21.10.1952, 'Verwoerd Blames PE for Native Riots'.

36 Schauder, for example, in a council in committee meeting, asked of the central government representative at the meeting whether he thought it 'advisable to enforce apartheid at New Brighton station', and in a letter to the council ten days after the incident he complained that he 'mistakenly tolerated a "hush-hush" policy' which had now harmed the reputation of the town. But he also reiterated the views expressed by other councillors that 'We believe that if you could stop the agitators and all those meetings and business which has been carried on for the past five or six years [you could give that control].' PEIA PEM 25/169 February 1952 to November 1952. 28.10.1952 Minutes of Proceedings of Council Meeting in Committee.

37 EPH Editorial 20.10.1952 wholeheartedly agreed with the ANC leadership which 'strongly dissociated itself from resort to violence

and condemned this unfortunate, restless and ill-considered return to jungle law'.

38 PEIA PEM 25/169 February 1952 to November 1952. 21.10.1952 Minutes of Special Meeting of Council. *Advance* 13 November 1952.

39 C.W.M. Gell to the Editor EPH 21.12.1955. Christopher Gell was by all accounts a remarkable man who was paralysed from poliomyelitis and confined to bed in an 'iron lung'. He collected information, wrote articles, launched *Africa X-Ray Digest* and gave valued advice to many activists and other politically involved people (*The Observer* 28.4.1957).

40 Evidence to Fagan Commission, UG.28–1948; Interview with Mr G.Young, Port Elizabeth, 27.7.1989.

41 Port Elizabeth Publicity Association 1952 *Port Elizabeth: City of Industry*.

42 Stultz (1974: 92–6) and Moodie (1975: 237) discuss more generally the importance of demographic shifts in the national and municipal election process in the 1940s and 1950s.

43 EPH 1.9.1945. In a resolution passed at a protest meeting attended by up to 2,000 people on 30 August 1945, the following was stated: 'This mass meeting of non-European citizens of Port Elizabeth: 1. Demands that the City Council should change the tenancy of all its economic and sub-economic houses from weekly to monthly, and to restore to the residents of Dowerville, Schauder Township, Holland Park, Stuart and Hoy Townships, McLeanville, Upper Valley Road and Forest Hill Township the vote which has been unjustly taken away from them.' Pinnock (1989) discusses the significance of these measures in Cape Town.

44 PEIA PEM 25/279 7.4.1941. Native Affairs Committee, Notes on Discussion between Sen. J.D. Reinallt-Jones and members of the City Council on the Question of the Registration of Native Service Contracts. The seasonality of much casual labour work in the town (harbour, wool, fruit packing) was stressed in order to explain why a large pool of reserve labour was necessary.

45 EPH, 1.2.1946; Hindson (1987: 56).

46 Schauder, quoted in EPH 1.2.1946.

47 EPH 2.2.1946.

48 PEIA PEM 25/279 No. 1 MOH Report 9.3.1943. Reports solicited by the town clerk from other towns show that this aspect of Influx legislation was more generally recognized, for example: Town Clerk East London to Town Clerk Port Elizabeth, 15.10.1945.

49 Ibid. 6.6.1944 Town Clerk's Memorandum.

50 MM 1950.

51 MM 1949; C.T. Boast, 'The Development of an Urban Bantu Community', manuscript prepared on the occasion of the

Municipal Centenary, 1961. Schauder claims credit for this innovation, as the *Journal of Municipal Affairs* notes in an interview with him that when, after the war, slums making use of motor car packing case timber began to emerge in Korsten, 'With his usual ingenuity he killed two birds with one stone: he first persuaded the city to use the packing-case timber for the building of houses for Natives; and he then obtained the consent of the Ford Motor Co. to allow the Council to have free of charge all the company's packing-case timber, thus preventing it from being used for the erection of shacks' (January 1964: 61–2). The ingenuity however surely lay with the African people themselves who solved a housing crisis not of their own making in an original way, only to have it removed again in the interests of political domination.

52 MM 1951; Boast, ibid.
53 MM 1951.
54 PEIA PEM 25/279 No. 1 24.1.1951 Minutes of Conference held in Connection with the Registration of Natives in Port Elizabeth and Surrounding Areas.
55 PEIA PEM 25/383 No. 1 25.8.1952 Address by Mr van Heerden of Union Native Affairs Department to meeting of PE City Council in the City Hall.
56 Ibid. 29.11.1952 NAC Meeting; 15.12.1952 Council Meeting.
57 Ibid.
58 Ibid. As Brand, the Urban Areas Commissioner, Cape Eastern Area, King William's Town commented during the course of this meeting: 'It has always been the policy of my Department to interfere reluctantly with the domestic affairs of an Urban Area...we have allowed your City Council a free hand to conduct your Native Administration as you think best. It has always been there to co-operate with your Council. The Minister now feels.. that these controls have most probably failed and wonders whether your Council should not, in the light of recent events, examine the position.'
59 EPH 21.10.1952.
60 PEIA PEM 25/279 No. 1 Native Commissioner PE to Town Clerk PE. The Minister of Native Affairs stressed that Sections 10, 10bis, 11, 12, 14, 23, 19 and 29 should have been implemented from 27 June 1952 and asked, 'May I have your Council's assurance that the provisions of the Act will be implemented and carried out not later than during the course of the first week in January 1953 at the latest.'
61 Ibid. 11.11.1952. Chief Native Commissioner to Town Clerk PE.
62 Ibid. SNA to Chief Native Commissioner King William's Town 20.11.1952; Native Commissioner PE to Town Clerk PE 24.12.1952.

63 EPH 21.10.1952: Verwoerd is reported to have said that 'the PE City Council had believed it could handle Native Affairs better in its own way...Proper controls would have to be enforced in PE in future, even if this meant passing special legislation.'

64 PEIA PEM 25/279 No. 1 14.1.1953 Memo by His Worship the Mayor for Consideration by Members of the City Council.

65 PEIA PEM 25/383 No. 1 15.1.1953. Minutes of Council Meeting.

66 PEIA PEM 25/383 No. 1 Memo NAD to Manager PE NAD 1955 'Implementation of Reference Books'.

67 PEIA PEM 25/169 28.10.1952 Minutes of Proceedings of Council in Committee.

68 PEIA AB BS1 Vol. 2 Town Clerk to City Engineer 28.12.1955.

69 PEIA AB BS1 Agenda and Town Clerk's Report for Meeting of Sub-Committee of Heads of Departments in Connection with Site and Service Scheme for Natives, 1955.

70 Ibid. Notes for Briefing of Enumerators.

71 Ibid. Housing and Slum Elimination Agenda 9.6.1955.

72 PEIA AB BS1 Vol. 2 City and Water Engineers Report 10.9.1955.

73 PEIA AB BS1 Vol. 2. Manager of Native Affairs to Town Clerk 14–11–1955: 'further shack erections will soon render the survey results ineffective.' Also Senior Urban Areas Inspector (Inspectorate Section, Native Registration and Labour Bureau) to Registering Officer PE 20.12.1955. The figure given for single women in the area seems incredibly unrealistic, suggesting significant biases in their survey methods.

74 MM 1955.

75 Manager of Native Affairs to Town Clerk 17.1.1958 PEIA AB A31 Vol. 2, 1955–1970.

76 Town Clerk to Manager of Native Affairs 14.10.1957 PEIA AB A31 Vol. 2 1955–1970.

77 PEIA AB S92 NAC Agenda 20.10.1954 Proposed Reorganization of Native Administration Department.

78 PEIA AB BS1(vi) C.T. Boast to Superintendents 23.6.1958.

79 PEIA AB BS1 Vol. 2 Manager of Native Affairs to Town Clerk 14.11.1955.

80 Ibid.

81 PEIA AB BS1 Vol. 2 Town Clerk Benoni to Town Clerk Port Elizabeth *re* Propaganda to Natives 22.8.1955.

82 PEIA AB BS1 Vol. 2 August 1955 Town Clerk to Medical Officer of Health; August 1955 Town Clerk to the Editor *Bantu*; Report of the Manager of Native Affairs to the Special Site and Service Committee No.1 1956 no date.

83 PEIA AB BS1 Vol. 2 Report of the Manager of Native Affairs to the Special Site and Service Committee No.1 1956 no date.

84 Interview with Mr John Poppleton 23.5.1988.
85 PEIA AB BS1(v) Site and Service Committee Agenda 10.6.1957.
86 Personal communication with Residents. PEIA A26 Manager of BA to Town Clerk 12.8.1969. Two-roomed houses in KwaZakele were still being converted into four-roomed houses.
87 PEIA AB BS1 (Vol. 1) 27.4.1955 Notes of the Meeting of the Housing and Slum Elimination Committee with the Central Government Urban Areas Commissioners.
88 Ibid., Councillor Young. EPH 16.2.1955.
89 EPH 9.2.1955; EPH 17.2.1955.
90 MM, 1957, p. 55, 'The Site and Service Scheme has made it possible to continue slum clearance on a scale which would have been quite impossible had this new approach to the Native housing problem not been employed.'
91 PEIA AB BS1 Housing and Slum Elimination Committee Minutes 8.3.1955.
92 PEIA AB BS1 (Vol. 1) 27.4.1955 Notes of the Meeting of the Housing and Slum Elimination Committee with the Central Government Urban Areas Commissioners.
93 MM 1955, 1956.
94 EPH 27.5.1958; 26.2.1957; 10.6.1957.
95 PEIA AB BS1(v) Manager of Native Affairs to District Commandant Korsten Police 21.6.1957.
96 PEIA AB BS1(vi) Housing and Slum Elimination Committee Agenda 2.12.1957. Interview with Mr John Poppleton 23.5.1988.
97 PEIA AB BS1(v) Site and Service Committee Agenda 10.6.1957.

7

A burgeoning state apparatus: the Port Elizabeth Native Affairs Department, 1955–1972

During the 1950s the stance of the city council and the face of native administration in the town hardened with the implementation of influx control in the town and the local authority's complicity in repressing African political movements. But the growth of African resistance from the mid 1940s as well as the huge rise in the population of the location made the task of securing control much more difficult. As a result the practice of native administration in the town was significantly trans- formed until, in 1972, the central state itself assumed this politically sensitive task of governing urban African people. Changes took place in legislation and in the ideology of administration as well as in the polit- ical role of the administrative apparatus. The strength, organization and effectiveness of the administration also had to be improved. Thus the formal administrative arrangements, as well as the more informal administrative style or ideology of the administrators, had to change substantially. As Mr McNamee (Junior) commented, 'implementation of ... draconian new legislation meant a shift from our old functions of assisting people to one of controlling people'.[1] Nonetheless, even in this period the ambivalence of the administrators is apparent. Caught between their old style of 'sympathetic' administration and the new regime in which the room for administrative discretion was minimal, some of the older administrators found their work increasingly difficult.

With the substantial extensions of New Brighton township during the 1950s, both the territorial ordering of the town and the internal organization of the township were central to the exercise of adminis- trative power. But the vastly increased demands placed upon the small, paternalist administration by the new circumstances highlight the importance of administrative capacity in building state power. For it is not enough to consider only the evolution of legislation or policy directives: the administrative complexities involved in enacting government decisions play an important role in shaping outcomes and in determining the meaning of the legislation. Securing political domination and routine governance are not as easy as designing suitable legislation or strategies – even when the strategy in question was as well tried and tested as the location strategy. Transforming state apparatuses also involves transforming people and working out the administrative micro-strategies which would make these apparatuses effective. Not only did the PE Native Affairs Department have to be vastly increased in size, then, but the tactics employed in the execution of their duties had to be rethought. And once again, the significance of spatiality in the exercise of power was not lost on these men.

Augmenting the apparatus of power

Between 1923 and 1960 the population living in the area of New Brighton and its various extensions increased from several thousand to almost 100,000 people (see Table 7.1). The staff whose task it was to control this population increased from a total of 45 people in 1927 – some administrative, some labourers and others medical personnel – until by 1948 the total number in the department was 66. An administrative expansion at the end of the 1950s resulted in a staff complement of 307 people. This fivefold growth reflected not only population growth and the extension of the township, but also an increase in the tasks and scope of the administration. This is signified, for example, by the 46 staff members who had been employed by 1959 to implement labour registration which had only been introduced in 1953.[2] The expansion of the staff was also accompanied by a change in the ethos and style of administration. This placed a strain on those administrators who had become accustomed to a particular mode of operation, and also bred a new type of administrator who was more likely to have an academic qualification, less likely to speak an African language and more inclined to pursue bureaucratic efficiency than to forge strong personal relationships with those living in the township.

When Mr McNamee retired in 1945, pleased to avoid the stigma of the incipient rent protests of the time (he had repeatedly urged the council not to implement rent increases since, in his opinion, people could not afford to pay any more), Mr Charles Travis Boast was appointed as his successor. Previously a magistrate and public prosecutor in Natal, by the accounts of his staff he brought a unique style to the administration. He prided himself on always being available to any

TABLE 7.1 *Distribution of Port Elizabeth's African population, 1911–1960*

Year	Total PE	Location	Other urban
1911	5,058[2]	3,414[3]	1,644[1]
1921	7,148[2]	5,299[4]	1,849[1]
1936	25,800[1]	7,827[3]	17,973[5]
1946	43,883[1]	26,381[3]	17,502[5]
1951	60,396[1]	36,760[3]	23,636[5]
1956	109,161[3]	68,428[3]	40,733[3]
1960	108,315[1]	96,990[3]	11,325[5]

Sources: [1] Census data; [2] calculated, location + other urban; [3] Mayor's Minutes estimates; [4] Baines, 1987: 45; [5] calculated, total PE–location

member of the township and he apparently would spend much of his time during the day in consultation with residents who came to him with various problems. His second in command, Mr Ivan Peter commented:

> At that time Mr C.T. Boast's policy was that we didn't turn anyone away if they came to us at head office to complain about something that was going on in the townships; we didn't say *voetsak* [get lost] go and see your Superintendent, we dealt with it and you helped them as far as you thought that some injustice had been done...we helped a lot of people who had difficulties.[3]

Another employee, though, noted that this 'probably got in the way of him managing the place',[4] and Mr Boast himself wrote that it was a time-consuming process interviewing (in 1962) some 2,463 members of the 'Bantu public' on matters such as eviction, domestic quarrels, rent payments, endorsements out of the area, dwelling defects or improper conduct by officials.[5]This approach of spending many hours listening to the grievances of the population proved most useful to an administration faced with a highly organized and politicized community. In the increasingly tense political climate of the 1950s and 1960s, Boast's administrative style served partially to hide the political face of the administration, and probably helped to defuse some tense situations in the township. But the records again suggest that even if the administration did have an inclination to 'help' some individuals it was still the vehicle for implementing state policy. The administrators often pointed out that they tried to deal with the people 'as human beings, regardless of their being black or white'. But their sympathy for the residents did not extend to include organized political activity and was clearly conditional upon what they defined to be 'good behaviour'. Politically active residents do not recall his administration with much affection, though, for Boast and his staff were deeply involved in policing and informing on African political organization in New Brighton.[6]

The white employees who worked for Mr Boast were primarily men who had had some encounters with black people during their youth: Mr Peter, for example, had grown up on a farm; Mr Reynolds' father had been the labour registering officer in East London's townships; Mr Mundell grew up in the Transkei 'amongst black people'; and Mr Boast himself was the son of a magistrate in a rural area. They generally spoke Xhosa or Zulu fluently, and this language requirement was the basic qualification for the job along with 'knowledge of the black man'. The men were not specially trained for the job, although it was expected that the manager would have some expertise in the fields of law or public administration. As a magistrate, then, Mr Boast was well qualified to interpret and to apply the numerous and changing laws applicable to the black population of Port Elizabeth. Mr Poppleton was something of an exception in this department. He had studied at the University of Natal, Durban, taking native administration as a major subject, and then worked in the Durban Native Affairs Department before moving to Port Elizabeth. Other senior members of the staff (apart from Mr Boast with his legal qualifications) were not so highly educated, and even matriculation was not considered essential for appointment to the post of superintendent.[7]

But the crucial factor was experience, and here the department was strong. Mr Peter, for example, had worked for many years with the central government's Native Affairs Department and then as a labour controller on the mine compounds. After this he had moved to East London as a superintendent in the municipal Native Affairs Department, from where he took up the position in Port Elizabeth in 1961. Mr Reynolds was employed as the registering officer in Port Elizabeth soon after the Labour Bureau was established. He had worked from about the age of fourteen in the East London Native Affairs Department after his father had 'pulled him in to help during the strikes of 1929/30' (the ICU strikes).[8] Mr D.B. Naude claimed 35 years' experience in urban native administration by 1955, 17 of which had been in Port Elizabeth,[9] while Mr A.P. McNamee (appointed in 1955) was the son of J.P. McNamee, the previous superintendent in the township, and had actually grown up in Red location.[10]

With the shift in the political and administrative situation through the 1950s and 1960s, this profile of superintendents also changed. These employees recall that they became 'a rare breed': men who had specific knowledge and experience of dealing with black people or who were prepared to work in the townships.[11] As the staff grew, so more technical and administrative employees were engaged, and these new officials did not need to have the personal interaction with the people in the township which had been so crucial to the superintendent's job. And as the numbers in the townships grew, even the superintendents found it ever more difficult to maintain this sort of relationship with the population. In addition, the rules and regulations of the township were substantially reinforced by national pass legislation which enlarged the means available for policing the population. Popular resistance to the administration became more focused and more clearly linked into a national anti-apartheid struggle. The staff could no longer hide behind a pretence at political neutrality. In addition, Mr Boast's successor, Mr Louis Koch, and the body which succeeded the Port Elizabeth Native Affairs Department, the Bantu Affairs Administration Board, both represented a fundamental change in the form of the state apparatus dealing with the urban administration of black people in Port Elizabeth, and marked a definite end to the particularity of the local administration.

Redrawing the administrative map: local strategies of control

The rapid growth of Port Elizabeth after the Second World War began to force a rethink of the format for administering the township. The earlier removals from Korsten to McNamee Village (1938–42) had created some administrative difficulties, which had been resolved by the appointment of additional headmen who were assigned wards of around 250 dwellings each to supervise. Extensions to the McNamee scheme, though, meant that the existing ten headmen proved insufficient and further expansion was required.[12] This expansion conformed to the system which had prevailed since the township had first come under the municipality's jurisdiction in 1923, with the familiar administrative hierarchy of superintendent of the location, from 1947 designated as Manager of Native Affairs, and several African headmen or wardsmen under his supervision. But the continued growth of the township meant that this formula was no longer functional to achieving 'proper control', and changes were duly made in two directions. The first involved the addition of several (white) superintendents below the manager. These men became responsible for particular areas of the township, and were required to report to the manager who retained overall control. The other change saw the African headmen designated first as 'inspectors' and later as 'constables', and the territorial nature of their responsibilities diluted. While an important motivation behind these changes was the growing size of the township, another was most certainly the difficulty of controlling a population whose social cohesion was diminishing and whose political resistance, increasingly directed at the administration, was growing apace.

The manager's first report to the city council on the 'Proposed Reorganization of the Native Administration Department' in 1946 made the point that

> apart from minor changes...the staff of my department is precisely the same as
> it was 12 years ago when Mr McNamee was Superintendent and the location had
> about 17,000 inhabitants.[13]

He felt that the situation had now reached serious proportions, and argued that unless the staff was strongly reinforced neither the efficient management of the location nor the performance of various other functions to do with native affairs would be possible. The reasons he gave for this were the large (threefold) increase in the population and the related growth of revenue collection duties and general administrative work, as well as the 'spate of legislation' relating to native affairs that had been passed in the preceding few years.[14] His suggested solutions concentrated on providing relief for the workload which was falling on his own shoulders, though, and he recommended appointing a deputy manager and a principal clerk to assist with public and office work respectively. But these efforts did not really begin to meet the problem for – apart from the misfortune of hiring some unsuitable people to fill these positions – the system remained largely unchanged and the effectiveness of control was not improved.[15]

However, on a visit to East London in 1955 the manager was impressed with the system of administration which had been implemented there. European superintendents had been appointed to take charge of different areas of the township, and beneath them served a number of Bantu constables. In his next report on department reorganization, it was this system which the manager recommended, since in East London it had apparently 'had a marked effect and much closer co-ordination of location administration had resulted than ever existed before'.[16] Radical changes were now essential, in his view, and this time they were implemented with much more success.

During the first round of administrative reorganization the whole location was split into three sections, with the manager, deputy manager and assistant manager each responsible for a section of the location. Within each of these areas several wards were demarcated, and a headman was allocated to each ward in order that each of the managers would have 'an effective overall system of control over [their] respective areas'.[17] In addition to this, the administration decided to divide the existing headmen into three 'action groups' to deal with (a) illicit liquor traffic and hooliganism, (b) unlawful structures and (c) unlawful occupation of premises, illegal trading and nuisances. Each group was required to make regular patrols through the location and to seek out those contravening the particular location regulations.[18] This represented the first signs of a distinct shift in the administration from the earlier area-based 'headman' arrangement to the use of 'constables' with more general responsibilities. This change was the object of some deliberation on the part of the management.

In 1959 Mr Poppleton, then deputy manager in New Brighton, delivered a paper to a regional meeting of the Institute of Administrators of Non-European Affairs entitled 'The Headman System as Opposed to a Municipal Police or Any Other Efficient System of Control'. The headman system had many advantages, he claimed, mostly to do with the opportunities that it offered for the headman to gain the trust and respect of the inhabitants of the area over which he had control. A particular headman remained in the one area and so could 'assimilate a thorough knowledge of all the residents of that particular area', and in the process could gain their confidence, become acquainted with their 'most intimate problems' and thereby address their problems more effectively. The disadvantages of this system from the point of view of the administration included the high degree of independence of action which the areal responsibility gave to the headman: he could act as an individual and perhaps even interpret the legislation incorrectly, possibly harming the administration as a consequence. The other danger of this arrangement was the possibility of the headman collaborating with the inhabitants of the area for his own gain. Clearly, then, an administration had to weigh up the advantages of building up trust with the community and the valuable access to detailed information which the headmen offered, against the disadvantages of the rather looser control that the superintendent could exercise through the headmen in such circumstances and the ever present opportunities for corrupt practices which the headman's position offered.

The proposal of a municipal constable system on the other hand was indicative of the strains which the traditional administrative ideology of local knowledge and approachability had been experiencing for some time. In place of the advantages of local familiarity and the opportunity to gain the confidence of the community (as offered by the system of headmen), it was felt that constables could operate as an 'organized body of men especially where strength of numbers were required' – such as in situations of conflict and resistance from the population. They could apply regulations more efficiently, carry out security patrols and be ascribed specific tasks, unlike the headmen who often 'roamed around aimlessly'. But Poppleton was concerned that this form of control would lead to 'a breach between the inhabitants of a location and administrative policy'. This was not just because the new system threatened good relationships with the community but because the headmen were efficient elements of a broader control system that depended upon their local knowledge to furnish information which was otherwise unavailable to the administration.[19] As Mr Peter remarked,

these headmen were the superintendent's sort of eyes and ears in the ward, they used to know the actual goings-on in each ward, and if a superintendent wanted to know something in a certain area he'd go to his headman.[20]

Changes in the designation of these African employees of the Native Affairs Department were not simply occasioned by the need for administrative reform prompted by the growing population within the location boundaries. In addition, resistance to the administration had been growing since the late 1940s, as had the strength of political organization in the township. The manager thus reported in 1955 that

> The headman system whereby 24 headmen assisted in the management of the location and the collection of rents had failed, principally due to subversive elements and that as a result there was a lack of supervision and arrears rentals had accumulated.[21]

'Subversion' was blamed for much of the administrative disorder which existed in the township at the time, and – whilst this may have been an exaggeration – the extent of political organization in New Brighton makes it not unlikely that allegations about headmen being 'excessively influenced by subversive elements' (the ANC) were correct. The method which was used to replace headmen by inspectors gave the administration the opportunity to replace almost half of its staff, as only 14 out of the 24 former headmen were re-employed as inspectors.[22]

In their actual reorganization of the New Brighton department the administration combined the two methods of territorial and general responsibility. A force of inspectors was assigned in groups of seven to superintendencies, and each inspector was also allocated a ward for which he was responsible.[23] The virtues of place-specific knowledge were hence retained, but the inspectors were also co-ordinated into teams who could embark on raids and searches more effectively than could the individual headmen. The manager hoped that this would ensure 'useful results as a joint body where individual efforts would have failed'.[24] The officers wore uniforms, an innovation designed to improve their visual effect in the community, and were designated as 'peace officers' with powers approaching those of police, although at this stage the council baulked at the idea of creating too close an association with the police and refused permission for them to be termed 'constables'.[25]

It took some time for the manager to create a force of 'Bantu officers' suitable to his purposes. After three years he wrote that 'there are indications that a body of reliable and efficient inspectors has now been established', although in his view many were still in the unsatisfactory position of living outside the areas for which they were responsible, which meant that they 'weren't in constant touch with developments in their own wards'.[26] Furthermore, the new body of inspectors occasioned some controversy concerning malpractices on the part of headmen, who were accused of unnecessarily evicting people and 'searching' houses when the occupants were absent.[27] The manager

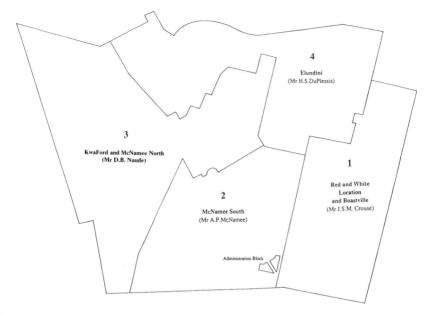

Figure 7.1 New Brighton administrative sub-divisions, 1945 (PEIA 25/391 No. 2)

politely noted that there were 'many temptations awaiting the unwary Bantu Inspector', and that 'considerable strength of character' was required to resist these.[28] But at the end of 1959 one of the superintendents had occasion to observe that 'some Bantu Inspectors are still irresponsible and require continual strict supervision', and reports of misconduct and corruption continued to be filed.[29] In their turn, however, the white officials also represented additional problems for the manager in his efforts to secure 'efficient control'.

In place of the old headman system the location had been divided first into four and later into eight 'control areas', each with a superintendent and several Bantu inspectors (see Figures 7.1 and 7.2).[30] New appointments had to be made for these posts, and not only did the men require on-the-job training and careful supervision but they were also severely hampered in their tasks by the conditions of township life at the time. The older areas were experiencing physical decay, having been in use for much longer than was ever planned and with only minimal attention ever paid to much needed repairs. In addition, the new areas of KwaZakele were poorly provisioned in terms of services, and the population was both socially and physically dislocated as a result of the circumstances surrounding their removal from Korsten. For the new superintendents, translating the formal system of administrative control into effective order proved difficult, if not impossible,

A   Administration Block

B   Bay Transport

Figure 7.2 New Brighton administrative sub-divisions, 1959 (MM 1960)

especially within the constraints of the municipality's insistence upon financial parsimony.

The turnover of staff in the KwaZakele area was of some concern to the manager, and in his 1958 annual report he commented on the 'serious staff difficulties' experienced in the site-and-service scheme.

He wrote that in KwaZakele, apart from the usual frustrations of the superintendent's job, 'the official must apply control measures to a population which has known no control, and where no effective regulations exist and office accommodation is very poor'.[31] Various social and physical environmental hindrances to effective administration plagued many areas of the township. The roads in many parts, including New Brighton, KwaFord, Elundini, Boastville and sections of the new site-and-service scheme, were in very poor repair owing to inadequate stormwater drainage, the proximity of parts of KwaZakele to the flood-plains of the Swartkops River and the general absence of tarred roads. Not only did this cause great inconvenience to the residents in that their homes were frequently 'damp, flooded or surrounded by large pools of stagnant water',[32] but it also made the roads impassable for the officials and interfered with routine administrative and policing activities and with service provision such as sewerage removal.[33] It exposed the officials to the discontent of the population, and J.S.M. Crouse (superintendent of area 1) commented that 'it is disturbing to face the same disgruntled delegation after every heavy rain'.[34] The lack of action from the council on this issue necessitated extreme measures on the part of the superintendents. Rather than leave areas uncontrolled, four-wheel-drive vehicles were purchased so that control could be exercised irrespective of the condition of the roads. Where roads were improved, the superintendents considered that this would 'enable the Patrols to operate quickly and efficiently, [and] crime should be more efficiently stamped out'.[35]

Another physical problem hampering control was the lack of electric light, which meant that most areas were totally devoid of illumination after dark. As one superintendent wrote, street lights in isolated areas 'would be a commendable proposition from a control point of view, bearing in mind the difficulties experienced in effecting some measure of control in these areas at night time'.[36] In 1964 the adjacent area of Veeplaas was incorporated into the location, and here the general problems of control were compounded by the absence of lighting.[37] According to the superintendent, 'the darkness [was] serving as a useful ally to the multifarious misdemeanours' of the unruly element.[38] Patrols were very dangerous to undertake, and members of the public apparently felt threatened by unruly elements. But the concern with 'control' did not extend to a desire to secure the safety of the ordinary residents. When the residents of KwaZakele requested that the police force be enlarged in order to prevent a rising tide of crime, the city council refused to oblige, citing the earlier objections of residents to the council's handling of security (political) matters through augmenting the police presence (as well as stressing the financial impossibility of meeting this request).[39]

As both physical neglect of the environment and poverty amongst the people became worse over the years, the superintendents found themselves in an increasingly contradictory position. Political grievances aside, their self-understanding of their role remained one of trying to 'promote peace and goodwill amongst all sections'[40] and to meet the basic requirements of the inhabitants as best they could. Over time this became ever more difficult, especially with the township running on a self-financing basis, but also because the most public face of the administration shifted from being that of the superintendent to become that of the much less flexible influx control machinery.

Extending the administrative compass: influx control – a new bureaucracy

In 1953, after considerable deliberation, the Port Elizabeth city council implemented central government legislation to control the movement of African people into the town. In addition to the Labour Bureau opened in March 1953, Section 10 of the Urban Areas Act was made applicable in the town from January 1953 and was enforceable from June 1953 when the first urban areas permits were printed.[41] Despite the fact that the compulsory registration of service contracts had not yet been introduced, and that not everyone had yet to acquire an urban areas permit to remain in Port Elizabeth, the Labour Bureau in effect provided the machinery for the application of influx control. Those who did not qualify in terms of Section 10 of the Act for permission to live and work in Port Elizabeth[42] were required to obtain temporary permission to seek a job, and this could be refused if it was felt that there was a labour surplus in the town. Clearly this was a very complicated set of rules, and for the many thousands of people who had recently come to settle in Port Elizabeth, or who needed to seek work in the town, they were likely to cause an immense amount of hardship. And although for a time long-standing male residents of the town and women in general received some shelter from the full force of this legislation, legal and administrative rights to remain in the town did not exempt people from police harassment and arrest in the course of raids and random checks. Indeed, as this point illustrates, influx control was designed not only to keep African people out of the towns, but also to enhance the surveillance capacities of the state.

Enforcing these laws was quite a different matter from declaring their applicability, though, and several difficulties confronted the local administration as it sought to give effect to government decree. The first of these was the problem of territorially ordering the African population which, as we saw in Chapter 6, was considered a prerequisite to applying influx control.

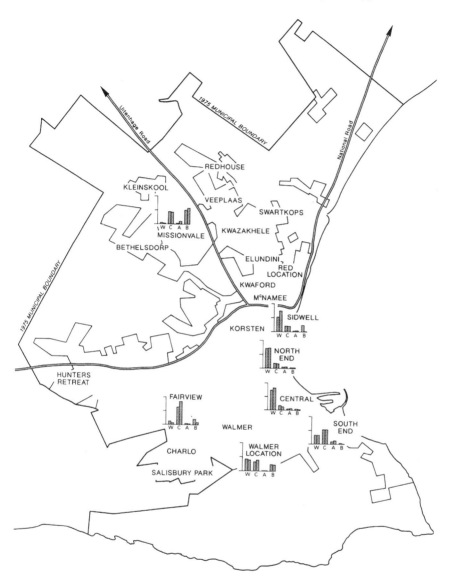

Figure 7.3 Percentage population changes in selected areas subject to influx control surveillance, 1951–1960: W, white; C, Coloured; A, Asian; B, black (Davies, 1971)

Giving evidence before a Commission of Enquiry in 1930 Mr McNamee, then superintendent, had commented that he only knew what was happening in New Brighton, and that he had no idea of events elsewhere in the city. By 1968 his successor, Mr Boast, could report that 'the Department is fully committed to preventing shack development over a 20 mile front. Dozens of shacks are demolished every week in Fairview, Salisbury Park, Veeplaas, Kleinskool and other areas to prevent the influx of unauthorized persons' (see Figure 7.3).[43] The sphere of influence of the local Native Affairs Department had been dramatically expanded and, as the above quotation suggests, the primary reason for this was the need to implement influx control. In order to prevent the 'unauthorized influx' of African people to the town, the long-standing law that all African people had to reside in the designated location was finally being fully enforced and the complex interactions between territorial and more general means of control were confirmed. The application of influx control measures depended upon the ordering of the urban landscape, both to confine African people to a specified area and, within the bounds of that area, to provide the means for effective surveillance and supervision. This manoeuvre also allowed for the closer regulation of the movements of African people into and out of urban areas.

But the vision of absolute control was once again very far from the reality, especially in the early days of labour registration and influx control in the town. Although they potentially wielded immense powers over the lives of ordinary people, the officials in the administration faced an enormous task in their effort to force thousands to leave the town and to encourage industry to refrain from employing 'illegals'. Mass political resistance to these regulations was reinforced by many individual actions, and the efforts of African people to escape the net of influx control caused many a headache for the officials. Part of the problem was indeed the uncontrolled areas in town, where people could escape the eye of the authorities. This included the many individuals and families scattered all over the town in racially mixed areas, small shack developments and the last large shack area to be incorporated into Port Elizabeth (in 1965), Veeplaas. And even within the township itself spaces emerged where people could, for a time anyway, hide away from the officials.

In addition to these efforts at securing the administratively efficient segregation of the population, the creation of a new bureaucracy designed to implement this legislation – completely new to Port Elizabeth – was a mammoth task. One of the reasons for the long delay in the council's agreeing to apply influx control was their concern over the costs and the problems associated with setting up a new bureaucracy of this nature.[44] At this stage of the evolution of influx control legislation the expenses were easily covered by both the fee charged for the registration of labour and the newly introduced native services levy, but the practical details were not so easily resolved.

Perhaps the most fundamental of these difficulties was the inade-quate local state apparatus which was available to implement the intentions of the legislation. The Port Elizabeth NAD was, as we saw above, a relatively inefficient organization, struggling to make the transition from a small paternalistic administration to the effective bureaucracy it was now required to be. The Labour Bureau presented additional challenges to the manager, who found it difficult to acquire suitable staff to operate this bureau, especially at the wages set by a parsimonious council. The Labour Bureau was established in hired premises on Theale Street, North End, and at first it employed only four European clerks and a few African staff.[45] But within two years of its foundation the administration was recommending that a staff of 34 Europeans and 18 Africans was necessary,[46] since the rising volume of work could not be dealt with by the small establishment then in operation.[47] In fact, only nine months after their introduction a backlog of about 7,000 applications for work-seekers' permits (or urban areas permits) had built up. This generated a lot of controversy, in that police were entitled to arrest anyone found in the town without such a permit, and many cases soon emerged of people being arrested and fined because their application for a permit had not yet been processed.[48] The central government was especially perturbed at the ineffectiveness of the influx control measures being applied in Port Elizabeth. The council's attitude was to deny its responsibility to police this legislation, and it therefore only maintained a small staff primarily for the routine administrative work of issuing permits.[49] The inspectorate division of the Labour Bureau was severely understaffed.

The quality of staff was also problematic. The Labour Bureau was, according to the manager, in the hands of very junior members, and in his opinion it was 'in danger of getting out of hand should the staff position be allowed to remain in its present precarious state'.[50] Indeed, one European clerk had absconded from his job, leaving a trail of 'irregularities' behind him, and several African clerks were charged with the fraudulent issuing of work-seekers' permits for personal financial gain.[51] Problems of this nature were endemic to the system of influx control in all centres, in part because the benefits of avoiding enforced repatriation to a rural area were extremely large. While people continued to struggle against this exceptionally severe legislation, the authorities had to make a concerted effort to eradicate the system's inefficiencies. A departmental investigation in 1959 made the following observation about the inspectorate staff in the Labour Bureau: 'their general background and standard of education is such that their capabilities are extremely limited, to the detriment of the control actually required in the urban areas.' In addition to their lack of supervision and direction, understaffing meant that 'the result of the inspectors' efforts is infinitesimal in regard to the volume of the many important aspects with which they should deal'.[52] Reorganization was most definitely in order, and – although the council placed financial restraints on the ambition of officials to improve control – the growing revenue which the Labour Bureau and the native services levy were earning made the council less sensitive to the costs involved in implementing the schemes necessary for securing both influx control and general political order.[53]

In 1955 there was a new thrust at reorganization as a consequence of the council's decision to implement legislation enforcing compulsory registration of service contracts. The previous system had generated some loopholes,[54] and had also not been able to deal with the volume of work involved in registering all those living in Korsten in order to facilitate the clearance of the slum area.[55] Under the new scheme every adult African male in the town would have to register for employment at the Labour Bureau, and women were also encouraged to do so, although this was not yet complusory for them.

One of the consequences of the implementation of the compulsory registration of service contracts in the town from 1 October 1955[56] was that appropriate accommodation for the expanding bureaucracy had to be found. The first Labour Bureau had consisted of only two rooms in a hired building. Its position in the centre of town, while supposedly convenient for both labourers and employers, and close to the new law courts where the magistrate and district commissioner were situated, was very inconvenient in other respects. Firstly, the long queues and large crowds gathering for registration were the subject of several complaints from neighbouring firms and the general public.[57] Secondly, the central site was quite problematic for large industrial concerns who were mostly located near the black township. Labourers seeking a job or registering a contract had to travel all the way into town and then out again before they could take up an appointment. This was especially a problem for casual or daily labour, since this bureaucratic requirement consumed a large portion of the working day.[58]

A new purpose-built Labour Bureau was eventually constructed in KwaFord on the edge of New Brighton. The design of the building and the system of operation which was implemented were the result of a detailed investigation of other centres which had established registration and influx control systems.[59] In their effort to place the Labour Bureau on a proper footing, the manager and two of his employees visited East London, Germiston, Pretoria, Benoni and Johannesburg in order to inspect the Labour Bureau systems which were in operation there. Compared with the other centres the Port Elizabeth registration department was clearly understaffed, and the manager proposed a complete overhaul of the system and the construction of a purpose-built office. Mr Poppleton, delegated the task of investigating the Labour

Bureau's operation, declared it to have been a 'shambles'. His proposals for its improvement envisaged an exceptionally efficient and highly regulated system of record-keeping and internal office surveillance. Since a key problem with the earlier Labour Bureau had been the fraudulent issuing of documents, in this new system hardly any office staff were to have access to the records. Counter staff (to be 'European') would order the records pertinent to an individual application from the records section situated on a raised platform. The record card would then be sent down to the counter on overhead wires. As Mr Poppleton explained, they

> used to fly over the heads of all the blacks congregated there – too high to touch – and then be taken off by clerks behind the counter. So they were never touched, no one had to carry them back and forth. I suppose things still happened though.[60]

But even once a relatively efficient administrative system was in place, there were further obstacles to overcome, including opposition from both employers and popular organizations.

The relationship between the implementation of influx control and labour regulation and the interests of capital has been the subject of considerable debate (Posel, 1988). Unfortunately the subject at hand does not permit an extensive assessment of these matters in the Port Elizabeth context, but available evidence suggests that businesses in the town did not unambiguously support or oppose the introduction of this legislation.

Relations between capital and the local state in Port Elizabeth were severely stretched in the early 1950s, especially when the local state's punitive response to the 'paint riot' led to the declaration of an unlimited general strike in protest.[61] On top of the absenteeism caused by the campaign itself, the local business community was distinctly annoyed with the council's handling of the situation. They minuted that 'the City Council should be urged in future to consult with Commerce and Industry before taking any major decisions affecting labour matters'.[62] Some consultative bodies were set up as a consequence, and the council certainly lent business a sympathetic ear, but a measure of conflict between the two persisted, exacerbated by the new influx control requirements.

As the authorities struggled to apply government legislation, the employers became increasingly annoyed at the difficulties which the Labour Bureau was causing them, and also at the extra expense which they were incurring.[63] In addition to the registration fee, which considerably increased the costs of what was usually an ultra-cheap workforce, the Labour Bureau created an artificial shortage of casual (daily or seasonal) labour. Both the wages and the conditions of work in some industries made employment in them an unattractive prospect for workers who felt that they had an alternative, especially if they felt that their long-term residence in the area made them immune to deportation (Posel, 1987). Furthermore, many of the people most desperate for jobs were unlikely to be eligible for the urban areas permits required by the Labour Bureau. Even in a town with the loosest influx control some of the larger industries (most likely to be noticed for irregular employment practices) still experienced urgent labour shortages. Whilst the employers blamed this situation upon inefficiencies in the Labour Bureau, the manager in turn pointed to the wages and conditions of work in industries such as timber, construction, cement and canning. He observed that labourers were very critical of these jobs, and that they usually failed to proceed to take up such employment when instructed to do so by the bureau.[64] Although there were clearly enough people in Port Elizabeth to satisfy the labour requirements, an artificial shortage was created by enforcing the dual restrictions of influx control – which gave some people the privilege of legal residence in the town not connected to their employment status – and labour registration, which prevented the in-migration of labourers willing to take on the least attractive jobs. As the Native Affairs Committee noted, this shortage was 'likely to continue...while influx control operated in Port Elizabeth'.[65]

The employers made some efforts to force official action to remedy this labour shortage, but the central government was unwilling to allow labour to be requisitioned from the rural areas while the council was not yet adequately controlling the general influx of African people to the town.[66] Many employers resorted to hiring illegal labour, and with an admission of guilt fine of only £1 the consequences were not too severe (although for employees, deportation or fines of over £5 were the usual punishment).[67] While the inspectorate facilities of the bureau remained so restricted (this was the case until well into the 1960s), it was difficult to police employers, who continued to disregard the regulations where to do so seemed profitable. The common administrative practice of registering a service contract after a labourer had been hired also eased the difficulties for capital.[68]

Early constraints on the labour supply motivated the chambers of commerce and industry to support efforts by the council to tighten up the regulations by implementing the compulsory registration of service contracts, in the hope that a more rigorous application of the law would force labourers to take on jobs under conditions chosen by capital.[69] Having undermined the rights of African people to organize themselves into trade unions, the strict application of this legislation – while in theory 'protecting the local native' from outside competition – potentially deprived African people of even the limited competitive powers of the labour market (cf. Roux, 1964: 330). Thus, those employers offering the worst conditions of employment probably benefited most out of the system because their supply of labour, although initially retarded, was later secured by the harsher and more efficient application of the same regulations (such as ensuring the transport of workers to their appointed employers) and also through the practice of meeting unfilled labour needs in the worst jobs by using migrant labour.

In addition to the opposition of employers, ordinary African people in the town resisted the application of this legislation both individually and through collective action. At every opportunity African people had objected to the suggestion that the city council enforce these laws, and when passes were finally issued they were greeted by demonstrations and protest meetings. The focus of opposition to the implementation of this legislation took the form of anti-pass campaigns. Locally, protests had been registered by unions and popular organizations whenever it was made known that the council was considering implementing 'pass laws',[70] and there was also strong support for the various national campaigns launched to oppose passes for Africans (Lodge, 1983). The strongest organized opposition to passes came from the women, who – having first been granted exemptions from these provisions – were required to carry passes from 1 February 1963. Women throughout the country had always protested vigorously against the application of pass laws on the grounds that the arbitrary arrest of mothers and wives would endanger their children and undermine home life (Walker, 1983). In Port Elizabeth women staged a number of protests against the legislation.[71]

But the state embarked upon a careful campaign to ensure that passes were issued, and one example of the care taken can be seen in their encouraging employers to make arrangements for their employees to acquire the relevant documents. Despite intense state repression of activists in the area,[72] people continued to object to the unjust and harsh application of apartheid laws.[73] And when the political opposition turned to violent methods of resistance, the Labour Bureau was a key target for attacks,[74] as were the administration offices and headmen's homes.[75] However, political organization in the area was severely undermined by the extensive bannings and imprisonments of leaders during the course of 1962 and 1963. At the end of 1963 the Manager of Native Affairs could report a 'significant decline in political activity'.[76] Individual evasions of the law persisted, but the pass laws were imposed and served as more or less effective weapons for routine political and population control until their abolition in 1986 (see Greenberg, 1987).

There were also some loopholes in the application of influx control. In Port Elizabeth the process of rehousing from Korsten to KwaZakele seems to have ensured that some people managed to escape the requirements of the legislation. A number of Korsten slum dwellers, especially women who were exempt from influx control legislation at the time, were able to acquire and retain housing in KwaZakele, despite the fact that they were technically illegally in the town.[77] The tightening up of influx control legislation in the early 1960s (Posel, 1987) made it substantially more difficult to escape the regulations.[78] By the 1960s, then, the influx control and labour registration bureaucracy had come to represent the public face of the administration far more than the superintendents, and this face was no longer paternalistic or humanitarian even though the superintendents continued to insist that 'they tried to help as many people as possible'.[79] Clearly they were constrained by the legisation (although they were not hesitant to use it to dispense with, amongst others, political activists).[80] Aside from the rare individuals who may have persuaded them of the value of their case, the Native Affairs Department officials generally supported the application of the law rather than a humane interpretation of the cases brought before them. There is some evidence that the registering officer was unwilling to make exceptions, although by virtue of their more 'personal' contacts with local people the superintendents and the manager occasionally argued with him for the application of 'discretion' in certain cases.[81] On the whole, though, the administration's powers over the daily lives of African people in the town were multiplied several-fold by these legislative measures, not withstanding the fact that (as we have seen) their application was not always as straightforward as the government may have wished. And in this regard, the ambivalence of some of the administrators is worthy of note – even if this was vastly overshadowed by the efforts of African people to subvert their administrative and legal powers.

The politics of administrative ambivalence

In contrast to the protestations of superintendents, who frequently explained their role in terms of 'helping' location residents, the history of 'native administration' in Port Elizabeth has shown that the growth and changing strategies of its Native Affairs Department were also related to the broader South African political context. In some senses, the intrinsic purpose of this state apparatus, irrespective of the particular mechanisms that it utilized, had always been to ensure the domination and to enable effective governance of African people. However, we have also seen how it was only from the 1950s that urban 'native' administration in Port Elizabeth came to be closely articulated to the projects of the central government. And even then, the particularly local character of location administration meant that attachments to the interests and needs of the locality and the people who lived there remained important. Bekker and Humphries (1985), for example, cite cases of township administrators resisting central directives even after all urban African residential areas had come under the jurisdiction of the central government – just as, during the days of municipal administration of townships, location superintendents and managers of native affairs frequently found themselves torn between the demands of residents and the intransigence of frugal town councils. But such ambivalences were also reflected in the administrators' relationships with location residents themselves.

The relationship which emerged between the administrators and African political organizations was curiously at odds with the professed concern of administrators for the needs of those whom they governed. Indeed, it is in the expressly political moments of administration that a certain functionality of a paternalistic administration can be observed. We saw, for example, how in the late 1920s the personal intervention of Paddy McNamee (Senior) in a dispute over the use of the single men's quarters had defused a potentially explosive situation (Chapter 4). Similarly, resistance to a much later removal of people (1960s) from Red location kitchens was dealt with by the area superintendent (McNamee Junior), who agreed to postpone the removals, and then slowly effected them once the dispute had died down. On a much larger scale, though, during the 1950s while the city council was generally refusing to interview the ANC on the grounds that all representation was to occur through the Native Advisory Board, and the administration in New Brighton was involved in surveillance of political organizations, the manager was receiving regular and vociferous deputations from the local ANC Women's League. These deputations were also 'handled' with a brand of paternalism. The women made strong demands of the administration and of the council which were entertained with patience by the administrators, but which received very short shrift from the city council.

A particularly striking example occurred in July 1956 when some 200 women met with various administration officials for some 90 minutes. Many detailed grievances were discussed and a clear, strongly worded memorandum was submitted by the women to the manager for transmission to the council. The women concluded their memorandum with the statement that

> We are not prepared to be sent from pillar to post by the powers that be. We therefore call upon you to convey our grievances to the City Council...you will not doubt our state of frustration and despondency.[82]

This suggests that the administration's tactic of patient and attentive listening, with no action on the matters of complaint, was being firmly rejected. But it also implies that the superintendents did know and did understand at least some of the difficulties of township life. The incident in question led to a public denouncement of the council's neglect of the location from a number of superintendents.[83] Nevertheless, the council refused to take serious measures to remedy these complaints, hampered as ever by its demand that the location be self-financing.[84]

In this case the administrators played a contradictory role, aware as they were of many of the legitimate grievances of individual residents. Their sympathies did not extend to grievances concerning the denial of basic political rights, however, and political activists were subjected to careful administrative surveillance as well as to police harassment. Activists from popular or banned political organizations were often punished through the powers of the township administration, who showed inflexibility in a variety of areas, including housing, employment and pass legislation. The council made use of these administrative tactics to encourage or to force activists to leave the town. Increases in administrative efficiency enhanced the possibilities for political surveillance, as the Manager noted in 1968:

> the effectiveness in establishing a special Section 29 Unit...has had a very important result. It has enabled this Department to co-operate with the Security Police concerning internal security measures.[85]

As the administration moved into the 1970s and became incorporated into the central government apparatus, its governing ideology and organization conformed more easily to prevailing government policies. Although earlier paternalistic administrative strategies were steadily replaced by a large and increasingly distant bureaucratic administration, the administrators continued with clientist or corporatist strategies, attempting to secure support within important (non-political) domains of township life. Nonetheless, in their efforts to ensure the 'impartial' application of legislation, Port Elizabeth was brought more into line with other black townships around the country, particularly as the next manager – Louis Koch – moulded the administration into this new form.

Koch introduced a council monopoly of beer brewing in 1968 in an effort to redress the growing deficit on the native revenue account, reformed the inefficient Registering Office, so central to the effectiveness of the new administrative regime, and embarked upon a detailed investigation and reorganization of the entire administration. He discontinued the tradition of always being available for township residents to discuss their problems and to plead special cases, although colleagues suggest that he attempted to preserve an image of such paternal concern and accessibility (and he himself presents his administration in this light). But in an ever growing community, personal relations were replaced with an attempt to foster influence with different (non-political) groups in the township – sporting, religious or charity groups. The administration claims some success in this regard,[86] but the extent of support for radical community organizations throughout the 1970s and 1980s suggests that they failed to win popular endorsement (Cooper and Ensor, 1981; Labour Monitoring Group, 1986).

Continuity and discontinuity in histories

This case study, spanning some five decades, has enabled us to take note of the persistence of the territorial aspects of administrative power through a broad sweep of historical time, especially as concretized in the location strategy. A variety of different modern technologies of power combined to make the location a familiar part of the South African urban landscape. But we have also seen how the modern politics of disciplinary power in South Africa's cities was closely entwined with the construction of racial and gender identities, and with the negotiation of power relations in particular localities. The disconti-nuities in the history of the location – both spatial and temporal – have also emerged from this study. For Port Elizabeth's enactment of the location strategy in different periods may have borne strong resem-blances to such histories in other towns, but it was quite specific to that place. From the early days of enlightened neglect, through a vigorous liberal interpretation of the location, to an at first ambivalent adoption of even more intrusive national legislation governing the movement and lives of African urban residents, the tale of spatial politics in Port Elizabeth is as unique as it is familiar.

These power relations, though, were also negotiated. The resistances and strategies of African people, as much as the incentives of state power, shaped and gave meaning to the administrative histories I have been recounting. Both those who sought personal and collective advancement in closer relations with the location administration, and those who very early perceived the administration's complicity in the broader racist strategies of disenfranchisement and exclusion, were intimately involved in the political and spatial outcomes recounted here. While this study has focused much more on the administrative strate-gies than on the resistances of those the state sought to control, this was partly done to redress a rather fortunate imbalance in recent South African historiography towards writing a 'history from below'. But history from above has also failed to move its glance away from the centre. Thus I hope that my account has given us some insight into important strategies for domination at the more dispersed sites of their execution and elaboration. How power works, then, is much more complicated than is suggested by a view from the centre. It is even more messy, though, than this view from a decentred, but still dominator-centric position has allowed. The task for the future is to be able to mesh these two histories together – from 'above' and from 'below' –, to grasp the negotiated outcomes which were the result of even such a brutally repressive regime as apartheid.

It is in the present moment – during the intermediate and difficult phase in which the rulers and the ruled have been negotiating a future in which they are both to share power – that the dynamics of negotiation which have always shaped the history of our cities, and our country, can be readily observed, even as they have been institutionalized and partly hidden away in various negotiation forums. Conflicts and mediation have moved from the superintendent's office or the mass meeting, the protest march or the prison cell, to the boardroom table, making it difficult for us to ignore the complex and exceptionally mediated dynamics which have produced South Africa's cities. Historically these dynamics have included not only the conflicts and compromises embodied in negotiations between representatives of African communities around the country and those who have ruled them, but, as I hope I have demonstrated, also the evolution of the tactics of modern government. No longer entwined with a state intent on maintaining racial domination, the imperatives of governing and ordering the city are likely to remain important, if now quite differently articulated, motivations for both local and central states in a post-apartheid South Africa.

The postscript traces the trajectory of urban government in South Africa through its growing crisis in the 1970s until the breakdown of control in African urban areas during the 1980s. The search for a negotiated settlement in the face of a deep crisis of urban order in the 1990s, and the new discourses of urban government and administration which are being created in the process of reshaping the post-apartheid local state enable us the luxury of drawing out both continuities and discontinuities which these emerging new forms of government might have with the strategies of government under apartheid. This is a luxury which is made all the more joyous by the meaning which looking back on apartheid has now – compared with the desperate days in which I began this study. The postscript, I hope, gestures towards the emerging places in a post-apartheid world from which we can begin anew the task of evaluating our pasts.

Notes

1   A.P. McNamee, Unpublished Manuscript, p. 59.
2   MM, Report of the Superintendent of Natives (or Manager of Native Affairs), 1927, 1948, 1959.

3 Interview with Mr Ivan Peter, 14.4.1988.
4 Interview with Mr John Poppleton, 23.5.1988.
5 Report of the Manager of Native Affairs, MM 1962, p. 198.
6 A source who has to remain anonymous insisted that Boast's administration was not at all sympathetic to the African residents of Port Elizabeth. There are also tales of Boast personally policing banning and restrictive orders on activists confined to the New Brighton Location area.
7 Interviews with Mr L.C. Reynolds, 26.6.1988; Mr Ivan Peter, 14.4.1988; Mr Poppleton, 23.5.1988; Mr Mundell, 6.5.1988.
8 Interview with Mr L.C. Reynolds, 26.6.1988; PEIA A31 Vol. 4 1 February 1961 to 2 December 1963, 20.3.1962 Town Clerk to Chief Bantu Affairs Commissioner.
9 PEIA 25/100NB No.10. D.B. Naude to Town Clerk 27.5.1955.
10 A.P. McNamee, Unpublished Manuscript.
11 Interview with Mr Ivan Peter 14.4.1988.
12 PEIA 25/186 No. 9. Manager of Native Affairs: Estimates of Expenditure and Income for the Native Affairs Department 1946.
13 Ibid.
14 PEIA 25/100NB No. 10. Confidential Report by Manager of Native Affairs 30.9.1954.
15 Bouchier (deputy manager) resigned after only three months, and B.C. Bauer absconded and several irregularities were later discovered in the accounts for which he was responsible. PEIA 25/100NB, D.G. Bouchier to Manager Native Affairs 24.3.1955, Report of the Location Superintendent 4.3.1955.
16 PEIA 25/100NB No.10. C.T. Boast to Town Clerk 17.5.1955.
17 PEIA A1(i). Native Affairs Committee Agenda 4.3.1955. Reorganization of New Brighton Administration.
18 Ibid.
19 PEIA A1(iii). Minutes of a Meeting of the Cape Provincial Division of the Institute of Administrators of Non-European Affairs (Southern Africa), held on 30-10-1959, Grahamstown.
20 Interview with Mr. Ivan Peter 14.4.1988.
21 PEIA 25/100NB No.10. Town Clerk's Memo to Finance and General Purposes Committee 20.5.1955.
22 PEIA 25/100NB No.11. Town Clerk PE to Town Clerk Somerset East 26.8.1955, Interview with Anonymous Township Activist of the 1950s.
23 Interview with Mr Ivan Peter 4.4.1988.
24 PEIA 25/100NB C.T. Boast to Town Clerk 17.5.1955.
25 PEIA 25/100NB No. 11. Town Clerk PE to Town Clerk Somerset East, 26.8.1955.
26 MM 1959. Annual Report of the Manager of Native Affairs, p. 149.

The reason for their being separate from their wards was the absence of four-roomed houses in KwaZakele at the time and the manager's unwillingness to transfer them to two-roomed houses, since 'they would find it quite impossible to accommodate their furniture'. MM 1958, Annual Report of the Manager of Native Affairs, p. 170.

27   PEIA A1(i). P.J.B. Kwaza (an ex-Advisory Board member and journalist) to Manager of Native Affairs 17.5.1956; Kwaza to J.S.M. Crouse 23.5.1956; Kwaza to the Editor *Evening Post* 25.5.1956 and 1.6.1956; C.W.M. Gell to the Editor, *Evening Post* 6.6.1956.

28   MM 1958. Annual Report of the Manager of Native Affairs, p. 171.

29   PEIA A26. 1959 Annual Report of Superintendency No. 7, G.A. Warnecke. PEIA A26 Annual Reports Vol. 5. Report for 1967, Area 5.

30   PEIA A1(i) Native Affairs Committee Agenda 5.3.1956.

31   MM. 1958. Annual Report of the Manager of Native Affairs, p. 171.

32   PEIA A26 Vol. 1 1959 Annual Reports of Superintendencies Nos 1, 3 and 5. June 1962 Annual Report of Superintendency No. 5: 75 houses were flooded in the April rains of that year.

33   Ibid. Reports of Superintendencies Nos 5,6,7 and 8 (KwaZakele areas).

34   PEIA A26 Vol. 1 Annual Report of Superintendency No. 1. for Year Ending 30.6.1962.

35   PEIA A26. Annual Report for Year Ending 30.6.1965 Area 7.

36   PEIA A1(ii) Native Affairs Committee Agenda 6.8.1956.

37   PEIA A26 Vol. 5. Annual Report for Year Ending 30.6.1968. Area 5.

38   PEIA A26 Vol. 3. Annual Report for Year Ending 30.6.1965, Area 9 (KwaZakele Extension). Baines (1994) notes that during the blackouts of the Second World War, crime in New Brighton had escalated considerably.

39   *Evening Post* 1.6.1957. Schauder commented that he was surprised by the request for more police and said, 'we are still trying to live down criticism against the former Mayor for his appeal to Dr Verwoerd to try to maintain law and order in New Brighton.'

40   PEIA A26 Vols 1 and 2. Annual Report of Superintendency No. 7. G.A. Warneke.

41   PEIA 25/383 No. 1. Town Clerk to Native Commissioner 16.1.1953.

42   Section 10 of the Act provided four categories of qualification which could be granted to (a) those born in the area, (b)wives and children of such people, (c)those who had worked continuously for one employer for ten years or for more than one for fifteen years, and (d) those who were given permission to remain as long as they were employed. Section 23 of the Native Urban Areas Act of 1945 made it an offence for an employer to engage any African person who did not have permission to be in the proclaimed area and to

seek work, or to employ anyone except through the Labour Bureau. (Section 27 made it compulsory for unemployed African people to register at the Labour Bureau.)

43 PEIA BS1(vi). Bantu Affairs Agenda 12.2.1968.
44 PEIA 25/383 No. 1. NAC Minutes 8.5.1952.
45 MM 1953, Annual Report of the Manager of Native Affairs.
46 PEIA 25/100NB No.11. Report by Mr Nefdt and Mr Poppleton 30–6–1955.
47. PEIA 25/100NB No. 10. Town Clerk's Report 17.2.1955. The daily numbers reporting at the Labour Bureau had increased from 200 in 1953 to 400–600 by this time.
48 PEIA 25/383 No. 2 Native Affairs Committee 26.11.1953; Port Goods Superintendent SAR&H to Town Clerk 20.11.1953; Director MCI to Town Clerk.
49 PEIA 25/279 No. 3. Minister of Native Affairs to the Town Clerk Port Elizabeth 9.12.1953. PEIA 25/100NB Vol. 16. New Brighton Staff. Investigation into the Administration and Organization of the Native Administration Department, New Brighton, Port Elizabeth, September 1959.
50 PEIA25/100NB. No. 10. Report of the Location Superintendent 4.3.1955.
51 PEIA 25/100NB No. 10. Report of the Location Superintendent. 4.3.1955. Statement by J. M. Mpati, permit clerk at Native Labour Bureau, confessing to accepting a bribe of £5 for issuing a record card and a work-seekers' card. He requested that he be placed in a 'less tempting position' but was summarily dismissed. Manager of Native Affairs to Mayor 2.3.1955. Eight more clerks were dismissed the following month for similar activities. Inspector Native Affairs Department to Manager of Native Affairs, 29.4.1955.
52 PEIA 25/100NB No. 16. Investigation into the Native Administration and Organization of the Native Administration Department, New Brighton, Port Elizabeth.
53 PEIA 25/100NB No. 10. Report of the Manager of Native Affairs, New Brighton 30.9.1954.
54 The issuing of urban areas permits after six months' continuous employment allowed people to leave their employer but retain an apparently valid permit.
55 Interview with Mr John Poppleton 23.5.1988.
56 PEIA 25/279 No. 3. Chief Native Commissioner (King William's Town) to PE Town Clerk 22.9.1955. *Government Gazette*, 30.9.1955.
57 PEIA 25/383. No. 1. Town Clerk to Native Affairs Committee 5.6.1953 Native Affairs Committee Minutes 4.9.1953.
58 PEIA 25/383 No. 1. PE Chamber of Commerce to the Town Clerk 6.11.1953.

59 PEIA 25/100NB No. 11. Report by Mr Nefdt and Mr Poppleton 'Registration of Service Contracts, Accommodation, Staff, Office Systems and Documentation' 30.6.1955.
60 Interview with Mr John Poppleton 23.5.1988.
61 *Advance* 6.11.1952.
62 Minutes of Chamber of Commerce meeting 4.8.1952 (These minutes are housed in the Library of the University of Port Elizabeth. They represent only a small selection of the chamber's general archives to which I was denied access.)
63 The first complaints came from those who depended upon large numbers of casual or seasonal workers. In response to complaints the council permitted the fees for casual labourers to be paid on the average number of workers employed over the year, but after substantial losses were experienced as a result the Council withdrew this arrangement before a year had passed. PEIA PEM 25/383. Director Midland Chamber of Industries to the Town Clerk 7.4.1953; NAC 4.9.1953; Council Minutes 1.10.1953; Council Minutes, 17.12.1953.
64 The city engineer, offering jobs cleaning and in construction, was angry that no African people would take these jobs. He wrote that 'if these people won't take work then they are of no value to Port Elizabeth and steps should be taken to have them removed' PEIA 25/383 No. 1 Establishment of Native Labour Bureau 8.1.1954. Town Clerk to Manager of Native Affairs.
65 PEIA 25/383. NAC Minutes 26.11.1953.
66 PEIA 25/279 No. 3 Manager of Native Affairs to Town Clerk 9.12.1953.
67 PEIA 25/383. No. 1 NAC Minutes 7.1.1954.
68 In response to a survey questionnaire in 1970, the manager of native affairs estimated that, of the registered male work-seekers in the town, 45% were hired at the Labour Bureau, 35% were hired by employers from work-seekers sent on by the Labour Bureau and then registered later, and 20% were employed first independently of the Labour Bureau and registered at a later date. The estimates for female work-seekers were 30%, 50% and 20% respectively. PEIA A31 Vol. 7. Responses to University of Pretoria, Department of Economics, Questionnaire on Labour Bureau 21.7.1970.
69 PEIA 25/279 No. 3. Chamber of Commerce to Town Clerk, 17.2.1954; Director of the MCI to Town Clerk 17.2.1954.
70 For example, after the council's decision in January 1953 to implement influx control, a meeting of some 20,000 African people in Port Elizabeth expressed their opposition and suggested that the city council had 'shed the last vestige of its once boasted liberalism'. *Advance* 22.1.1953.

71 *New Age* 20.8.1959; 13.10.1960; 11.10.1962.

72 Many people were banned, arrested and tried on various charges, including treason. *New Age* 19.4.1962; 23.8.1962; 11.10.1962; 8.11.1962.

73 *New Age* 1.10.1959; 5.7.1962.

74 PEIA AB F1(ii) 19.12.1961, Boast to Town Clerk, reporting a bomb attack on the bureau on 16-12-1961. This was a symbolic holiday for the whites, celebrating their defeat of the Zulu people over 100 years before.

75 PEIA AB F1(ii) 11.10.1962, Boast to Town Clerk 2.3.1959 reporting an effort to burn down the superintendent's offices and the homes of headmen.

76 MM 1963 Manager of Native Affairs Report.

77 The manager reported on 21.6.1957 that he was clearing people from areas in Korsten 'regardless of their qualification to be in the area'. PEIA BS1(v) MNA to District Commandant Korsten Police.

78 *New Age* reports this from the point of view of the African population who experienced increased harassment during pass raids (5.7.1952) and women who were deported to rural areas (11.10.1962).

79 Ibid. Native Registration and Labour Bureau Annual Report for 1959: 'the attitude of officials in this particular section is interpreted by the Native population attending as the attitude of the Department as a whole and that the Influx section is considered one of the most important focal points in the whole Department.'

80 By the end of the 1960s, the administration used any available reason to refuse permission for people to remain in the town. An ex-convict, for example, whose parents did not wish him to return to Port Elizabeth, was endorsed out, and all returning political prisoners were similarly treated. An officer responsible for one such decision commented, although he had no idea of what exactly the person in question was alleged to have done, that 'he was a member of an organization [he did not know which one] which supported the aims [of sabotage, terrorism and murder]' and therefore he 'would be very reluctant to agree to his admission into this area'. Rule by administrative fiat certainly resulted in some cruel decisions including one regarding an 80-year-old woman who was refused permission to come and live with her daughter since, the officer claimed, 'it is quite obvious that it is her aim to come and work in Port Elizabeth'. PEIA C69: Influx Control and Foreign Natives, 9.3.1971 to 30.8.1972.

81 Ibid., Superintendent A. P. McNamee's suggestions regarding the returning political prisoner mentioned in note 80 were directly contrary to those of the registering officer cited; Interview with Mr Ivan Peter 14.4.1988.

82 PEIA AB A1(i) Memorandum for Submission to the Manager of
Native Administration, New Brighton Administration 16.7.1956.
83 *Evening Post* 6.8.1956.
84 PEIA AB A1(i) NAC Minutes 6.8.1956. On his retirement, Mr
Boast commented that 'his only frustration during twenty-six years
in the municipal service had been lack of finance for projects under
his control. He expressed the hope that more benevolence would be
shown by the Council in future in providing more finance for
municipal projects. However, he paid tribute to the Council for the
work it had done in the past of promoting industry in PE and avoiding friction between the races.' EPH 1.5.1969.
85 PEIA AB A31 Vol. 7 Manager of Bantu Affairs to Chief Bantu
Affairs Commissioner 24.1.1968.
86 As Koch commented, 'There was a great co-operation between the
administration and the elected councillors and a previously political community turned into a very positive one': Interview,
30.8.1989. And Craig Charney's (1994) work suggests that the
measure of consent and co-operation in black politics through the
apartheid years has been much underestimated.

8

Postscript: post-apartheid, post-colonialism: negotiating apartheid urban spaces

Our yardstick should be the extent to which changes in local government, both now and in the future, improve the daily lives of the most disadvantaged sectors: black communities, women, the poor, the rural areas. (Moses Mayekiso, President SANCO, at launch of Local Government Negotiating Forum, 22 March 1993).

The language of critique is effective not because it keeps forever separate the terms of the master and the slave, the mercantilist and the Marxist, but to the extent to which it overcomes the given grounds of opposition and opens up a space of translation: a place of hybridity, figuratively speaking, where the construction of a political object that is new, neither the one nor the other, properly alienates our political expectations, and changes, as it must, the very forms of our recognition of the moment of politics. (Bhabha, 1993: 25).

Chaos and confrontation in the cities: the demise of the apartheid order

Many of the dynamics of the recent transformation of South African society have been played out in the urban arena. Indeed, one could make a stronger argument to the effect that the urban crisis has been at the centre of the crisis of apartheid, and that its resolution will be essential to the success of the new government. The resurgence of a nation-wide political movement contesting the legitimacy of the apartheid state in the 1980s was grounded in numerous urban communities and their struggles over the living conditions which apartheid planning and government had produced. The crisis of urban government was compounded by the evident failure of the state machinery to control the movement of African people to the cities. Both influx

205

control and the location strategy – linchpins of the apartheid state's urban policy – had proved unworkable by the 1980s (Greenberg, 1987). The apparatus of native administration, strengthened by its links to the central state, was nonetheless facing a growing financial crisis and in the 1980s was also confronted with an increasingly articulate and popular critique of the prevailing racist and undemocratic form of urban government. Where previously national and local struggles for change had been somewhat disconnected, the links between urban poverty, segregation and apartheid rule were being drawn by the opponents of apartheid to great strategic effect.

During the 1970s the state had attempted to balkanize the country along ethnic lines, excluding African people from political rights within 'white' South Africa. The centralization of urban native administration was also part of this process of drawing a stark dividing line between those inside white South Africa and those excluded from its wealth and privilege. Under Verwoerd's practical approach to apartheid in the 1950s, a large urban African population had been housed and granted rights to remain in white cities – in separate locations, with no political rights (Posel, 1987). But with the extension of the powers of the governing Nationalist Party during the 1960s, the vision of a racially fragmented territory, with African people exercising their rights in 'independent' segments of the country, came to dominate. Attempts to re-ethnicize the urban population (through education, for example), to repatriate unwanted workers to homelands and to clamp down on urbanization reached their height during the 1960s and 1970s.

The powers of the apartheid state were nonetheless precarious. Opposition to this profoundly oppressive regime began to re-emerge in the 1970s. Worker organization grew, and youths contested the language and education policies which were designed to keep them subordinated. Facing what Saul and Gelb (1981) have termed an 'organic' crisis (of economy, legitimacy and political control), the government began in the second half of the 1970s to search for new compromises which would perpetuate their rule. The urban question was at the centre of their reform initiatives – just as the urban arena formed the backdrop for many of the conflicts during this long period of crisis. The possibilities for effective urban government were, as we have observed throughout this study, crucially dependent upon state capacity. And in situations of relatively weak state capacity, territoriality had been a useful means for enhancing surveillance capabilities. But the old problems of physical order and routine governance, while playing a renewed part in cities facing an ever growing population and decaying infrastructure, were now compounded by increasing problems of social disorder.

Unemployment and youth disaffection, together with the obstacles put in the way of family life under the apartheid laws, and the illegitimacy of the authorities, combined to generate increasing lawlessness in townships. Together with the growing organizational and ideological sophistication of liberation movements, the old strategies of urban native administration were under severe strain. As Chaskalson (1988) has shown, some native administrators themselves began to search for alternative forms of managing African urban areas. These included pressurizing for a stronger measure of self-government than the state's reforms allowed. Domination perhaps always relied upon some measure of consensual negotiations (Atkinson, 1991); the survival of the regime in this period came to depend upon sleights of hand, offering the form of political power without the substance. A form of self-government was promoted in African townships, but the black local authorities which were created were never completely autonomous and lacked popular support since they were premised upon separation from the 'white' cities of which they were an intrinsic part. The territorial excision of African locations from the white city was not to be addressed until the passing of the Local Government Transition Bill in 1993.

The reform initiatives of the government were skilfully resisted by apartheid's opponents, who refused to participate in state structures – such as local urban councils – which did not meet the requirements of democracy and non-racialism. Faced with the failure of their reformist agenda, and with the breakdown of administrative capacity, the state came to rely increasingly upon violence to contain political opposition. Police shootings at mass meetings and marches, imprisonment of activists and finally the banning of political organizations represented the failure of the state's capacities for securing routine control over those they sought to dominate. Violence, then, represented a weakened state, unable to maintain control through the administrative and hegemonic strategies which had worked more or less effectively during previous decades.

This was most especially true in urban areas. Here community organizations around the country had formed in response to the deteriorating conditions in townships where the poor were to pay for all their own housing, services and infrastructure and where the population was rising inexorably, both naturally and as a result of in-migration from impoverished rural areas. During the mid 1980s some townships were rendered 'ungovernable' by activists – and a vision of a 'dual power' arrangement, whereby community organizations could assume power at the local level, became popular. But if the state was weakened in these areas, popular organizations did not have the capacity to deliver services and government. Nonetheless with the initiation of a rent boycott in many townships around the country (especially in the

Transvaal) in protest at the poor services and illegitimate black local authorities, the capacities of local authorities in black areas were decimated.

From the late 1970s, the urban crisis began to attract the attention of elements of capital who sensed that part of the wider political solution would involve a solution to the problems of order and governance in the cities. Once again, it was housing which was to be central to the problems of social and political order. But the Urban Foundation, formed by big business in response to the growing urban crisis, also pressured for influx control to be lifted. In the face of its unworkability the state abandoned this centrepiece of apartheid in 1986 – but attempted to legislate for what they called 'orderly urbanization' which made urban residence dependent upon housing availability (Watson, 1986). This was not effectively implemented, but reminds us that problems of urban governance have been associated with housing provision for many decades, and not only in South Africa. The state and liberal organizations such as the Urban Foundation once again turned their attention to resolving the housing crisis. This time around, the minimal provision of shelter was considered sufficient for the urban poor, and site-and-service schemes and squatter settlement upgrades began to take shape in the urban landscape. At the same time the once monotonous townships acquired a more varied appearance with the provision of better quality housing for the emerging black middle and upper class. Run-down inner-city housing also became targeted by both landlords and the poor as suitable accommodation in the midst of the urgent search for alternatives to overcrowded and inconveniently located township housing. The emerging 'toilet' (site-and-service) policy of the state and big business has been strongly criticized by professionals associated with community organizations (Bond, 1994), but without a strong commitment from the central government to putting together sufficient loan and subsidy funds for housing for the poor, the 1994 election promises of the ANC may well amount to nothing more. Nonetheless, as in earlier decades it is the provision of urban services and housing which is seen to be central to creating both political and social order. Hindson *et al.* (1992), for example, see the emerging differentiation between wealthy inner-city dwellers and the burgeoning shack settlements of poor, recent in-migrants as potentially explosive. Whether such a neat spatiality to the divisions between poor and rich is emerging in the ever more complex post-apartheid city (Simon, 1989) is questionable, but it is certainly apparent that access to urban services has become crucial to the success of the new political order. And, partly as a result of the politicization of urban services and government during the 1980s and 1990s, they certainly offer the scope to act as a potential fault-line in post-apartheid politics.

The crisis of apartheid, then, has been at least partly a crisis of urban government. It could be argued that the contradictions of black townships in the 1970s bore some strong resemblances to the contradictions of earlier decades which I have discussed in much more detail. Strategies of governance relying upon the location strategy (territorially based administration needing a measure of locally negotiated support from the population) persisted if in somewhat different guises. But the 1980s saw the breakdown of the location strategy. This territorial strategy had been once more overwhelmed by the housing crisis and the economic contradictions of providing housing for the poor. But perhaps more importantly, the articulation of local and national struggles within the broad democratic movement of the 1980s put to rest the possibilities for securing local consensus in the government of African areas or for reshaping the cities after segregationist ideals. The demand for 'one city' rather than the fragmented map of apartheid urban government and the call for an end to the self-financing of townships meant that an entirely new strategy of urban government became necessary. The nemesis of the location strategy in the military campaigns which confined access to conflict-ridden townships to police and army road blocks represented the breakdown of this spatial technology of power – rather than its realization, as some commentators suggested.

While I would not suggest that one will be able to draw too easy connections between apartheid and post-apartheid urban government, the account of the location strategy which I have offered here suggests that some elements of the normalizing discourses which combined to produce the location may well persist into the post-apartheid era.[1] Here one would need to look at emerging discourses of government and emerging practices of urban planning. Of course important new directions in both of these domains of urban practice will also be apparent. More significantly, perhaps, the process of negotiation itself may well produce compromises about urban government and planning which enable some elements of the previous urban order to persist. And new forms of power and government will produce their own relations to urban space as well as being forced to confront the elements of the past fixed in that space. With so many of these aspects of urban government still to be determined we cannot deal with these in any detail. What I can offer, though, is an account of the negotiations for interim local government structures, which give us some insights into the ways in which the landscapes of apartheid could be influential in shaping the post-apartheid city.

Negotiating spaces: compromise and continuity

Along with national-level negotiations which gave rise to the transfer of power from the white minority government to a government of

National Unity in May 1994, negotiations for a new form of local government were held during the course of 1993-4. These took the form of a Local Government Negotiating Forum (LGNF) at which representatives of local government associations, central and provincial local government organizations as well as national civic organizations (leading a delegation of extra-parliamentary groups) were represented.[2] The negotiations for this level of government were set up very differently from those for national government. Whereas the ANC's strategy of a two-sided table had failed at national-level negotiations (Friedman, 1993), at the local level the delegates to the LGNF agreed to divide into statutory and non-statutory delegations. The legislation governing the creation of local-level negotiating forums and interim local government structures, prior to the staging of the first non-racial elections for local government, also embodied this dualistic interpretation of stakeholders in local politics.

The non-statutory alliance in the LGNF was led by the South African National Civic Organization (SANCO), an umbrella body of civic organizations formed in 1992 to replace the disbanded United Democratic Front. SANCO had initiated the rent boycotts which had brought the authorities to the negotiating table in many different localities. During the course of the LGNF, though, SANCO consulted with and was joined in its delegation by members of the African National Congress (ANC) and the Congress of South African Trade Unions (COSATU) (principally the South African Municipal Workers Union, SAMWU). The hegemonic notions of non-racialism and anti-apartheid which cemented this 'side' of the forum were challenged by the settlement reached by the end of the negotiating process. New ambitions also became apparent amongst this grouping as the negotiations proceeded. These included the achievement of a peaceful and orderly transition, fiscal responsibility and sound government. Not that the agenda of non-racialism and equity was abandoned – far from it – but the negotiations did see some changes in the alliance platform. Objections from unions and from some local ANC groupings about the compromises reached shadowed emergent divisions within the anti-apartheid alliance. New and historically contingent criteria for political hegemony and coalition, both in the urban terrain and more generally, are therefore emerging as the oppositional movements shift into power.

For those already in power, the coherence of the formulation 'establishment' forces was also shown to be fragile – although as we will see this operated to promote the more conservative demands of this alliance. The establishment forces in local government included representatives from different levels of government (local, regional and national) as well as organizations representing officials, professional institutes, councillors and practitioners.[3] Some members of the establishment felt inclined to support the non-establishment forces on a number of issues (the Major Cities Association, for example), and the spread of political opinions within this camp meant that consensus was not easily achieved. It also meant that more favourable and conservative positions could be insisted upon in the interests of keeping reluctant negotiators in the process. This was especially the case with the conservative Transvaal Municipal Association (TMA) which represented the interests of smaller, more conservative towns in the province. Bilateral negotiations between individual members of both groupings proved necessary in order to establish consensus positions. Nonetheless the establishment side made repeated efforts to promote initiatives likely to preserve the status quo until the very last stages of negotiating new local government legislation.

Just as interesting for the purposes of understanding the emergent form of politics in the urban arena are the processes of exclusion whereby the forum was constituted. Who was left out of the forum, and what effect did this have upon its deliberations and outcomes? The definition of membership formalized by the already constituted forum was that an organization wishing to join the LGNF had to be nationally constituted, be a stakeholder in local government (or motivate its particular interest in local government), and be a part of either the statutory or non-statutory delegations. Political parties were not permitted to join on the grounds that they had representation at the Multi Party Negotiating Forum (MPNF), where constitutional discussions about local government would also take place.[4] Political parties, women's organizations, business groups and regionally based organizations were therefore excluded from the negotiations. While this meant that the ANC alliance had more control over the negotiations than otherwise might have been the case, it also meant that a variety of groupings with interests in local government could not make a contribution to the technical details and the compromises which were negotiated.

Unlike the national-level negotiations, where each political party had been pressurized into including women on their negotiation teams at all times, the local-level negotiations did not incorporate women into the negotiations in any structured way – and there were very few women included in the negotiating or advisory teams or working groups. Neither were gender issues addressed in any detail at all. Passing comments from key (male) spokespeople from the non-statutory organizations during the plenary sessions, or during caucus discussions to select representatives, and even the inclusion of the desire for a 'non-sexist' local government system in the mission statement of the LGNF, seem to have had no impact whatsoever on either the deliberations of the LGNF or the final recommendations and legislation produced.[5] A women's lobby group wrote to the forum requesting representation, but failed to meet the criteria for admission. Their arguments for inclusion are interesting. They wrote: 'We are deeply concerned that there may not be sufficient numbers of women involved in this planning. We fear that issues with which women are even more familiar and knowledgeable than men may be overlooked. Local development must have the input of women interacting with men to achieve fundamental changes and improvement.'[6]

Individual party agreements regarding women's representation on party lists (especially the ANC, where a hard-fought campaign from the ANC Women's League has guaranteed one-third representation for women) will probably ensure that a reasonable number of women do serve in local government structures. But a system of partial ward-based representation together with the persistent failure by all parties to seriously address gender issues (and not just women's participation) will probably mean that women's issues are sidelined from local councils and bureaucracies unless women's organizations challenge this. SANCO, the leading organization in the local government negotiations, has been strongly criticized for the predominantly male character of both local and national committees. And while senior leadership in the organization are taking these criticisms very seriously, comments from the podium will, unfortunately, not be enough to challenge this. Future research and political action will be well advised to focus upon increasing pressure to advance concern for gender issues in local government. Here at least is one unfortunate continuity with urban government under apartheid. But the compromises reached by the LGNF ensure that the spaces of apartheid will also continue to have political pertinence for some time to come.

The government had developed a policy platform in support of a measure of autonomy for communities within wider metropolitan areas. Delport (Minister for Local Government), for example, noted that 'local government will have to account for the need for sub-municipal units. The security that people find within their smaller communities and their pride in their own environment, should be seen as a positive phenomenon and be applied to serve as building blocks of stability.'[7] These ideas attempted to ensure that wealthy white communities could protect their privileges through setting zoning and planning norms which would preserve the character of their neighbourhood and possibly prevent the kinds of changes in urban form envisaged by the representatives of the poor black majority.[8] Further government proposals included a second ballot for property owners, ward-based elections (as opposed to proportional representation which did not offer the same opportunity for over-weighting wealthier white communities), and local options where the electorate wish to deviate from nationally agreed guidelines for the unification of fragmented apartheid local government (to allow for pre-existing negotiated agreements under the government's legislation and for the participation of traditional leaders). High on their list of priorities as they entered the negotiations was the cessation of the payments boycott.[9]

As chief protagonist in the payments boycotts in the Transvaal, and with a great deal of perceived legitimacy amongst township residents and political observers, SANCO was in a strong position to demand that the government enter into negotiations about local government. They also had an interest in ensuring that the balance of power in the local, urban terrain was not manipulated against their interests – as the government was attempting to do through its legislative initiatives.[10] And while their allies did at times refer to the potential problem of legitimacy involved in having SANCO spearhead the non-establishment delegation, this formulation of the representation was generally accepted as strategically useful.[11] Consultation between the ANC, SANCO and SAMWU (on behalf of COSATU) did take place, in the form of a high-level National Working Group on Local Government and various consultative workshops and forums. Delegates to the LGNF were also split amongst the alliance organizations. A National Consultative Conference was held on 7 March 1993 to prepare for the launch of the forum, and here the different organizations put forward their visions of the process of local government negotiations.

COSATU's position stressed the importance of consultation and caucusing amongst the allies, and they were concerned that decision-making could too easily become the preserve of only the political parties. They also insisted that a legitimate pre-interim[12] form of local government should be elected rather than appointed, as many people in the alliance were arguing: 'The mere removal of illegitimate political structures at local level does not bring us closer to legitimacy – on the contrary in the first place it merely strengthens the autonomous control of the managers of the administrations.'[13] In their opinion, appointed structures should operate for no more than 6 months.

The ANC's submission was more concerned with ensuring that changes at the local level were in tandem with the national-level transition, as it was being negotiated amongst the different political parties. The pre-election phase was, in their opinion, to be used to ensure the 'normalization' of the situation at the local level. This would include an end to the suspension of various services, the provision of central government finance to support local administration, and a moratorium on evictions and sales of state housing stock. But their concern with ensuring that there were no contradictions between national and local transitions led them to propose a transitional scenario in which 'local and regional government structures will stay in place and certain checks and balances will be put in place to descale (or reduce) the powers and functions of these structures to administration of day-to-day affairs...the checks and balances in question would include sub-council/commission for local and regional government and the regional co-ordinating/monitoring commissions and reconstituted local negotiating forums.'[14] This scenario, the authors suggested, was 'based on the idea of constitutional continuity already adopted at Codesa', namely the appointment of a Technical Executive Committee to oversee government actions in the run-up to the elections. Part of the thinking here was ensuring that any failure to re-incorporate ex-homelands at the national-level negotiations would not jeopardize local government arrangements where these areas formed part of functional urban areas. The other concern was with the difficulties embodied in persuading the present government (as opposed to a new, ANC-led government or constitutional assembly) to abandon apartheid at the local level. 'In short it is suggested that there should be no appointed or elected interim local government structures during the pre-election phase. The non-statutory bodies should consider the appointment or election of interim structures only under a new constitution which will have empowered the national liberation movement.'

By contrast, SANCO argued that the state of crisis in the urban areas demanded an urgent and immediate response. The lengthy delays involved in the national-level negotiations made Mayekiso and his advisers anxious that holding the local processes hostage to national-level time frames could prolong the crisis on the ground in townships around the country. They found previous state efforts at restructuring local government unacceptable 'because they [simply] entrench separate and segregated apartheid local government structures'. They referred to an emerging consensus amongst SANCO, organized local government and the central government that there was a need for new interim measures to address the local government crisis. They felt that a new Interim Measures Act for Local Government, negotiated amongst the relevant parties, should be implemented 'as rapidly as possible' and regardless of delays in national-level negotiations. Local options should not be allowed, and for them the key aim was to ensure the resumption of service delivery on the ground, and the resolution of the problem of the illegitimacy of existing local governments. The proposals put to the LGNF by the non-statutory delegation at the launch of the forum broadly followed SANCO's position and, in a later submission to a Technical Sub-committee of the MPNF, the ANC had changed its position to suggest that 'while the process of local government is to some extent dependent on, and will need to be co-ordinated with, national multi-party negotiations, delays in such negotiations should not prevent the introduction of pre-interim measures at local government level'.[15]

Despite these initial differences in terms of process (which were to be resolved in practice during the course of the negotiations) the civics and the ANC brought to the negotiating table some well-formulated ideas as to what a post-apartheid city and urban government should look like. The demand for 'one city, one tax base' had been made for a number of years, calling upon central white local authorities to spread the benefits of the high industrial and commercial property taxes they collected to black areas which had been cut off from municipal responsibility since 1971, and which, as we have seen, had almost always been managed on a self-financing basis. The bounds of the 'one city' were imagined on a functional basis, integrating all who lived and worked within broader metropolitan areas.[16] Within these new, integrated metropolitan areas, the demand was for a more equitable rendering of basic services to all living in the municipal area on an affordable and, if necessary, subsidized basis. This was central to the civic movement's mobilization of township residents, as was the general demand for local government to be organized on a non-racial, democratic (and later nonsexist and financially sound) basis. Detailed research on various aspects of local government and urban planning was being conducted within the progressive academic networks in order to support these broad political demands with technical analysis.[17]

The two sides therefore came to the early stages of the negotiations with quite specific, and different, demands. SANCO was interested in putting an end to unilateral control of urban processes and policy formulation[18] whereby the state had the capacity to mobilize the very considerable resources of urban government for their own political ends. SANCO's primary demand was for interim appointed local councils on a non-racial and one-city basis to end the rule of illegitimate apartheid local councils as soon as possible. The government on the other hand, insisted that an ending to the payments boycott was a crucial first step,[19] and moreover asserted that any new local authorities should be elected, or suffer from the same lack of legitimacy as present councils. Elections would clearly take a very long time, and in the absence of voters' rolls in many black areas they could work to the disadvantage of the non-establishment forces.

The first meetings of the negotiations and working group deliberations therefore revolved around finding a trade-off between SANCO's willingness to deliver a call to end the payments boycott and the government's conceding appointed councils in the interim. These the statutory team presented in the form of a 'package deal'.[20] Agreements on pre-interim appointed structures were directly traded against an agreement on SANCO's part to call for an ending to the payments boycott and for steps to be taken to address the financial crisis which had resulted at the local level. By the time of the second plenary session on 30 June 1993, a joint news release was produced announcing the intentions of the forum to replace local authorities with non-racial governments. No mention was made about the financial agreements being negotiated in one of the working groups.

However, the statutory delegation had persistently referred to the absence of legitimacy on the part of SANCO (as well as the established local government structures) and asked: 'how...the proposed Interim Local Councils and Interim Metropolitan Councils [could] be made more broadly representative and responsible'.[21] This attempt to discredit their negotiating partners was much more strongly articulated by the conservative Transvaal Municipal Association (TMA) who wrote in a submission regarding the contested services and finances working group that 'it often seems that the leaders of these civic organizations are self-appointed leaders who do not enjoy the support of the majority of the residents' and that 'there can be no talk of a new system of local government until order and discipline comes to the black towns. Civic associations such as SANCO should devote all their energy to bringing black towns to order so that the process of governing can continue.'[22] The TMA was insisting on retaining separate local authorities but allowing for an overarching structure on a confederal basis – the notion underpinning the conservatives' vision for national (non-integration) whereby service delivery and some limited (10%) redistribution of white city revenues could be facilitated. The non-statutory delegation's demands, however, included that 'the effect of pre-interim structures must be to ensure that a single local government structure exercises authority over all resources in a single jurisdiction, based on non-racial boundaries'.[23]

The notion of a government of local unity entered into the discussions of the LGNF during a meeting on 13 June 1993 seeking a compromise on the pre-interim period. Here Thozamile Botha mooted the idea of a government of local unity which could be achieved through the allocation of council portfolios and through a combination of ward and proportional representation. As Andrew Boraine explained, they were seeking a solution which would 'address the aspirations of people who have been deprived and allay the fears of the "haves" while not undermining the democratic process'.[24] It was also noted here that business interests needed to have a say in the process of urban government as well, although the non-statutory delegation ensured that their opposition to the highly undemocratic notion of a second 'property' vote for property owners stood firm. However, in the months following the June plenary session, where a number of resolutions had been taken, it became apparent that in fact very little had been agreed. Even the news release claiming that appointed non-racial councils would replace the current racial councils proved to be still up for negotiation.

The sense of agreement fostered by the plenary resolutions was therefore short-lived, as many of the detailed negotiations still remained. The political desire to neutralize the disruptive threats of conservative local governments together with the passage of the LGNF proposals through the Multi Party Negotiating Forum and bilateral negotiating process meant that many of the demands and apparent non-negotiables of the non-statutory delegation were not met. Not unexpectedly, in July the conservative TMA rejected the 'package deal' drawn up in agreement with the rest of the statutory delegation.[25] The government also made use of this deadlock to trade agreement on pre-interim appointed councils for power-sharing (or a government of local unity) during the interim phase, even though non-racial appointed pre-interim authorities had effectively been agreed upon during the June plenary.[26] Indeed, the consolidation of a position in support of lengthy power-sharing arrangements at the national negotiations strengthened the government's hand at the LGNF. The pressure of timing became important as well. In a report to the regions, the non-statutory delegation noted that 'Delport has indicated that if there is no agreement on local government power-sharing, the government will not agree to the Interim Constitution, and the April elections will therefore be in jeopardy. It is not clear whether this position is shared by the rest of the government.'[27]

The strategies for power-sharing at the local level were complex. The compromises embodied in the bill used the apartheid structure of the cities to create councils in which white representation would be disproportionately high. Together with the extremely high ceilings set for agreement in these councils, the white population in most cities would have a large and potentially disabling veto on many key decisions in the new local governments. As an ANC member from the Eastern Cape wrote, 'I spoke to a number of PE ANC people yesterday *re*: the voting procedures in the Interim Councils. All are horrified at the possibility for 2/3 voting majorities, and believe that will be the recipe for permanent paralysis. Please don't concede that.'

Various proposals for effecting a government of local unity were put forward by the government during the course of discussions. These included: delimitation of wards on the basis of loaded votes, establishment of ward councils/committees, separation of legislative and executive powers, increased majorities for decision-making, council structures (a multiple committee system), a second chamber, direct participation by the electorate, local judicial procedures, integration of standards and norms.[28] The position of the non-statutory grouping as regards these was that establishing a government of local unity should not detract from democracy, and should not undermine non-racialism or the ability of the local authorities to address the backlog of services and housing; and, while they should address white fears, they should not pander to racist ideologies.[29]

Significantly, however, demands for a property or business vote were deflected by means of the formulation of a government of local unity – although the government tried to insert these requirements until the final stages of drafting the Bill. But the demand for local options to appease the recalcitrant Conservative Party negotiators in the LGNF and also government representatives meant that the pre-interim was to see potentially very little change in those areas unwilling to oversee their own demise. And the agreement on the interim phase (a long five years during which the government of National Unity was to negotiate a final constitution for the country) saw a strong compromise on the question of racial representation in local government.

The combination of ward and proportional representation was widely seen as a useful way of accommodating both the usual black majority interest in most cities as well as the wealthier and more geographically dispersed white ratepayers. The final compromise, though, was premised upon exactly the apartheid geography which the local government negotiations were designed to transform. The spatial structuring of urban politics was to persist, if in the quite different form of a 'gerrymandered' spatial electoral politics. The final legislation agreed that 50% of the wards in any local government election would be composed of previously white, coloured and Indian local authority areas (as defined in earlier legislation), and the other 50% would be delimited in other areas. With 60% of the votes for a new local authority coming from ward representation, and 40% from proportional representation, most cities would end up with a minimum of 30% representation from white areas. Some anomalies were produced by this system: in Cape Town, for example, where black people form a minority of the population, they would be strongly advantaged relative to the more numerous Coloured population who would share their 30% of ward-based votes with the white population. And of course any changes in the apartheid urban form on the ground, such as the racial integration of neighbourhoods, would affect the racial nature of this compromise. Together with high voting majorities required on many sensitive issues, the Conservative Party had carefully negotiated (or extorted by means of the threat of violence) a system which gave whites an effective veto over many areas of local government for quite a long time – and potentially laid the grounds for a persistence of these agreements into the future as well. There was likely to be substantial room for manoeuvre on the part of conservative or wealthy white councils wishing to avoid the redistributive consequences of a unified metropolitan or city government. And the spatial form of the apartheid city, predominantly shaped by the legacy of the location strategy, would continue to be central to government of the post-apartheid city in the interim, transitional phase.

Post-apartheid, post-colonialism

The demise of apartheid may have been occasioned by a breakdown in political power, particularly in urban areas, but it is in the urban areas that some aspects of this order may well persist, undermining efforts to transform this crucial political terrain. The spatial dimensions of race, privilege and wealth in the apartheid city have been translated into the interim local government legislation, in ways which could once again affect the outcomes of state actions. For while a post-apartheid state (both local and central) must be concerned with re-establishing the basis for governance, this will now be disproportionately influenced by the powers of those whose personal, economic and financial concerns have been privileged by apartheid. Of course the implications of this will vary around the country, and the dynamics of local government will once again be a product of particular histories and local discourses – as we saw so clearly in Port Elizabeth over the years. Post-apartheid urban areas will also be shaped by new modernizing discourses of government and planning which will produce new political subjects as well as new mechanisms for achieving social and political order.

The visions of liberation, then, have appeared in the world in a very mediated form. Thus while one of the most revered township activists from 1940s Port Elizabeth, Raymond Mhlaba, is now Prime Minister of the new Eastern Cape region, and the language of township resistance has become the hopeful language of urban reconstruction around the country, every town council will also be contending with an over-representation of white citizens, a treasurer as eager as ever to contain excessive spending and maintain existing council assets, and an international development discourse urging that housing the urban poor is best understood in terms of its impact upon the local economy rather than in terms of its benefit to human welfare.[30] Post-colonial experiences around the world have perhaps already warned us of the difficulties of revolution, of the persistence of the old order in so many guises. But it is the interpretations of the post-colonial which remind us of the intrinsic doubleness of the world after colonization and which are perhaps more hopeful. Indeed, even aspects of apartheid – so frequently used as a talisman for all that is evil in the world and clearly so destructive of so many opportunities for those who lived through it – turn out to be curiously ambivalent, as some of the evidence I have been discussing here has suggested. And if the colonized are (albeit uncomfortably) embedded in the modernizing world of the colonizer, the menaces of the post-apartheid era should come as no surprise. This doubleness, though, as Gilroy (1993) and others – especially Homi Bhabha (1993) – have demonstrated, also brings with it the possibilities for transformation. But this would be a transformation which is always open to critique, which avoids closing off the identities of participants around old stereotypes, and which is constantly interrogating both the present and the past for the contradictions and the slippages which give us hope for a better future.

Notes

1   I have briefly discussed some aspects of this in Robinson (1992).
2   I must thank Andrew Boraine of the Institute for Local Governance and Development, Bellville, for allowing me access to his excellent records of the Local Government Negotiating Forum (abbreviation AB in following).
3   As a briefing document for an ANC Workshop on Interim Measures towards a non-racial and democratic system of local and regional government noted, 'The definition of a "two-sided table" should not preclude being able to respond to differences within the establishment camp (for example, between central government and organized local government, and between local government in small towns and the big cities) or, for that matter, within the non-establishment side of the table.' AB, Non-Statutory 10.11.1992, Planact, p. 5).
4   AB, Report of Management Committee (Mancom) of LGNF: Membership and Participation in LGNF. 30.6.93.
5   AB, Moses Mayekiso, Opening Remarks to LGNF, Johannesburg Civic Centre, 22.3.1993. 'Secondly, we must ensure that more women participate in the process of restructuring local government in South Africa. Looking around I see that much work needs to be done by all parties to the forum in this regard. But more than participation in the negotiation process, we need to ensure that women become centrally involved in the running of local government itself.'
6   AB, The Women's Lobby to Deputy Director Local Authority Development (Dirk Strydom) 18.3.93.
7   Ibid.
8   In his April 1993 parliamentary address Delport listed the following as the likely functions and powers of ward councils: 'the regulation of norms and standards of the residential environment, arrangements relating to the use of property, the supply of community facilities, security affairs, civil protection, possibly education and welfare, and the levying of an additional rate on residents in

order to finance its own structure and to promote specific projects within its area of jurisdiction'.

9 As the director for local government and constitutional affairs in the Cape provincial Administration, Craythorne expressed his frustration with the situation: 'Nowhere has it been possible for a major slice of the population to live free of charge'. AB, Local Government. Beyond the Interim Measures Act: The Challenge of Local Government Restructuring, September 1992. One of the biggest concerns brought into the negotiations by the government was the payments boycott. They demanded that SANCO end the boycott, immediately, and blamed a multitude of social evils on SANCO's role in leading this action. The history behind the dreadful conditions in townships was conveniently forgotten: indeed, the reasons for the boycott in the first place or the political history which had created separate and vastly under-serviced areas for African people were elided. The present reality was evoked, innocent of its past and action to remedy the situation was seen as imperative. In this SANCO was cast in a recalcitrant light, withholding assurances on ending the boycott and being held responsible for the declining physical fabric in many townships as well as for the huge and growing fiscal burden which the payments boycott created. But as the boycott itself highlighted, order and routine government in the townships could not be secured without legitimacy. And it was for some resolution of this problem that the government was inclined to enter into negotiations with SANCO.

10 The Interim Measures for Local Government Act (No. 128 of 1991) was passed in 1991, prescribing various options as well as a timetable for local government unification. Major objections from the civics and the ANC concerning this Act were that it was premised upon the apartheid local government structures which were devoid of legitimacy, and that it prolonged the existence of these bodies.

11 As Mathole Motshekga, Deputy head of the Local Government Department in the ANC commented, 'it has been suggested that some elements may question the representivity of SANCO'. AB, Non-Statutory, M. Motshekga, 1992. A Critical Analysis of the Proposals of the Working Group of the Local Government Negotiating Committee. Once or twice SANCO were challenged to put their credentials on the table during the course of the LGNF, but these demands were never pressed. The usefulness in having SANCO spearhead the delegation included the fact that it could justify keeping other political parties out of the negotiations.

12 The timetabling of the transition came to be organized around three different periods: pre-interim structures were those in place

prior to elections; interim structures those in place between the
first elections held under the interim constitution (nationally in
April 1994, local elections in November 1995 except for some areas
in the Western Cape and all of KwaZulu-Natal where they are to
be held in 1996); and final structures those in place after the final
elections held under the final constitution agreed upon by the first
government of national unity.

13 AB, Non-Statutory, COSATU Position Paper on the LGNF and
Local Government Restructuring 7.3.1993.

14 AB, Managing the Transition to Non-Racial Democracy at the
Local Level, Discussion Paper Prepared by the ANC Department of
Local, Regional Government and Housing Presented at the
National Consultative Local Government Workshop, 7.3.1993.

15 AB, Plenary, Submission by the ANC to the Technical Sub-
Committee on TEC, 19.5.1993. This was based on the framework
adopted at the LGNF.

16 In one of the earlier statements about this matter in the LGNF,
the suggestion was that RSC boundaries could be followed, or
where these were too large, the 'natural/logical boundaries of each
city should be used'. Disputes could be resolved by a boundary
dispute commission of the LGNF where the following criteria
could be considered: municipal service provision, urban economic
considerations, means of communication, physical features, boundaries of existing electoral divisions, sparsity or density of population, probability of increase or decrease in population, local
authority and magisterial district boundaries. AB, Working Group
2 (WG2), National Guidelines for Local Negotiations. Also AB,
LGNF WG2 Services and Finances, Non-Statutory Side Proposals,
3.5.1993. A later formulation (agreed upon by both statutory and
non-statutory components) suggested that economic functional
areas should be the basis for new urban government, determined
by 'a. commercial/industrial linkages within the area; b. daily
commuting patterns within the area; c. RSC and magisterial
boundaries'. AB, WG2 Consolidated Proposals – Task Team,
14.5.1993).

17 Research was co-ordinated by Thozamile Botha (then Head of the
ANC's Local Government Department) based at the University of
the Western Cape.

18 As Planact wrote in their 1992 review of local government in transition: 'The government has consistently refused to involve democratic organizations in the determination of a nationally negotiated
framework for the transition of local government.' AB, Planact,
Local Government in the Transition and the Options for Interim
Administrative Arrangements.

19 AB, LGNF WG2 Consolidated Proposals – Task Team, 14.5.1993. The statutory delegation noted that they held the view 'that the ending of the rent and services boycott should be ended immediately the process of negotiation has commenced.' AB, Mancom 18.6.93, WG2 Report 18.5.1993 to the Management Committee. The statutory group felt that payments should end immediately, the non-statutory group that 'the ending of boycotts should be linked with the establishment of legitimate political structures. There has to be visible change.'

20 AB, Mancom, March-September 1993, 18.6.1993, WG1 Report to Mancom. On 7.6.1993 Consultative Committee on Local Government (representing most statutory groups) resolved '(a) that the principle of appointed local structures for the pre-interim period enjoys sufficient support (b) that the principle of nominated structures should be linked to a package approach and be based on 3 phases, namely the pre-interim, interim and final phases.'

21 AB, Plenary LGNF WG1 Preliminary Comments by Statutory Delegation Members of the Task Team on the Non-Statutory Delegation's Draft Proposals 26.4.93.

22 AB, WG1 TMA Submission to WG2 (Services and Finances).

23 AB, WG1 Non-Statutory Delegation Draft Proposals, Restructuring Local Government Political Structures during the Pre-Interim and Interim Period, 25.5.1993.

24 AB, WG1 13.6.1993, WG1 Task Team Informal Minutes.

25 AB, WG1 19.7.1993.

26 AB, Non-Statutory Report 30.9.1993.

27 AB, Non-Statutory Report 30.9.1993

28 AB, LGNF Co-ordination, Non-Statutory. Summary of Issues for Bilateral with Minister Delport 30.8.1993.

29 Ibid.

30. World Bank, 1991. Urban Policy and Economic Development. An Agenda for the 1990s.

Primary sources

Central government archives, Cape Town (CA)
Native affairs, Cape Colony
NA 656 New Brighton Location 1903–1906

Town clerk's files, Port Elizabeth (3/PEZ)
Correspondence

1/1498–1/1499 Native Advisory Board
1/1634–1/1635 and 1/1896 Native Affairs in the City 1927–1945
1/1711 Health Conditions in Urban Areas, Bethelsdorp Incorporation
1/1730 Housing New Brighton Village 1935–1936
1/1275–1/1278 New Brighton Location Departmental 1925–1930
1/1489 Staff New Brighton 1925–1930
1/1842 Staff New Brighton 1936–1947
1/1846 New Brighton Location Departmental 1941–1945

Committees and minutes

1/2/1/47–1/2/1/52 Minutes of Standing Committees
1/3/1/2/1 Minutes of Meetings of Health and Location Committee 1903–1906
1/3/2/15/1–1/3/2/15/7 Native Affairs Committee Agendas 1926–1945
1/3/2/11/2 Health and Abattoir Committee Agenda 1937
1/3/2/6/8 and 9 Housing and Slum Elimination Committee Agendas 1936–1937
1/3/2/3/1 Industries Agendas 1936
4/2/1/1/243 and 244 Native Affairs General 1939–1945
4/2/1/1/332 City Engineer's Department Housing and Slum Elimination Housing Schemes 1939–1944
4/2/1/1/360 Housing General. General Inquiries *re* Layout of Housing Schemes etc.

4/2/1/1/380 Land. General. Korsten. Industrial
4/2/1/1/422 New Brighton. Native Housing Schemes
6/1/1/1/428 Valuation Roll 1940
4/PEZ ADD 4/2/1. City of Port Elizabeth. Report of Town Planning
Committee in Relation to the City of Port Elizabeth. Provisional Town
Planning Scheme No. 1. Covering the Municipal Area as at 31
December 1951

Port Elizabeth Intermediate archives (PEIA)

Files under the control of the municipality

25/279 Nos 1–3 Registration of Natives and Influx Control/Service
Contracts 1947–1955
25/383 No. 1 Establishment of Native Labour Bureaux 1943–1955
25/169 Native Affairs in the City 1952
25/168 No. 9 Housing New Brighton Village 1944–1945
25/100NB Nos 9–19 New Brighton Staff 1955–1959
25/391 No. 2 New Brighton Location Boundaries 1954–1958

*Files under the control of the Cape provincial administration
(previously Bantu Affairs Administration Board)*

A1 (i)–(iii) Administration General 1955–1960
A1 Administration General 1960–1961
A1/1/9–A1/1/11 Veeplaas Administration 1966–1970
A26 Vols 1–5 Annual Reports 1959–1971
A/200/1 Municipal Labour Bureau Administration
A/300/6/1971–1973 Annual Reports
A31 Vols 1–7 Administration. Census and Statistics 1955–1970
A89 Newspaper Cuttings 1967–1973
A121 Extension of Location Boundaries (Bethelsdorp) 1960–1963
A500/2/1 Extension of Boundaries–Expropriation of Properties for
Zwide Development Vol. 1. 1971–1973
A118 Territorial and Tribal Representatives
BS1 Vols 1–7. S&S (Site and Service) General and Slum Clearance
1955–1968
BN1 New Brighton–General 1955–1970
BV1/2–BV1/3 Zwide IV Development Vols 1–2 1968–1973
C69 Control: Influx Control and Foreign Natives 1956–1972
C1 Control General 1960–1965
D10 Establishment of Urban Bantu Council, PE 1963–1969
F1(ii) Security General 1959–1961
F11 Security. Public Meetings and Gatherings 1958–1973
S92 Re–organisation 1954–1972

Documents housed in various libraries

Cory Library, Grahamstown

I.L. Griffiths. Unpublished and Incomplete Manuscript *c.*1961. Chapter 4 of a Study on Port Elizabeth with Maps. Conducted under the Auspices of the Institute for Social and Economic Research, Grahamstown

J. P. McNamee. Report on Native Urban Administration in the City of Bulawayo and the Implementation of the Natives (Urban Areas) Accommodation and Registration Act of 1946.

A. Schauder. Citation on Award of Honorary Doctorate to Adolf Schauder, Rhodes University

A. Schauder. 1964. Housing for All Races–the Basis for National Development. Address Delivered to the Annual Congress of the Local Government Association of Southern Rhodesia, Victoria Falls 19-5-1964

Cullinan Library, University of the Witwatersrand

SAIRR AD 843
26.3.2 McNamee and Schauder Plans
26.5.1 New Brighton Lecture Society
26.8.2 Correspondence *re* Korsten Removals
27.1 Records of Conferences
28.7.4 Details of Housing Schemes, 1943
4.5 Social and Economic Conditions, Especially Durban and Port Elizabeth
46.3.3 Correspondence with PE Joint Council
9.3 Correspondence with PE City and Water Engineer

AD 1433
Cg 4.7.1 Report on PE Visit
Aa1 Visit by M. Webb to PE
Cp5 Port Elizabeth Joint Council of European and Bantu
Cp5.6.10 New Brighton Location

Killie Campbell Africana Library, University of Natal

Oral History Project: Interview with S.B. Bourquin, 8.9.1980, by Iain Edwards.

Port Elizabeth Public Library

Port Elizabeth Mayor's Minutes 1899–1965
Africana Collection: Various Pamphlets and Directories

Rhodes House Library, Oxford, United Kingdom

A. Schauder. 1949. A Social and Housing Policy for the Urban Bantu.

Paper delivered to Annual Congress of Native Advisory Boards of the
Union of South Africa, Port Elizabeth, December 1949

Central government archives, Pretoria (TA)

K26 Vol. 7 Record of Evidence to the Natives Economic Commission. 18
March to 10 April 1931

Newspapers and journals

Eastern Province Herald (EPH) (Port Elizabeth) 1925–1928; 1945–1952
Cape Guardian 1945–1952
Advance 1952–1954
New Age 1954–1962
Bantu

Interviews conducted by the author

Mrs Boast (Port Elizabeth), 30.6.1988
Mr Louis Koch (Cape Town), 30.8.1989
Mr Barry Mundell (Port Elizabeth), 6.5.1988
Mr Ivan Peter (Port Elizabeth), 14.4.1988
Mr Pick (Port Elizabeth), 25.4.1988
Mr John Poppleton (Port Elizabeth), 23.5.1988
Mr L. C. Reynolds, 26.6.1988
Cllr J. G. Young (Port Elizabeth), 27.7.1989

Government Publications

Cape Colony

Report and Proceedings with Appendices of the Government
Commission on Native Laws and Customs. 1883. G.4–1983
Reports of Commissioners of Police of the Several Police Districts of the
Colony for the Years 1883–1891
Blue Book on Native Affairs 1874. G.27–1974
Labour Commission. Minutes of Evidence and Minutes of Proceedings.
Cape Town: Government Printers. 1894. G.3–1994.
Minutes of Evidence of the Select Committee on the Native Reserve
Location Bill. A22–1902.
Blue Books on Native Affairs 1901–1910 G.25–1902, G.29–1903,
G.12–1904, G.12*–1904, G.12*–1905, G.46–1906, G.36–1907,

G.24–1908, G.19–1909, G.28–1910
South African Native Affairs Commission (SANAC). 1903–1905. Report
and Minutes of Evidence

Union government

Report of the Commission Appointed to Inquire into Assaults on
Women. UG.39–1913
Report of the Tuberculosis Commission. UG.34–1914
Report of the Influenza Epidemic Commission UG.15–1919
Report of the Housing Committee Appointed by the Minister of Public
Works to Inquire into Matters Concerning Housing Accommodation in
Urban Areas and the Amendment of the Unhealthy Areas Bill.
UG.4–1920
Report of the Central Housing Board. UG.25–1921, UG.13–1922,
UG.31–1925
Reports of the Native Affairs Commission. UG.36–1923, UG.22–1932,
UG.48–1937, UG.54–1939, UG.42–1941, UG.14–1947, UG.36–1954,
UG.58–1954, UG.55–1955, UG.37–1958, UG.36–1961, RP.72/1962
Report of the Interdepartmental Committee on the Native Pass Laws
1920. UG.41–1922
Report of the Native Affairs Department 1921
Notes on Conference between Municipalities and Native Affairs
Department held at Pretoria 28–29 September 1937 to Discuss the
Provisions of the Native Laws Amendment Act (No. 46 of 1937).
UG.56–1937.
National Housing. A Review of Policy and Progress. 1947.
Report of the Native Laws (Fagan) Commission 1946–1948.
UG.28–1948

Other manuscripts/documents

McNamee, A. P., Unpublished memoirs (in author's possession)
British Parliamentary Papers. Colonies. Africa. Vol. 22 (Irish University
Press, Dublin). Correspondence with the Governor of the Cape of Good
Hope, 1849–1850. Correspondence relative to the state of the Kafir
tribes on the Eastern Frontier of the Colony.
No. 2. Copy of a despatch from Governor Sir H.G. Smith to Earl Grey.
March 15 1849. Enclosure: Instructions for Superintendents of Fingoes;
No. 4. Extract of a Despatch from Governor Sir H.G. Smith to Earl
Grey, October 21 1848;
No. 4. Copy of a despatch from Governor Sir H.G. Smith to Earl Grey.
May 24 1850. Enclosure No. 1: 'Notes on the Management of Native
Villages – more particularly the Fingoe, with a view to their own
improvement and the security of the Frontier' by Rev. C.H. Calderwood.

References

Adam, H. and Moodley, K. 1986. *South Africa without Apartheid.* Berkeley, Los Angeles, London: University of California Press.

Adler, G. 1987. 'Trying Not To Be Cruel': Local Government Resistance to the Application of the Group Areas Act in Uitenhage, 1945–1962. Institute of Commonwealth Studies, Southern African Seminar Series.

Adler, G. 1993. From the 'Liverpool of the Cape' to the 'Detroit of South Africa': the Automobile Industry and Industrial Development in the Port Elizabeth–Uitenhage Region. *Kronos* 20: 17–43.

Agnew, J. 1983. An Excess of 'National Exceptionalism': towards a New Political Geography of American Foreign Policy. *Political Geography Quarterly* 2: 151–66.

Agnew, J. 1987. *Place and Politics: the Geographical Mediation of State and Society.* London: Allen and Unwin.

Agnew, J. and Duncan, J. (eds) 1989. *The Power of Place.* London: Unwin Hyman.

Anderson, P. 1974. *Lineages of the Absolutist State.* London: Verso.

Appel, A. 1984. Port Elizabeth *c.* 1855–1875: Enkele Sosio–Ekonomiese Aspekte. *South African Historical Journal* 16: 101–17 .

Arendt, H. 1986. Communicative Power. In S.Lukes, (ed.) *Power.* Oxford: Basil Blackwell. pp. 59–74.

Atkinson, D. 1991. *Cities and Citizenship.* Unpublished PhD Thesis, Department of Politics, University of Natal, Durban.

Azarya, V. and Chazan, N. 1987. Disengagement from the State in Africa: Reflections on the Experience of Ghana and Guinea. *Comparative Studies in Society and History* 29: 106–31.

Baines, G. 1988. *The Port Elizabeth Disturbances of October 1920.* Unpublished MA Thesis, Department of History, Rhodes University.

Baines, G. 1989. The Control and Administration of Port Elizabeth's African Population *c.* 1834–1923. *Contree* 26: 13–21.

Baines, G. 1990a. The Origins of Urban Segregation: Local Government and the Residence of Africans in Port Elizabeth, *c.* 1835–1865. *South African Historical Journal* 22: 61–81.

Baines, G. 1990b. The Port Elizabeth Natives Advisory Board, 1912–1952. Paper presented to the History Workshop Conference, University of the Witwatersrand, July 1990.

Baines, G. 1994. *New Brighton, Port Elizabeth c. 1903–1953: a History of an African Community.* Unpublished PhD Thesis, Department of History, University of Cape Town.

Barbalet, J. 1988. Power and Resistance. *The British Journal of Sociology*. 36: 531–48.
Beinart, B. and Bundy, C. 1987. *Hidden Struggles in Rural South Africa*. London: James Currey.
Bekker, S. and Humphries, R. 1985. *From Control to Confusion*. Pietermaritzburg: Shuter and Shooter.
Bell, T. 1986. The Role of Regional Policy in South Africa. *Journal of Southern African Studies*. 12: 276–292.
Benton, T. 1981. 'Objective' Interests and the Sociology of Power. *Sociology* 15: 161–84.
Bhabha, H. 1993. *The Location of Culture*. London: Routledge.
Bickford-Smith, V. 1981. Dangerous Cape Town: Middle-class attitudes to poverty in Cape Town in the late Nineteenth Century. In *Studies in the History of Cape Town* Vol. 4: 29–65. UCT: Centre for African Studies.
Bieusheuvel, S. 1955. Mind, Manners and Morals. *Race Relations Journal* 22(3): 18–30.
Bloch, R. 1981. The Cost of Living: the Port Elizabeth Disturbances of October 1920. *Africa Perspective* 9: 39–59.
Block, F. 1977. The Ruling Class Does Not Rule: Notes on the Marxist Theory of the State. *Socialist Revolution* 33: 6–28.
Block, F. 1981. Beyond Relative Autonomy: State Managers as Historical Subjects. *New Political Science* 7: 33–49.
Bond, P. 1995. 'Fly-fishing' in *South African Review of Books*. May/June.
Bonner, P. 1982. The Transvaal Native Congress, 1917–1920: the Radicalisation of the Black Petty-Bourgeoisie on the Rand. In S. Marks and R. Rathbone (eds) *Industrialisation and Social Change in South Africa*. London: Longman.
Bonner, P. 1988. Siyawugobla, Siyawugebhola Umbhlaba ka Maspala ('We Are Digging, We Are Digging Great Chunks Of the Municipalities Land') Popular Struggles in Benoni, 1944–1952. Paper presented at the African Studies Institute Seminar Series, University of the Witwatersrand, Johannesburg.
Bonner, P. and Lambert, R. 1987. Batons and Bare Heads: the Strike at Amato Textiles, February 1958. In S.Marks and S.Trapido (eds) *The Politics of Race, Class and Nationalism in Twentieth Century South Africa*. London: Longman. pp. 336–65.
Bonner, P., Delius, P. and Posel, D. (eds) 1993. *Apartheid's Genesis 1935–1962*. Johannesburg: Ravan Press.
Borja, J. 1978. Urban Movements in Spain. In M. Harloe (ed.) *Captive Cities*. New York: Wiley.
Bourdieu, P. 1977. *Outline of a Theory of Practice*. Cambridge: Cambridge University Press.
Bowman, I. 1921. *The New World. Problems in Political Geography*. London: Harrap.
Bozzoli, B. 1978. Capital and the State in South Africa. *Review of African Political Economy* 11: 40–50.
Bradford, H. 1984. Mass Movements and the Petty Bourgeoisie: the Social Origins of the ICU Leadership 1924–1929. *Journal of African History* 25: 295–310.
Bradford, H. 1987a. `We Are Now the Men.' Women's Beer Protests in the Natal Countryside, 1929. In B. Bozolli (ed.) *Class, Community and Conflict*. Johannesburg: Ravan.
Bradford, H. 1987b. *A Taste of Freedom. the ICU in Rural South Africa, 1924–1930*. New Haven and London: Yale University Press.
Brewer, J. 1986. Adam Ferguson and the Theme of Exploitation. *British Journal of Sociology* 37: 461–78.
Brookes, E.H. 1974. *White Rule in South Africa, 1830–1910*. Pietermaritzburg: University of Natal Press.
Browett, J. 1982. The Evolution of Unequal Development within South Africa: an Overview. In D. Smith (ed.) *Living Under Apartheid*. London: Allen and Unwin.

Brown, R.H. 1957. *Political Areal Functional Organization with Special Reference to St Cloud, Minnesota*. Research Paper No. 51, Department of Geography, University of Chicago.

Burawoy, M. 1982. The Resurgence of Marxism in American Sociology. *American Journal of Sociology*. 88 (Supplement): 1–31, eds M. Burawoy and T. Skocpol.

Burchell, G., Gordon, C. and Miller, P. 1991. *The Foucault Effect: Studies in Governmentality*. London: Harvester.

Butler, J. 1985. Housing in a Karoo Dorp: A survey of sources and an examination of developing segregation before the Group Areas Act. *South African Historical Journal* 17: 93–119.

Butler, J. 1990. *Gender Trouble*. London: Routledge.

Calderwood, D. M. 1953. Native Housing in South Africa. PhD thesis, Faculty of Architecture, University of the Witwatersrand, Johannesburg.

Calderwood, D. M. 1959. Native Housing Policies and Problems. *Proceedings of the South African Institute of Town Planners Summer School*. Johannesburg, 2–6 February 1959.

Calderwood, Rev. H. 1858. *Caffres and Caffre Missions*. London: James Nisbet.

Cameron, R. 1986. *The Administration and Politics of the Cape Town City Council, 1976–1986*. Unpublished MPubAdmin Thesis. University of Cape Town.

Cameron, R. 1988. The Institutional Parameters of Local Government Restructuring in South Africa. In C. Heymans and G. Totemeyer (eds) *Government by the People?* Johannesburg: Juta.

Carter, P. 1987. *The Road to Botany Bay: an Essay in Spatial History*. London: Faber and Faber.

Castells, M. 1977. *The Urban Question*. London: Edward Arnold.

Cell, J.W. 1982. *The Highest Stage of White Supremacy*. Cambridge: Cambridge University Press.

Charney, C. 1994. 'A World of Networks': Power, Political Culture and Collective Action in Black South African Communities 1945–1965. Paper presented at the History Workshop Conference, University of the Witwatersrand, July 1994.

Chaskalson, M. 1987. The Road to Sharpeville: the Council and the Townships in Vereeniging, 1950–1960. Paper presented at the South Africa in the 1950s Conference, Oxford, 25–6 September.

Chaskalson, M. 1988. Apartheid with a Human Face: Punt Janson and the Origins of Reform in Township Administration, 1972–1976. African Studies Institute Seminar Paper, University of the Witwatersrand, Johannesburg.

Cherry, J. 1988. *Blot on the Landscape and Centre of Resistance: a Social and Economic History of Korsten*. Unpublished BA(Hons) Thesis, Economic History Department, University of Cape Town, South Africa.

Cherry, J. 1992. *The Making of an African Working Class: Port Elizabeth 1925–1963*. Unpublished MA Thesis, University of Cape Town.

Chisholm, L. 1986. The Pedagogy of Porter: the Origins of the Reformatory in the Cape Colony, 1882–1910. *Journal of African History* 27:481–95.

Chisholm, L. 1987. Crime, Class and Nationalism: the Criminology of Jacob de Villiers Roos, 1886–1918. *Social Dynamics* 13: 46–59.

Christopher, A.J. 1983. From Flint to Soweto: Reflections on the Colonial Origins of the Apartheid City. *Area* 15: 145–9.

Christopher, A.J. 1987. Race and Residence in Colonial Port Elizabeth. *South African Geographical Journal* 69(1): 3–20.

Christopher, A.J. 1988. Roots of Urban Segregation: South Africa at Union, 1910. *Journal of Historical Geography* 14: 151–69.

Clark, G.L. and Dear, M. 1984. *State Apparatus*. Boston: Allen and Unwin.

Clarke, S. 1978. Capital, Fractions of Capital and the State: 'Neo–Marxist' Analysis of the South African State. *Capital and Class* 5: 32–77.

Claval, P. 1984. The Coherence of Political Geography: Perspectives on its Past Evolution. and its future relevance. In P. Taylor and J. House (eds) *Political Geography: Recent Advances and Future Directions*. London: Croom Helm.

Clegg, S.R. 1989. *Frameworks of Power*. London: Sage.

Cobbet, W. 1986. 'Orderly Urbanisation': Continuity and Change in Influx Control. *South African Labour Bulletin*. 11(8): 106–21.

Cobbet, W., Glaser, D., Hindson, D. and Swilling, M. 1986. South Africa's Regional Political Economy: a Critical Analysis of Reform Strategy in the 1980s. In South Africa Research Service (eds) *South African Review 3*. Johannesburg: Ravan.

Cockburn, C. 1977. *The Local State. Management of Cities and People*. London: Pluto.

Cocks, J. 1989. *The Oppositional Imagination*. London and New York: Routledge.

Cohen, R. 1986. *Endgame in South Africa?* London: James Currey.

Cohen, S. 1982. A New Map of Global Political Equilibrium: a Developmental Approach. *Political Geography Quarterly* 1: 223–42.

Connel, P.H., Jonas, K., Wepener, F. J., Kantorowich, R. and Irvine-Smith, C. 1939. *Native Housing. A Collective Thesis*. Johannesburg: Witwatersrand University Press.

Connell, W. 1988. *Gender and Power*. Cambridge: Polity.

Connell, W. 1990. The State, gender and sexual politics: theory and appraisal. *Theory and Society* 19: 507–44.

Cooke, P. 1989a. *Localities: the Changing Face of Urban Britain*. London: Unwin Hyman.

Cooke, P. 1989b. Nation, Space and Modernity. In R.Peet and N.Thrift (eds) *New Models in Geography*. Vol. 1. London: Unwin Hyman. pp. 267–91.

Cooper, C. and Ensor, L. 1981. *PEBCO. a Black Mass Movement*. Johannesburg: South African Institute of Race Relations.

Cooper, F. 1981. *Struggle for the City*. Beverley Hills: Sage.

Cope, R. 1989. C.W. de Kiewiet, the Imperial Factor and South African 'Native Policy'. *Journal of Southern African Studies* 15: 486–505.

Cory, G.E. 1913. *The Rise of South Africa*. Vol. II. London: Longmans, Green.

CSIR. 1954. *Research Studies on the Costs of Urban Bantu Housing*. Pretoria: Council for Scientific and Industrial Research.

Cox, K. 1973. *Conflict, Power and Politics in the City: a Geographic View*. New York: McGraw-Hill.

Cox, K. and Mair, A. 1988. Locality and Community in the Politics of Local Economic Development. *Annals of the Association of American Geographers* 78: 307–25.

Croock, R. 1989. Patrimonialism, Administrative Efficiency and Economic Development in Cote d'Ivoire. *African Affairs* 88: 205–28.

Crow, G. 1989. The Use of the Concept of 'Strategy' in Recent Sociological Literature. *Sociology* 23: 1–24.

Crowder, M. 1962. *Senegal: a Study in French Assimilation Policy*. London: Oxford University Press.

Crowder, M. 1968. *West Africa under Colonial Rule*. London: Hutchinson.

Crush, J. 1993. Scripting the Compound: Power and Space in the South African Mining Industry. *Society and Space* 12: 301–24.

Curtis, L. 1951. *With Lord Milner in South Africa*. Oxford: Basil Blackwell.

Cutten, A. J. 1951. The Planning of a Native Township. *Race Relations Journal* 18(2): 74–95.

Daudi, P. 1986. *Power in the Organisation. the Discourse of Power in Managerial Praxis*. Oxford: Basil Blackwell.

Davenport, T.R.H. 1969. African Townsmen? South African Natives (Urban Areas) Legislation through the Years. *African Affairs* 68: 95–109.

Davenport, T.R.H. 1970. The Triumph of Colonel Stallard: the Transformation of the Natives (Urban Areas) Act between 1923 and 1937. *South African Historical Journal* 2: 77–96.

Davenport, T.R.H. 1971. *The Beginnings of Urban Segregation in South Africa. the Natives (Urban Areas) Act of 1923 and its Background*. Occasional Paper No. 15, Institute for Social and Economic Research, Rhodes University, Grahamstown.

Davenport, T.R.H. 1977. *South Africa: a Modern History*. Johannesburg: Macmillan.

Davies, R., Kaplan, D., Morris, M. and O'Meara, D. 1976. Class Struggle and the Periodisation of the State in South Africa. *Review of African Political Economy* 7: 4–30.

Davies, R.J. 1976. *Of Cities and Societies: a Geographer's Viewpoint*. Cape Town: University of Cape Town Inaugural Lecture Series.

Davies, R.J. 1981. The Spatial Formation of the South African City. *Geojournal Supplementary Issue* 2: 59–72.

Davies, W. 1971. *Patterns of Non–White Population Distribution in Port Elizabeth with special reference to the Application of the Group Areas Act*. Series B, Special Publication No. 1, Institute for Planning Research, University of Port Elizabeth.

Davies, W. 1990. *A Review of Socio–Economic Conditions in the Greater Algoa Bay Area*. Institute for Social and Economic Research, Rhodes University, Grahamstown.

Dear, M. 1981. The State: a Research Agenda. *Environment and Planning A* 13: 1191–6.

Dear, M. 1982. Research Agendas in Political Geography–a Minority View. *Political Geography Quarterly* 1: 179–80.

Dear, M. 1988. The Postmodern Challenge: Reconstructing Human Geography. *Transactions, Institute of British Geographers* 13: 262–74.

De Blij, H. 1967. *Systematic Political Geography*. New York: Wiley.

De Kiewiet, C.W. 1941. *A History of South Africa: Social and Economic*. Oxford: Oxford University Press.

Denoon, D. 1973. A Grand Illusion: the Failure of Imperial Policy in the Transvaal Colony during the Period of Reconstruction 1900–1905. London: Longman.

Dews, P. 1984. Power and Subjectivity in Foucault. *New Left Review*. 144: 72–95.

Dillon-Malone, C. M. 1978. *The Korsten Basketmakers*. Manchester: Manchester University Press for Institute of African Studies, University of Zambia, Lusaka.

Dreyfus, H. and Rabinow, P. 1982. *Michel Foucault: beyond Structuralism and Hermeneutics*. Brighton: Harvester.

Driver, F. 1985a. Theorising State Structures: Alternatives to Functionalism and Reductionism. *Environment and Planning A* 17: 263–73.

Driver, F. 1985b. Geography and Power: the Recent Work of Michel Foucault. Paper presented at the IBG Annual Conference, Leeds.

Driver, F. 1985c. Power, Space and the Body: a Critical Assessment of Foucault's *Discipline and Punish*. *Environment and Planning D: Society and Space* 3: 425–46.

Driver, F. 1987. *The English Bastille: Dimensions of the Workhouse System, 1834–1884*. Unpublished PhD Thesis, Department of Geography, University of Cambridge.

Driver, F. 1988a. Political Geography and the State: a Theoretical Discussion. Paper for the Anglo-Austrian Seminar in Geography and Social Theory. Zell/Moos.

Driver, F. 1988b. Moral Geographies: Social Science and the Urban Environment in Mid Nineteenth Century England. *Transactions, Institute of British Geographers* 13: 275–87.

Dubow, S. 1986a. *Segregation and 'Native Administration' in South Africa 1920–1936*. D.Phil Thesis, St Anthony's College, Oxford University.

Dubow, S. 1986b. Holding 'a Just Balance between White and Black': the Native Affairs Department in South Africa c. 1920–33. *Journal of Southern African Studies* 12(2): 217–39.

Dubow, S. 1987. Race, Civilization and Culture: the Elaboration of Segregationist Discourse in the Inter–War Years. In S. Marks and S. Trapido (eds) *The Politics of Race, Class and Nationalism in Twentieth Century South Africa*. London: Longman.

Dubow, S. 1989. *Racial Segregation and the Origins of Apartheid in South Africa, 1919–36*. London: Macmillan.

Duncan, S. and Goodwin, M. 1988. *The Local State and Uneven Development: behind the Local Government Crisis.* Cambridge: Polity.

Dunleavy, P. 1982. Is There a Radical Approach to Public Administration? *Public Administration* 60: 215–33.

Du Toit, A.E. 1954. The Cape Frontier: a Study of Native Policy with Special Reference to the Years 1847–1866. *Archives Year Book for South African History* 17(1).

Du Toit, A. 1993. The Micro–Politics of Paternalism: the Discourses of Management and Resistance on South African Fruit and Wine Farms. *Journal of Southern African Studies* 19: 314–36.

Edwards, I. 1987. Nurturing the soil to protect you from politics: the African Proletariat in Durban in the Early 1950s. Paper presented at the South Africa in the 1950s Conference, Oxford, 25–6 September.

Elphick, R. and Giliomee, H. 1989. The Origins and Entrenchment of European Dominance at the Cape, 1652–1840. In R. Elphick and H. Giliomee (eds) *The Shaping of South African Society, 1652–1840.* Cape Town: Maskew Miller Longman. pp. 521–66.

Elphick, R. and Malherbe, E. 1989. The Khoisan to 1828. In R. Elphick and H. Giliomee (eds) *The Shaping of South African Society, 1652–1840.* Cape Town: Maskew Miller.

Esping–Andersen, G., Friedland, R. and Olin Wright, E. 1976. Modes of Class Struggle and the Capitalist State. *Kapitalistate.* 4/5: 186–220.

Evans, I.T. 1986. *The Political Economy of a State Apparatus: the Department of Native Affairs in the Transition from Segregation to Apartheid in South Africa.* Unpublished PhD Thesis, Sociology Faculty, University of Wisconsin–Madison.

Evans, P.B. Rueschemeyer, D. and Skocpol, T. 1985. On the Road towards a More Adequate Understanding of the State. In P.B. Evans, D. Rueschemeyer and T. Skocpol (eds). *Bringing the State Back In.* Cambridge: Cambridge University Press.

Fekete, J. (ed.). 1988. *Life after Postmodernism.* London: Macmillan.

Ferguson, D. 1981. *Civilization for Africa.* Port Elizabeth: Walton.

Flowerdew, R. 1982. *Institutions and Geographical Patterns.* London: Croom Helm.

Floyd, T. B. 1951. *Township Layout.* Pietermaritzburg: Shuter and Shooter.

Floyd, T. B. 1959. Die Geskiedenis van Stadsbeplanning in Suid-Afrika. *Proceedings of the South African Institute of Town Planners Summer School.* Johannesburg, 2–6 February 1959.

Foucault, M. 1977. *Discipline and Punish.* Harmondsworth: Penguin.

Foucault, M. 1979. Governmentality. *Ideology and Consciousness* 6: 5–21.

Foucault, M. 1980. *The History of Sexuality.* Vol. 1. New York: Vintage Books.

Foucault, M. 1981. Omnes et Singulatim: towards a Criticism of 'Political Reason'. In S.M. McMurrin (ed.) *The Tanner Lectures on Human Values.* Cambridge: Cambridge University Press.

Foucault, M. 1982. Afterword. In H. Dreyfus and P. Rabinow (eds) *Michel Foucault: beyond Structuralism and Hermeneutics.* Brighton: Harvester.

Foucault, M. 1986. Disciplinary Power and Subjection. In S. Lukes (ed.) *Power.* Oxford: Basil Blackwell. pp. 229 –42.

Frankel, P. 1979. The Politics of Passes: Control and Change in South Africa. *Journal of Modern African Studies* 17: 199–217.

Fraser, N. 1982. Foucault on Modern Power: Empirical Insights and Normative Confusions. *Praxis International* 1: 272–87.

Fredrickson, G. 1981. *White Supremacy: a Comparative Study in American and South African History.* Oxford: Oxford University Press.

Freund, W. M. 1976. Race in the Social Structure of South Africa, 1652–1836. *Race and Class* 18: 53–67.

Freund, W. 1984. *The Making of Contemporary Africa.* London: MacMillan.

Freund, M. 1989. The Cape under the Transitional Governments, 1795–1814. In R.

Elphick and H. Giliomee (eds) *The Shaping of South African Society, 1652–1840*. Cape Town: Maskew Miller Longman. pp. 324–57.
Friedman, S. 1993. *The Long Journey: South Africa's Quest for a Negotiated Settlement*. Johannesburg: Ravan Press.
Fyfe, N. 1989. State, Power, the Police and Territory: a Geography of British Policing 1829–1989. Unpublished manuscript, Department of Geography, Cambridge University.
Gaitskell, D. 1979. 'Christian Compounds for Girls': Church Hostels for African Women in Johannesburg, 1907–1970. *Journal of Southern African Studies* 6: 44–69.
Galbraith, J.K. 1984. *The Anatomy of Power*. London: Hamish Hamilton.
Gale, T.S. 1980. Segregation in British West Africa. *Cahiers d'Etudes Africaines* 80: 495–507.
Gann, L. and Duignan, P. 1978. *The Rulers of British Africa 1870–1914*. London: Croom Helm.
Gelb, S. 1987. Making Sense of the Crisis. *Transformation* 5: 33–50.
Gelb, S. (ed.) 1991. *South Africa's Economic Crisis*. Cape Town: David Philip.
Gell, C. 1957. Port Elizabeth Diary. *Africa South* 1(4).
Giddens, A. 1981. *A Contemporary Critique of Historical Materialism*. London: Macmillan.
Giddens, A. 1985. *The Nation–State and Violence*. Cambridge: Polity.
Gilroy, P. 1993. *The Black Atlantic*. London: Verso.
Goldberg, D. 1993. 'Polluting the Body Politic': Racist Discourse and Urban Location. In M. Cross and M. Keith (eds) *Racism, the City and the State*. London: Routledge.
Goldin, I. 1987. *Making Race: The Politics and Economics if Coloured Identity in South Africa*. Cape Town: Maskew Miller Longman.
Gordon, C. (ed.). 1980. *Michel Foucault: Power/Knowledge*. Brighton: Harvester.
Gordon, C. 1987. The Soul of the Citizen: Max Weber and Michel Foucault on Rationality and Government. In S. Whimster and S. Lash (eds) *Max Weber, Rationality and Modernity*. London: Allen and Unwin.
Gottmann, J. 1973. *The Significance of Territory*. Charlottesville: University of Virginia.
Green, L.P. 1957. *History of Local Government in South Africa: an Introduction*. Cape Town: Juta.
Greenberg, S. 1980. *Race and State in Capitalist Development: Comparative Perspectives*. New Haven: Yale University Press.
Greenberg, S. 1987. *Legitimating the Illegitimate*. London: University of California Press.
Gregory, D. 1989. Areal Differentiation and Post–Modern Geography. In D. Gregory and R. Walford (eds) *Horizons in Human Geography*. London: Macmillan.
Gregory, D. and Urry, J. 1985. *Social Relations and Spatial Structures*. London: Macmillan.
Guenalt, P. H. and Randall, R. J. 1940. Urban Native Housing in South Africa. *Race Relations Journal* 7(4): 74–82.
Guy, J. 1980. Ecological Factors in the Rise of Shaka and the Zulu Kingdom. In S. Marks and A. Atmore (eds). *Economy and Society in Pre–Industrial South Africa*. London: Longman. pp. 102–19.
Habermas, J. 1976. *Legitimation Crisis*. London: Heinemann.
Habermas, J. 1984. *The Theory of Communicative Action*. Vol. 1. London: Heinemann.
Habermas, J. 1987. *The Philosophical Discourse of Modernity*. Cambridge, Mass.: MIT Press.
Hailey, Lord. 1951. *Native Administration in the British African Territories*. Part 4. London: HMSO.
Hall, J. 1985. *Powers and Liberties*. Oxford: Basil Blackwell.
Hall, J. (ed.). 1986. *States in History*. Oxford: Basil Blackwell.
Harries, P. 1987. Plantations, Passes and Proletarians: Labour and the Colonial State in Nineteenth Century Natal. *Journal of Southern African Studies* 13: 372–99.
Hart, D. and Pirie, G. 1984. The Sight and Soul of Sophiatown. *Geographical Review* 74: 38–47.

Hartshorne, R. 1950. The Functional Approach in Political Geography. *Annals of the Association of American Geographers* 11: 95–130.

Harvey, D. 1976. The Marxian Theory of the State. *Antipode* 8(2): 80–9.

Harvey, D. 1978. The Urban Process under Capitalism: a Framework for Analysis. *International Journal of Urban and Regional Research* 2: 101–31.

Harvey, D. 1982. *The Limits to Capital*. Oxford: Basil Blackwell.

Harvey, D. 1985. *Consciousness and the Urban Experience*. Oxford: Basil Blackwell.

Harvey, D. 1989. *The Condition of Postmodernity*. Oxford: Basil Blackwell.

Hector, A. R. and Calderwood, D. M. 1951. A New Native Township for Witbank Municipality. Reprint from *South African Architectural Record* 36(5). Pretoria: CSIR.

Held, D. 1984. Power and Legitimacy in Contemporary Britain. In G. McLennan, D. Held and S. Hall (eds) *State and Society in Contemporary Britain*. Cambridge: Polity.

Held, D. 1989. *Political Theory and the Modern State*. Cambridge: Polity.

Helliker, K. 1988. South African Marxist State Theory–A Critical Overview. *Politikon*. 15: 3–15.

Heper, M. (ed.) 1987. *The State and Public Bureaucracies: a Comparative Perspective*. London: Greenwood.

Hertslet, L. E. 1919. Some Essentials of a Native Policy. *South African Quarterly* 2(1): 14–15.

Heymans, C. 1988. The Political and Constitutional Context of Local Government Restructuring. in C. Heymans and G. Totemeyer (eds) *Government by the People?* Johannesburg: Juta. pp. 34–48.

Heymans, C. and Totemeyer, G. 1988. *Government by the People?* Johannesburg: Juta.

Hindess, P. 1982. Power, Interests and the Outcomes of Struggles. *Sociology*. 16: 498–511.

Hindson, D. 1983. The Role of Labour Bureaux in South Africa: a Critique of the Riekert Commission Report. In D. Hindson (ed.) *Working Papers in Southern African Studies*. Vol. 3. Johannesburg: Ravan.

Hindson, D. 1987. *Pass Controls and the Urban African Proletariat in South Africa*. Johannesburg: Ravan.

Hindson, D., Byerley, M. and Morris, M. 1994. From Violence to Reconstruction: The Making, Disintegration and Remaking of the Apartheid City. *Antipode* 26: 323–50.

Hobart Houghton, D. 1973. *The South African Economy*. Cape Town: Oxford University Press.

Hoernle, R. F. A. 1945. *South African Native Policy and the Liberal Spirit*. Johannesburg: Witwatersrand University Press.

Horvarth, R. J. 1969. In Search of a Theory of Urbanisation: Notes on the Colonial City. *East Lakes Geographer* 5: 69–82.

Houston, J. M. 1970. The Foundation of Colonial Towns in Hispanic America. In D. N. McMaster and J. M. Houston (eds) *Urbanization and its Problems*. Oxford: Basil Blackwell.

Humphries, R. 1982. *An Examination of the Finances of the East Cape Midlands Administration Board, 1973–1979*. Working Paper No. 8, Institute for Social and Economic Research, Rhodes University, Grahamstown.

Humphries, R. 1983. *The Origins and Subsequent Development of Administration Boards*. Unpublished MA Thesis, Department of Political Studies, Rhodes University, Grahamstown.

Hyslop, J. 1993. 'A destruction coming in': Bantu education as response to social crisis in Bonner, P., Delius, P. and Posel, D. (eds) *Apartheid's Genesis 1935–1962*. Johannesburg: Ravan Press. pp. 393–410.

Inggs, J. 1986. Liverpool of the Cape: Port Elizabeth Trade 1820–1870. *The South African Journal of Economic History* 1: 77–98.

Innes, D. and Plaut, M. 1978. Class Struggle and the State. *Review of African Political Economy* 11: 51–61.

Institute of Administrators of Non-European Affairs (Southern Africa). *Records of Proceedings of the Annual Conferences 1952–1963.*

Jackson, P. (ed.) 1987. *Race and Racism.* London: Allen and Unwin.

Jackson, R.H. and Rosberg, C.G. 1982. Why Africa's Weak States Persist: the Empirical and the Juridical in Statehood. *World Politics* 35: 1–24.

James, W. and Simons, M. (eds) 1989. *The Angry Divide: Social and Economic History of the Western Cape.* Cape Town: David Philip.

Jameson, F. 1984. Postmodernism, or the cultural logic of late capitalism. *New Left Review* 146: 53–92.

Janisch, M. 1940. Health and Social Welfare Services for Natives in Urban Areas. *Race Relations Journal* 7(4): 83–7.

Jeater, D. 1993. *Marriage, Perversion and Power: The Construction of moral discourse in Southern Rhodesia, 1894–1930.* Oxford: Clarendon Press.

Jessop, B. 1983. Accumulation Strategies, State Forms and Hegemonic Projects. *Kapitalistate* 10/11: 89–111.

Jessop, B. 1984. *The Capitalist State.* Oxford: Basil Blackwell.

Jessop, B. 1985. *Nicos Poulantzas: Marxist Theory and Political Strategy.* London: Macmillan.

Jessop, B. 1990. *State Theory: Putting the Capitalist State in its Place.* Cambridge: Polity.

Johnston, R. J. 1980. Political Geography without Politics. *Progress in Human Geography.* 4: 439–46.

Johnston, R. J. 1982. *Geography and the State: an Essay in Political Geography.* London: Macmillan.

Johnston, R.J. 1989. The State, Political Geography, and Geography. In R. Peet and N. Thrift (eds) *New Models in Geography.* Vol. 1. London: Unwin Hyman.

Jones, S.B. 1954. A Unified Field Theory of Political Geography. *Annals of the Association of American Geographers* 44: 111–23.

Kaplan, D.E. 1976. The Politics of Industrial Protection in South Africa, 1910–1939. *Journal of Southern African Studies* 3: 70–91.

Kearns, G. 1988. History, Geography and World–Systems Theory. *Journal of Historical Geography* 14: 281–92.

Keegan, T. 1987. Dispossession and Accumulation in the South African Interior: the Boers and the Thlaping of Bethulie, 1833–1861. *Journal of African History* 28:191–207.

King, A. 1976. *Colonial Urban Development: culture, social power and environment.* London: Routledge and Kegan Paul.

King, A. 1990. *Urbanism, Colonialism and the World-Economy.* London: Routledge.

Kinkead-Weakes, B. 1985. *Africans in Cape Town: the Origins and Development of State Policy and Popular Resistance to 1936.* Unpublished MSocSc. Thesis, Department of Sociology, University of Cape Town.

Kirk, J. 1987. The African Middle Class, Cape Liberalism and Resistance to Residential Segregation at Port Elizabeth, South Africa, 1880–1910. Unpublished PhD Thesis, University of Wisconsin–Madison.

Kirk-Greene, A. H. M. 1980. The Thin White Line: the Size of the British Colonial Service in Africa. *African Affairs* 79: 25– 44.

Kuper, L., Watts, H. and Davies, R. 1958. *Durban: a Study in Racial Ecology.* London: Gray.

Labour Monitoring Group. 1986. The March Stay–Aways in Port Elizabeth and Uitenhage. *South African Labour Bulletin* 11: 10–35.

Lacey, M. 1982. *Working for Boroko: the Origins of a Coercive Labour System in South Africa.* Johannesburg.

Laclau, E. 1994. The Politics of the Empty Signifier. In J. Weeks (ed.) *The Lesser Evil and the Greater Good.* London: Rivers Oram Press.

Laclau, E. and Mouffe, C. 1985. *Hegemony and Socialist Strategy*. London: Verso.
La Hausse, P. 1982. 'Drinking in a Cage': the Durban System and the 1929 Beer Hall Riots. *Africa Perspective* 20: 60–72.
La Hausse, P. 1993. So who was Elias Kuzwayo? Nationalism, Collaboration and the Picaresque in Natal. In Bonner, P., Delius, P. and Posel, D. (eds) *Apartheid's Genesis 1935–1962*. Johannesburg: Ravan Press. pp. 195–228.
Language, F. 1950. Native Housing in Urban Areas. *Journal of Racial Affairs* 1(2): 27–38.
Lazar, J. 1986. The Role of the South African Bureau of Racial Affairs (SABRA) in the Formulation of Apartheid Ideology, 1948–1961. Seminar Paper, Institute of Commonwealth Studies, London.
Leftwich, A. 1983. *Redefining Politics*. London: Methuen.
Leftwich, A. (ed.) 1989. *What is Politics?* Oxford: Basil Blackwell.
Legassick, M. 1973. The Rise of Modern South African Liberalism: its Assumptions and its Social Base. Unpublished Paper, Institute of Commonwealth Studies, Southern African Seminar Series.
Legassick, M. 1974. Legislation, Ideology and Economy in Post–1948 South Africa. *Journal of Southern African Studies* 1: 253–91.
Legassick, M. and Wolpe, H. 1976. The Bantustans and Capital Accumulation in South Africa. *Review of African Political Economy* 7: 87–107.
Leigh, R.L. 1966. *The City of Port Elizabeth: from a Border Garrison Town to a Modern Commercial and Industrial City*. Port Elizabeth: Chamber of Commerce.
Leonard, S. 1982. Urban Managerialism: a Period of Transition? *Progress in Human Geography* 6: 190–215.
Levy, N. 1982. *The Foundations of the South African Cheap Labour System*. London: Routledge and Kegan Paul.
Lipietz, A. 1987. *Mirages and Miracles*. London: Verso.
Lipton, M. 1986. *Capitalism and Apartheid*. Aldershot: Wildwood.
Lodge, T. 1981. The Destruction of Sophiatown. *Journal of Modern African Studies* 19: 107–32.
Lodge, T. 1983. *Black Politics in South Africa since 1945*. Johannesburg: Ravan.
Lodge, T. 1987. Political Mobilisation during the 1950s: an East London Case Study. In S. Marks and S. Trapido (eds) *The Politics of Race, Class and Nationalism in Twentieth Century South Africa*. London: Longman. pp. 310–35.
Logan, J. and Molotch, L. 1987. *Urban Fortunes: the Political Economy of Place*. Berkeley: University of California Press.
Lovering, J. 1987. Militarism, Capitalism, and the Nation–State: towards a Realist Synthesis. *Environment and Planning D: Society and Space* 5: 283–302.
Lowder, S. 1986. *Inside Third World Cities*. London: Croom Helm.
Lukes, S. 1974. *Power: a Radical View*. London: Macmillan.
Lupton, M. 1994. Collective consumption and urban segregation in South Africa: The case of two colored suburbs in the Johannesburg region. *Antipode* 25, 1: 32–50.
Mabin, A. 1986a. Labour, Capital, Class Struggle and the Origins of Residential Segregation in Kimberley, 1880–1920. *Journal of Historical Geography* 12(1)): 4–26.
Mabin, A. 1986b. The Rise and Decline of Port Elizabeth, 1850–1900. *International Journal of African Historical Studies* 19: 275–303 .
Mabin, A. 1987. The Land Clearances at Pilgrim's Rest. *Journal of Southern African Studies* 13: 400–16.
Mabin, A. 1988. Does Geography Matter? A Review of the Past Decade's Books by Geographers of Contemporary South Africa. *South African Geographical Journal* 71: 121–6.
Mabin, A. 1991. Origins of Segregatory Urban Planning in South Africa, 1900–1940. *Planning History* 13: 8–16.

Magnusson, W. and Walker, R. 1988. De-Centring the State: Political Theory and Canadian Political Economy. *Studies in Political Economy* 26: 37–71.

Maharaj, B. 1992. The Group Areas Act in Durban: central-local state relations. PhD thesis, Department of Geography, University of Natal, Pietermaritzburg.

Manicom, L. 1991. Ruling relations: rethinking state and gender in South African history. Paper presented to the Conference on Women and Gender in Southern Africa, University of Natal, Durban, January 1991.

Manion, T. and Flowerdew, R. 1982. Institutional Approaches in Geography. In R. Flowerdew (ed.) *Institutions and Geographical Patterns*. London: Croom Helm. Chapter 1.

Mann, M. 1984. The Autonomous Power of the State: its Origins, Mechanisms and Results. *Archives européenes de sociologie* 25: 185–213.

Mann, M. 1986. *The Sources of Social Power*. Vol. 1. Cambridge: Cambridge University Press.

Mann, M. 1993. *The Sources of Social Power*. Vol. 2. Cambridge: Cambridge University Press.

Marks, S. 1978. Natal, the Zulu Royal Family and the Ideology of Segregation. *Journal of Southern African Studies* 4:172–94.

Marks, S. 1986. *The Ambiguities of Dependence in South Africa: Class, Nationalism and the State in Twentieth Century Natal*. Baltimore and Johannesburg: Johns Hopkins University Press.

Marks, S. and Trapido, S. 1979. Lord Milner and the South African State. *History Workshop* 8: 50–73.

Marks, S. and Trapido, S. 1987. The Politics of Race, Class and Nationalism. In S. Marks and S. Trapido (eds) *The Politics of Race, Class and Nationalism in Twentieth Century South Africa*. London: Longman. pp. 1–70.

Marquard, L. 1968. *South Africa: People and Policies*. Oxford: Oxford University Press.

Massam, B. 1975. *Location and Space in Social Administration*. London: Edward Arnold.

Massey, D. 1984. *Spatial Divisions of Labour*. London: Macmillan.

Matravers, D.R. 1980. It's All in a Day's Work. In G. Cook and J. Opland (eds) *Mdantsane: Transitional City*. Grahamstown: Institute of Social and Economic Research.

Matthewson, J. E. 1956. Recent Developments in Urban Native Administration. Parts I, II, III. *Bantu* March, April, May.

Mawby, A. 1974. Capital, Government and Politics in the Transvaal, 1900–1907. *Historical Journal* 17: 387–415.

Maylam, P. 1982. 'Shackled by the Contradictions': the Municipal Response to African Urbanisation in Durban, 1920–1950. *African Urban Studies* 14: 1–18.

Maylam, P. 1989. The Rise and Decline of Urban Apartheid. Paper presented to the Biennial Conference of the South African Historical Society, University of Natal. Pietermaritzburg, January.

McCarthy, J. 1983. The Political Economy of Urban Land Use: towards a Revised Theoretical Framework. *South African Geographical Journal* 65(1): 25–48.

McCarthy, J. and Friedman, M. 1983. On the Social Construction of Urban Problems. In K. Tomaselli and R. Tomaselli (eds) *Culture, Ideology and the Media in South Africa*. Johannesburg: Jonathan Ball.

McCarthy, J. and Swilling, M. 1985. South Africa's Emerging Politics of Bus Transportation. *Political Geography Quarterly* 4: 235–49.

McGee, T. 1967. *The Southeast Asian City*. London: Bell.

McGee, T. 1971. *The Urbanization Process in the Third World*. London: Bell.

McMaster, D. N. 1970. The Colonial District Town in Uganda. In R. P. Beckinsale and J. M. Houston (eds) *Urbanization and its Problems*. Oxford: Basil Blackwell.

McMillan, W.M. 1917. *The Place of Local Government in the Union of South Africa*. Johannesburg: Hirtor.

McMillan, W.M. 1963. *Bantu, Boer and Briton: the Making of the South African Native Problem*. Oxford: Clarendon Press.

Mellor, R. 1989. *Nation, State and Territory: a Political Geography*. London: Routledge.

Merle Frean, R. 1957. Aesthetics in the Planning and Lay–Out of Low–Cost Native Housing. Reprint from the *South African Architectural Record* 42(1). Pretoria: CSIR.

Miliband, R. 1969. *The State in Capitalist Society*. London: Quartet.

Miliband, R. 1983. State Power and Class Interests. *New Left Review* 138: 35–68.

Miller, D., Rowlands, M. and Tilly, C. (eds). 1989. *Domination and Resistance*. London: Unwin Hyman.

Miller, P. 1987. *Domination and Power*. London and New York: Routledge and Kegan Paul.

Mitchell, T. 1988. *Colonising Egypt*. Cambridge: Cambridge University Press.

Moffat, J.S. 1901. The South African Natives. *Contemporary Review*. 129: 318–25.

Moll, T. 1990. From booster to brake? Apartheid and economic growth in comparative perspective. In N. Nattrass and E. Ardington (eds) *The Political Economy of South Africa*. Cape Town: Oxford University Press. pp. 73–87.

Moodie, A.E. 1949. *Geography Behind Politics*. London: Hutchinson.

Moodie, T. Dunbar. 1975. The Rise of Afrikanerdom: Power, Apartheid and the Afrikaner Civil Religion. Berkeley: University of California Press.

Morril, R. L. and Donaldson, O. F. 1975. Geographical Perspectives on the History of Black America. In E. Jones (ed.) *Readings in Social Geography*. Oxford: Oxford University Press.

Morris, M. and Padayachee, V. 1989. Hegemonic Projects, Accumulation Strategies and State Reform Policy in South Africa. *Labour, Capital and Society* 22, 1: 65–109.

Morris, M. and Padayachee, V. 1989.

Morris, P. 1981. *A History of Black Housing in South Africa*. Johannesburg: South Africa Foundation.

Moulakis, A. (ed.) 1986. *Legitimacy/Légitimite*. Berlin, New York: Walter de Gruyter.

Moyer, R.A. 1974. The Mfengu, Self–Defence and the Cape Frontier Wars. In C. Saunders and R. Derricout (eds) *Beyond the Cape Frontier*. London: Longman.

Muthien, Y. 1987. Pass Controls and Squatting in Cape Town during the 1950s. Paper presented at the South Africa in the 1950s Conference, Oxford, 25–6 September.

Nattrass, J. 1981. *The South African Economy: its Growth and Change*. Johannesburg:Juta.

Nattrass, N. 1989. The Falling Rate of Profit in South Africa, 1948–1984. *Transformation* 9: 24–51.

Nel, J. 1986. *Die Geografiese Impak van die Wet op Groepsgebiede en verwante wetgewing op Port Elizabeth*. MA Thesis, Department of Geography, University of Port Elizabeth.

Nettl, J. 1968. The State as a Conceptual Variable. *World Politics* 20: 168–91.

Newton, A. 1968. *Select Documents Relating to the Unification of South Africa*. London: Frank Cass & Co.

Nimocks, N. 1968. *Milner's Young Men: the 'Kindergarten' in Edwardian Imperial Affairs*. Durham, NC: North Carolina UP.

Odendaal, A. 1985. *African Political Mobilisation in the Eastern Cape, 1880–1910*. Unpublished PhD Thesis, University of Cambridge.

Offe, C. and Ronge, V. 1975. Theses on the Theory of the State. *New German Critique* 6: 137–47.

Ogborn, M. 1989. Gender Identities and the State: an Historical Geography of the Contagious Diseases Act, 1864–1883. Paper presented at the Conference on Feminism and Historical Geography, University College London, November.

Ogilvie, G. C. W. 1946. *The Housing of Africans in the Urban Areas of Kenya*. Nairobi: Kenya Information Office.

O'Loughlin, J. 1984. Geographic Models of International Conflicts. In P. Taylor and J. House (eds) *Political Geography: Recent Advances and Future Directions*. London: Croom Helm.

O'Loughlin, J. 1989. Political Geography: Coping with Global Restructuring. *Progress in Human Geography* 13(3): 412–26.

O'Neill, J. 1986. The Disciplinary Society: from Weber to Foucault. *British Journal of Sociology* 37, 1: 42–60.

Paddison, R. 1983. *The Fragmented State.* Oxford: Basil Blackwell.

Pahl, R. 1975. *Whose City?* Harmondsworth: Penguin.

Palmer, I. 1985. State Theory and Statutory Authorities: Points of Convergence. *Sociology* 19: 523–40.

Parnell, S. 1987. *Council Housing Provision for Whites in Johannesburg: 1920–1955.* Unpublished MA Thesis, University of the Witwatersrand, Johannesburg.

Parnell, S. 1988. Land Acquisition and the Changing Residential Face of Johannesburg 1930–1955. *Area* 20: 307–14.

Parnell, S. 1991. Sanitation, Segregation and the Natives (Urban Areas) Act: African exclusion from Johannesburg's Malay Location. *Journal of Historical Geography* 17: 271–88.

Parnell, S. 1993. Creating Racial Privilege: the Origins of South African Public Health and Town Planning Legislation. *Journal of Southern African Studies* 19: 471–88.

Pateman, C. 1988. *The Sexual Contract.* Cambridge: Polity.

Peach, C., Robinson, V. and Smith, S.(eds). 1981. *Ethnic Segregation in Cities.* London: Croom Helm.

Peake, H.J.E. 1930. Geographical Aspects of Administrative Areas. *Geography* 15: 531–46.

Pearcy, G. and Fifield, R. 1948. *World Political Geography.* New York: Crowell.

Peckham, L. 1990. Ons Stel Nie Belang Nie/We Are Not Interested In: Speaking Apartheid. In R. Ferguson *et al* (eds) *Out There: Marginalisation and Contemporary Cultures.* Cambridge, Mass.: MIT Press.

Peires, J. 1989. The British at the Cape, 1814–1834. In R. Elphick and H. Giliomee (eds) *The Shaping of South African Society, 1652–1840.* Cape Town: Maskew Miller Longman. pp. 472–520.

Pennant, T. 1983. Housing the Urban Labour Force on Malawi: An Historical Overview, 1930–1980. *African Urban Studies* 16: 1–22.

Phillips, R. E. 1930. *The Bantu are Coming.* London: SCM Press.

Philo, C. 1988. 'Enough to Drive One Mad': The Organisation of Space in Nineteenth Century Lunatic Asylums. In J. Wolch and M. Dear (eds) *The Power of Geography.* London: Unwin Hyman.

Pickles, J. 1987. *The Re–Internationalisation of Apartheid: Information, Flexible Production and Disinvestment.* Research Paper 8717, Regional Research Institute, West Virginia University.

Pinnock, D. 1989. A Blueprint for a Garrison City. In W. G. James (ed.) *The Angry Divide.* Johannesburg: Ravan.

Pirie, G.H. 1984. Race Zoning in South Africa: Board, Court, Parliament, Public. *Political Geography Quarterly* 3: 207–21.

Poggi, G. 1978. *The Development of the Modern State.* London: Hutchinson.

Posel, D. 1987. *Influx Control and the Construction of Apartheid, 1948–1961.* Unpublished DPhil Thesis, Nuffield College and Faculty of Social Studies, Oxford University.

Posel, D. 1988. Providing for the Legitimate Labour Requirements of Employers: Secondary Industry, Commerce and the State in South Africa in the 1950s and early 1960s. In A. Mabin (ed.) *Organisation and Economic Change: Southern African Studies.* Vol. 5. Johannesburg: Ravan. pp. 199–220.

Poulantzas, N. 1973. *Political Power and Social Classes.* London: Verso.

Poulantzas, N. 1978. *State, Power, Socialism.* London: New Left Books.

Pratt, G. 1992. Editorial: Spatial Metaphors and Speaking Positions. *Society and Space* 10: 241–44.

242   References

Prescott, J.R.V. 1968. *The Geography of State Policies*. London: Hutchinson.
Prinsloo, C. W. 1950. Bantoehuise vir die Bantoe. *Journal of Racial Affairs* 1(3): 12–18.
Prior, L. 1988. Architecture of the Hospital: a Study of Spatial Organisation and Medical Knowledge. *British Journal of Sociology* 39: 86–114.
Rabinow, P. 1984. (ed.) *The Foucault Reader*. Harmondsworth: Penguin.
Rabinow, P. 1989a. Governing Morocco: Modernity and Difference. In *International Journal of Urban and Regional Research* 13: 32–46.
Rabinow, P. 1989b. *French Modern: Norms and Forms of the Social Environment*. Cambridge, Mass. and London: MIT Press.
Rabinowitz, H. N. 1978. *Race Relations in the Urban South 1865–1890*. New York: Oxford University Press.
Radcliffe-Brown, A. R. 1922. Some Problems of Bantu Sociology. *Bantu Studies* 1(3): 38–46.
Radford, J. 1976. Race, Residence and Ideology: Charleston, South Carolina in the Mid–Nineteenth Century. *Journal of Historical Geography* 2: 329–46.
Raeff, M. 1975. The Well–Ordered Police State and the Development of Modernity in Seventeenth and Eighteenth Century Europe: an Attempt at an Alternative Approach. *American Historical Review* 80: 1221–43.
Redgrave, J.J. 1947. *Port Elizabeth in Bygone Days*. Wynberg: Rustica.
Reinallt-Jones, J. D. 1919. Editorial. *South African Quarterly* 2(1): 1.
Reinallt-Jones, J. D. 1920. Native Studies in South Africa. *South African Quarterly* 2(3): 4–6.
Reinecke, P. 1959. Contribution to Discussion on Native Housing Policies and Problems. *Proceedings of the South African Institute of Town Planners Summer School*. Johannesburg, 2–6 February 1959.
Rex, J. 1974. The Compound, the Reserve and the Urban Location: the Essential Institutions of Southern African Labour Exploitation. *South African Labour Bulletin* 1: 4–17.
Rex, J. and Moore, R. 1967. *Race, Community and Conflict*. London: Oxford University Press.
Rice, R. L. 1968. Residential Segregation by Law, 1910–1917. *Journal of Southern African History* 34: 179–99.
Rich, P.B. 1978. 'Ministering to the White Man's Needs': the Development of Urban Segregation in South Africa 1913–1923. *African Studies* 37(2): 177–91.
Rich, P.B. 1980a. The Origins of Apartheid Ideology: the Case of Ernest Stubbs and Transvaal Native Administration, c. 1902–1932. *African Affairs* 79: 171–94.
Rich, P.B. 1980b. Administrative Ideology, Urban Social Control and the Origins of Apartheid Theory, 1930–1939. *Journal of African Studies* 7: 70–82.
Rich, P.B. 1984. *White Power and the Liberal Conscience: Racial Segregation and South Africa Liberalism*. Johannesburg: Ravan.
Rich, P. B. 1987. The Politics of Race Relations in Britain and the West. In P. Jackson (ed.) *Race and Racism*. London: Allen and Unwin.
Riordan, R. 1989. African Unemployed in Port Elizabeth–Its Extent and Causes. Paper for Idasa Symposium, 31 July 1989, Port Elizabeth.
Robinson, J. 1990. A perfect system of control? Territory and Administration in early South African locations. *Environment and Planning D: Society and Space* 8: 135–62.
Robinson, J. 1992. Power, space and the city: historical reflections on Apartheid and post-Apartheid urban orders. In D. Smith (ed.) *The Apartheid City and Beyond*. London: Routledge.
Robinson, J. 1993. The Politics of Urban Form: Differential Citizenship and Township Formation in Port Elizabeth 1925–1945. *Kronos* 20: 44–65.
Robinson, R. and Gallagher, J. with Alice Denny. 1981. *Africa and the Victorians: the Official Mind of Imperialism*. London: Macmillan.

Roemer, J. 1988. *Free to Lose*. Cambridge, Mass.: Harvard University Press.

Rogers, A. and Uto, R. 1987. Residential Segregation Retheorized: a View from Southern California. In P. Jackson (ed.) *Race and Racism*. London: Allen and Unwin.

Rogers, H. 1949. *Native Administration in the Union of South Africa*. Pretoria: Government Printer.

Roux, E. 1964. *Time Longer than Rope*. Madison: University of Wisconsin Press.

Sack, R.D. 1983. Human Territoriality: a Theory. *Annals of the Association of American Geographers* 73: 55–74.

Sack, R.D. 1986. *Human Territoriality*. Cambridge: Cambridge University Press.

Sapire, H. 1987a. Political Mobilisation in Brakpan in the 1950s. Paper presented at the South Africa in the 1950s Conference, Oxford, 25–6 September.

Sapire, H. 1987b. The Making of Class: African Settlement and Segregation in Brakpan, 1920–1927. Paper presented at the History Workshop, University of the Witwatersrand, July.

Sarakinsky, A. 1989. State, Strategy and the Extra–Parliamentary Opposition in South Africa, 1983–1988. Paper presented at the Annual Conference of the Association for Sociology in Southern Africa, Johannesburg, University of the Witwatersrand, July.

Saul, J. and Gelb, S. 1981. *The Crisis in South Africa: class defence, class revolution*. New York: Monthly Review Press.

Saunders, C. 1978. Segregation in Cape Town: the Creation of Ndabeni. In *African Seminar, Collected Papers*. Vol. 1. Cape Town: University of Cape Town. pp 43–62.

Saunders, C. 1980. Africans in Cape Town in the Nineteenth Century: an Outline. In C. Saunders and H. Phillips (eds) *Studies in the History of Cape Town*. Vol. 2. Cape Town: University of Cape Town.

Saunders, P. 1985. *Social Theory and the Urban Question*. London: Unwin Hyman.

Saunders, W. 1920. *The Municipal Control of Locations*. Grahamstown: Grocott and Sherry.

Savage, M. 1986. The Imposition of Pass Laws on the African Population in South Africa 1916–1984. *African Affairs* 85: 181–205.

Schreuder, D. 1976. The Cultural Factor in Victorian Imperialism: a Case Study of the British 'Civilising Mission'. *Journal of Imperial and Commonwealth History* 4: 283–317.

Schutte, G. 1989. Company and Colonists at the Cape, 1652–1795. In R. Elphick and H. Giliomee (eds) *The Shaping of South African Society, 1652–1840*. Cape Town: Maskew Miller Longman.

Scott, D. 1982. A review and analysis of urban planning theory with application in Natal. Final Report prepared for the Natal Town and Regional Planning Commission. Pietermaritzburg: Town and Regional Planning Commission.

Scott, D. 1992. In D. Smith (ed.) *The Apartheid City and Beyond*.

Scott, J. 1985. *Weapons of the Weak: Everyday Forms of Peasant Resistance*. New Haven: Yale University Press.

Scott, P. 1955. Cape Town: a Multi–Racial City. *Geographical Journal* CXXI.

Seegers, A. 1988. Extending the Security Network to the Local Level. In C. Heymans and G. Totemeyer (eds) *Government by the People?* Cape Town: Juta.

Shannon, P. 1982. Bureaucratic Initiative in Capitalist New Zealand: a Case Study of the Accident Compensation Act of 1972. *American Journal of Sociology* 88 (Supplement): 154–75.

Sider, G. 1987. When Parrots Learn to Talk, and Why They Can't: Domination, Deception, and Self-Deception in Indian–White Relations. *Comparative Studies in Society and History* 29(1): 3–23.

Simkins, C. 1981. Agricultural Production in the African Reserves of South Africa, 1918–1969. *Journal of Southern African Studies*. 7: 176–95.

244   *References*

Simon, D. 1984. Third World Colonial Cities in Context. *Progress in Human Geography* 8: 493–514.
Simon, D. 1989. Crisis and Change in South Africa: Implications for the Apartheid City. *Transactions Institute of British Geographers* 14: 189–206.
Simons, J. and Simons, R. 1983. *Class and Colour in South Africa, 1850–1950* (1968). London: IDAF.
Skocpol, T. 1977. Wallerstein's World Capitalist System: a Theoretical and Historical Critique. *American Journal of Sociology* 82: 1075–90.
Skocpol, T. 1979. *States and Social Revolutions*. Cambridge: Cambridge University Press.
Skocpol, T. 1985. Bringing the State Back In: Strategies of Analysis in Current Research. In P. Evans, D. Rueschemeyer and T. Skocpol (eds) *Bringing the State Back In*. Cambridge: Cambridge University Press. pp. 3–37.
Smalberger, J.W. 1974. I.D.B. and the Mining Compound System in the 1880s. *South African Journal of Economics* 42(4): 398– 414.
Smith, A. 1985. State-Making and Nation-Building. In J. Hall (ed.) *States in History*. Oxford: Basil Blackwell. pp. 228–63.
Smith, D. (ed.). 1982. *Living under Apartheid*. London: Allen and Unwin.
Smith, G. 1985. Political Geography. In L. Robins (ed.) *Introducing Political Science*. London: Longman.
Smith, N. 1984. Isaiah Bowman: Political Geography and Geopolitics. *Political Geography Quarterly* 3: 69–76.
Smith, S.J. 1989. *The Politics of 'Race' and Residence: Citizenship, Segregation and White Supremacy in Britain*. Cambridge: Polity.
Soga, J.H. 1930. *The South-Eastern Bantu*. Johannesburg: University of the Witwatersrand Press.
Soja, E. 1971. *The Political Organisation of Space*. AAG Commission on College Geography, Resource Paper No. 8, AAG, Washington DC.
Soja, E. 1989. *Postmodern Geographies: the Reassertion of Space in Critical Social Theory*. London: Verso.
Spence, B. 1950. How Our Urban Natives Live. Reprint from *South African Architectural Record* 35(10). Pretoria: CSIR.
Spittler, G. 1983. Administration in a Peasant State. *Sociologia Ruralis* 23(2): 130–44.
Stadler, A. 1979. 'Birds in the Cornfield: Squatter Movements in Johannesburg, 1944–1947. *Journal of Southern African Studies* 6: 93–123.
Stadler, A. 1987. *The Political Economy of Modern South Africa*. Cape Town: David Philip.
Stanford, W. 1962. *The Reminiscences of Sir Walter Stanford*. Vol. 2. Ed. J. W. McQuarrie. Cape Town: Van Riebeeck Society.
Stepan, A. 1979. *The State and Society: Peru in Comparative Perspective*. Princeton: Princeton University Press.
Stepan, A. 1985. State Power and the Strength of Civil Society in the Southern Cone of Latin America. In P. Evans, D. Rueschemeyer and T. Skocpol (eds). *Bringing the State Back In*. Cambridge: Cambridge University Press. pp. 317–43.
Stokes, E. 1962. Milnerism. *Historical Journal* 5: 47–60.
Stokes, F. 1946. *Problems of Liquor Control as Illustrated by Conditions in a Seaport Town over the Period 1934–1943*. MA Thesis, Department of Sociology, Unisa.
Stokes, F. 1953. *The Rehabilitative Value of Sub-Economic Housing as Illustrated by Schauder Township, Port Elizabeth*. PhD Thesis, Department of Social Science, Rhodes University, Grahamstown.
Strachey, Sir John. 1911. *India: its Administration and Progress*. London: Macmillan.
Stultz, N. 1974. *Afrikaner Politics in South Africa, 1934–1948*. London: University of California Press.

Sutcliffe, M. 1986. The Crisis in South Africa: Material Conditions and the Reformist Response. *Geoforum* 17: 141–60.

Swanson, M. 1968. Urban Origins of Separate Development. *Race* 10(1):31–40.

Swanson, M. 1976. The Durban System: Roots of Urban Apartheid in Colonial Natal. *African Studies* 35: 159–76.

Swanson, M. 1977. The Sanitation Syndrome: Bubonic Plague and Urban Native Policy in the Cape Colony, 1900–1909. *Journal of African History* 18(3): 387–410.

Swilling, M. and Phillips, M. 1989. The Powers of the Thunderbird: Decision–Making Structures and Policy Strategies in the South African State. In *South Africa at the End of the Eighties*. Centre for Policy Studies, University of the Witwatersrand, Johannesburg.

Swyngedouw, E. The Heart of the Place: the Resurrection of Locality in an Age of Hyperspace. *Geografiska Annaler B* 71: 31–42.

Tatz, 1962. *Shadow and Substance in South Africa*. Pietermaritzburg: University of Natal Press.

Taylor, A. 1976. A Systems Approach to the Political Organisation of Space. *Social Science Information* 14: 7–40.

Taylor, B. 1989. A Social History of Port Elizabeth. Unpublished Project Progress Report, Institute for Social and Economic Research, Rhodes University, Grahamstown.

Taylor, P. 1981. Political Geography and the World Economy. In A. Burnett and P. Taylor (eds) *Political Studies from Spatial Perspectives*. Chichester: Wiley. pp. 157–72.

Taylor, P. 1983. The Question of Theory in Political Geography. In N. Kliot and S. Waterman (eds) *Pluralism and Political Geography: People, Territory and State*. London: Croom Helm. pp. 9–18.

Taylor, P. 1985. *Political Geography: World-Economy, Nation-State and Locality*. London: Longman.

Thomas, N. 1990. Sanitation and Seeing: the Creation of State Power in Early Colonial Fiji. *Comparative Studies in Society and History* 32: 149–70.

Thompson, L. 1971. The Unification of South Africa. In *The Oxford History of South Africa*. Oxford: Oxford University Press.

Tilly, C. 1975. Reflections on the History of European State-Making. In C. Tilly (ed.) *The Formation of National States in Western Europe*. Princeton: Princeton University Press.

Tipple, A. G. 1981. Colonial Housing Policy and the 'African Towns' of the Copperbelt: The Beginnings of Self-Help. *African Urban Studies* 11: 65–85.

Todes, A. and Watson, V. 1986. Local Government Reform, Urban Crisis and Development in South Africa. *Geoforum* 17(2): 251–66.

Torr, L. 1985. *The Founding of Lamont*. Unpublished MA Thesis, Department of History, University of Natal, Durban.

Torr, L. 1987. Providing for the 'Better-Class Native'. The Creation of Lamont, 1922–1933. *South African Geographical Journal* 69(1): 31–46.

Trapido, S. 1980. 'The Friends of the Native': Merchants, Peasants and the Political and Ideological Structure of Liberalism in the Cape, 1854–1910. In S. Marks and A. Atmore (eds). *Economy and Society in Pre–Industrial South Africa*. London: Longman.

Turrell, R. 1984. Kimberley's Model Compounds. *Journal of African History* 25: 59–75.

Turrell, R. 1987. *Capital and Labour on the Kimberley Diamond Fields 1871–1890*. Cambridge: Cambridge University Press.

Union of South Africa. 1924. *Industrial Development in South Africa*. Pretoria: Government Printer.

van Aswegen, H.J. 1971. Die Versteedeliking van die Nie–Blanke in die Oranje–Vrstaat, 1854–1902. *South African Historical Journal* 2: 19–37.

van Onselen, C. 1979. Crime and Total Institutions in the Making of Modern South Africa: the Life of 'Nongoloza' Mathebula 1867–1948. *History Workshop* 19: 62–81.

van Onselen, C. 1982. *New Nineveh, New Babylon*. London: Longman.

Vasey, E. A. 1950. *Report on African Housing in Townships and Trading Centres*. Nairobi: Kenya.

Wade, R. C. 1964. *Slavery in the Cities. the South 1820–1860*. New York: Oxford University Press.

Walby, S. 1989. Theorising Patriarchy. *Sociology* 23(2): 213–34.

Walker, C. 1983. *Women and Resistance in South Africa*. London: Onyx.

Walker, C. (ed.) 1990. *Women and Gender in southern Africa to 1945*. Cape Town: David Philip.

Wallerstein, I. 1984. *The Politics of the World–Economy*. Cambridge: Cambridge University Press.

Walton Jameson, F. 1937. The Housing of Natives by Public Bodies. *Race Relations Journal* 4(1): 27–34.

Waters, M. 1989. Patriarchy and Viriarchy: an Exploration and Reconstruction of Concepts of Masculine Domination. *Sociology* 23(2): 193–211.

Watson, V. 1986. South African Urbanisation Policy: Past and Future. *South African Labour Bulletin*. 11(8): 77–90.

Weber, M. 1948. *From Max Weber: Essays in Sociology*. Ed. H.H. Gerth and C. Wright Mills. London: Routledge and Kegan Paul.

Weber, M. 1968. *Economy and Society*. Vol. 3. New York: Bedminster.

Welsh, D. 1971. *The Roots of Segregation*. Cape Town: Oxford University Press.

Werlen, B. 1993. *Society, action and space: an alternative human geography*. London: Routledge.

Western, J. 1978. Knowing One's Place. In D. Ley and M. Samuels (eds) *Humanistic Geography: Prospects and Problems*. London: Croom Helm.

Western, J. 1981. *Outcast Cape Town*. London: Allen and Unwin.

Whitney, J.B.R. 1970. *China: Area, Administration and Nation–Building*. Research Paper No. 123, Department of Geography, University of Chicago.

Whittlesey, D. 1935. The Impress of Effective Central Authority upon the Landscape. *Annals of the Association of American Geographers* 25: 85–97.

Whittlesey, D. 1939. *The Earth and the State: a Study of Political Geography*. New York: Henry Holt.

Williams, G.F. 1902. *The Diamond Mines of South Africa: some Account of their Rise and Development*. London: Macmillan.

Williams, P. 1978. Urban Managerialism: a Concept of Relevance? *Area* 10: 236–40.

Williams, P. 1982. Restructuring Urban Managerialism: towards a Political Economy of Urban Allocation. *Environment and Planning A* 14: 95–105.

Wilson, D. 1987. Urban Revitalisation on the Upper West Side of Manhattan: an Urban Managerialist Assessment. *Economic Geography* 63(1): 35–47.

Wilson, D. 1989. Toward a Revised Urban Managerialism: Local Managers and Community Development Blockgrants. *Political Geography Quarterly* 8(1): 21–41.

Wolch, J. and Dear, M. (eds) 1989. *The Power of Geography: How Territory Shapes Social Life*. Boston: Unwin Hyman.

Wolpe, H. 1974. Capitalism and Cheap Labour Power in South Africa: from Segregation to Apartheid. *Economy and Society* 1: 425–56.

Wolpe, H. 1988. *Race, Class and the Apartheid State*. London: James Currey.

Worger, W. 1983. Workers as Criminals: the Rule of Law in Early Kimberley, 1870–1885. In F. Cooper (ed.) *Struggle for the City*. Beverley Hills: Sage. Chapter 2.

Wrong, D. 1979. *Power: its Forms, Bases and Uses*. Oxford: Basil Blackwell.

Yudelman, D. 1983. *The Emergence of Modern South Africa*. Westport: Greenwood.

Index